Social Class and Marxism

Social Class and Marxism

Defences and Challenges

Edited by

NEVILLE KIRK

Published by
SCOLAR PRESS
Gower House
Croft Road
Aldershot
Hants GU11 3HR
England

Ashgate Publishing Company
Old Post Road
Brookfield
Vermont 05036–9704
USA

British Library Cataloguing in Publication Data

Social Class and Marxism: Defences and
Challenges
  I. Kirk, Neville
  305.50941

  ISBN 1–85928–142–7

Library of Congress Cataloging-in-Publication Data

Social class and Marxism: defences and challenges/edited by Neville Kirk.
     p.   cm.
   Includes index.
   ISBN 1–85928–142–7
   1. Social classes. 2. Communism. 3. Socialism. I. Kirk, Neville,
   1947–   .
   HT609.S622   1996   95–25341
   305.5—dc20   CIP

ISBN 1 85928 142 7

Typeset in Sabon by Raven Typesetters, Chester and printed in Great Britain by the University Press, Cambridge

Contents

List of figures and tables   vii

List of contributors   ix

Editor's introduction   1

Part One   Social Class

1   The 'new structuralism': class politics and class analysis   15
     Fiona Devine

2   Space, networks and class formation   58
     Michael Savage

3   Class and the 'linguistic turn' in Chartist and post-Chartist
     historiography   87
     Neville Kirk

Part Two   Marxism

4   The logic of social democracy: Adam Przeworski's
     historical theses   137
     Robert Looker

5   Class struggle, capitalist democracy and rational choice:
     Przeworski's analytical theses   165
     Robert Looker

6   Roger Scruton and the New Left   194
     David Coates

7   Reading Alastair Reid: a future for labour history?   214
     David Howell

Index   237

List of figures and tables

Figure 1.1   The patterning of production and consumption   22
             sector cleavages
             Source: Dunleavy and Husbands (1985), Figure 1.4,
             p. 25

Table 1.1   Voting in the 1983 general election by overall   24
             consumption sector and social class
             Source: Dunleavy and Husbands (1985),
             Table 6.15, p. 142

Table 1.2   Voting in the 1979 and 1983 general elections   33
             by social class, household production sector
             and household consumption sector
             Source: Edgell and Duke (1991), Table 3.3, p. 65

Table 1.3   Voting in the 1987 general election by social class, 34
             household production sector and household
             consumption sector
             Source: Edgell and Duke (1991), Table 3.4, p. 66

Table 1.4   The association between an index of privatised   42
             consumption (excluding housing) and voting
             intention (excluding non-votes)
             Source: Saunders (1990), Table 4.3, p. 225

Table 1.5   The association between an index of privatised   43
             consumption (including housing) and voting intention
             (excluding non-votes)
             Source: Saunders (1990), Table 4.4, p. 226

Table 1.6   The relationship between housing tenure and voting   45
             intention, controlling for social class
             Source: Saunders (1990), Table 4.7, p. 233

Contributors

David Coates is Professor of Government and co-director of the International Centre for Labour Studies at the University of Manchester. His writing includes a number of studies of the UK labour movement including *The Labour Party and the Struggle for Socialism* (1975); *Labour in Power? A Study of the Labour Government 1974–79* (1980).

Fiona Devine is a Lecturer in Sociology at the University of Manchester, having previously taught at the University of Liverpool. She is the author of *Affluent Workers Revisited* (1992) and *Social Class in Britain and America* (1996, forthcoming) both published by Edinburgh University Press.

David Howell teaches politics at the University of York. He has published widely in the field of labour movements with special reference to Britain and Ireland. His books include *British Workers and the Independent Labour Party 1888–1906* (1983).

Neville Kirk is Reader in Economic and Social History at Manchester Metropolitan University. He is author of *The Growth of Working Class Reformism* (1985) and *Labour and Society in Britain and the USA 1780–1939*, 2 vols (1994).

Robert Looker lectures in politics at the University of York. He was written widely on socialist politics and labour movements and parties. He is currently working on a volume concerning the comparative analysis of labour movements in the western world.

Michael Savage is Professor of Sociology at the University of Manchester, having previously worked at the Universities of Keele and North Carolina at Chapel Hill. Among his other publications are *Property, Bureaucracy and Culture* (1992) and *Urban Sociology, Capitalism and Modernity* (1993).

Editor's introduction

In recent years scholars working in the humanities and social sciences have widely questioned the continued methodological, philosophical and substantive utility of the notion of social class. Whether as historical relationship, sociological and historical means of analysis and structure, or as a major practical influence upon political ideas and behaviour, class has increasingly been seen as deficient; as mainly incapable of meeting the epistemological and disciplinary tests of empirical adequacy and comprehension and theoretical rigour and consistency.

This questioning process has manifested itself in a number of ways and in a variety of areas. For example, welcome, and in many cases long overdue, current attention to identities revolving around race, gender and ethnicity is not infrequently accompanied by the claim that such identities have, in both past and present, largely taken precedence over that of class.[1] In related fashion, post-structuralist and post-modernist concerns with discourse and subjectivity frequently lead to a denial of the existence of a reality 'out there', as external to consciousness and intention, and as situated in mainly unwilled class and social structures and interests.[2] On a more concrete level, the very successes of the Conservative Party since 1979, combined with the weaknesses and failures of the labour movement, have moved several historians and political scientists fundamentally to reconsider the general nature of connections between the 'social' and the 'political' and the specific relations between the working class and socialist and Labour politics.[3] Furthermore, differential experiences concerning patterns of opportunity, choice and consumption within social classes in post-1979 Britain have also induced many journalists and academics to posit a loosening or even the dissolution of 'traditional' class collectivities and solidarities and the triumph of 'modern' individualistic attitudes and behaviour. As was the case with 'embourgeoisement' theorists of the 1950s and 1960s, affluence is seen as the necessary harbinger of a mass, middle-class society rooted in the politics of choice, opportunity and the relentless pursuit of private interests.[4]

To pose questions and raise serious doubts concerning the continued utility and explanatory power of class is of course not an invention of the 1980s and 1990s. Historians, for example, have long debated the extent to which concerns such as levels of income and skill and allegiances rooted in occupation, locality, religion, politics, culture and consumption, united rather than divided nineteenth-century British workers.[5] Within the social sciences the relative merits and frequently competing claims of class and status, class and power, class and nation, and production- and distribution-based theories of class have been hotly debated for much of this century.

What is, arguably, of novel and major importance, at least in terms of the history of the social sciences and humanities in Britain during the past 30 years, is the sheer force, momentum and appeal currently exercised by these distinct, if often interrelated, anti-class trends. While class has never been – even during the 'radical sixties' and in the wake of the publication in 1963 of E.P. Thompson's classic, *The Making of the English Working Class* – the undisputed 'master narrative' of modern British history; nevertheless there can be little doubt of the growing influence among academics and the massive appeal to students of radical and Marxist class-based approaches during the 1960s and early 1970s. As David Coates argues in his chapter in this volume, there has occurred 'a definite shift in the balance of intellectual forces from that evident only 15 to 20 years ago'. 'Then', suggests Coates:

> Marxism was a self-confident intellectual current. Though almost always a minority element in history departments, it was . . . much more dominant in the social sciences . . . The work of the Marxist historians (from Christopher Hill and Eric Hobsbawm, through Edward Thompson and John Saville, to Perry Anderson and Tom Nairn) was widely recognised as rich and important; as, in social science, were the writings of Raymond Williams, Ralph Miliband, Nicos Poulantzas, Herbert Marcuse, Jurgen Habermas and so on.

By way of marked contrast:

> These days less radical intellectual frameworks prevail. New icons hold the undergraduate imagination; and the writing off of Marxism is highly fashionable.[6]

Class, as a central component of the Marxist method of analysis, has been a casualty, at least in the eyes of influential sectors of academic and public opinion in Britain, of the failure of 'Marxian socialism' in eastern Europe. However, as anyone familiar with their work will immediately know, leading Left practitioners of class-based analysis, such as Thompson, Saville and Miliband, have for many years been unrelenting critics of Stalinism and the 'communist' regimes in eastern Europe. So any adequate explanation of the declining influence of class must cast its net wider and deeper.

In so doing, the following factors merit inclusion and careful evaluation. In terms of politics and economics, the growth of the New Right; the crisis of social democracy and severe labour movement defeats and retreats in the face of right wing successes; the globalisation of capital and the restructuring of the labour force in the interests of flexibility; enhanced managerial control; and reduced labour costs are of manifest importance. Furthermore, globalisation and deindustrialisation, accompanied in Britain by the serious contraction of the manufacturing labour force, the mushrooming importance of the tertiary sector and part-time and casual employment (especially for women) have exerted a profoundly adverse effect upon the 'traditional' working class, complete with its habits and values of mutuality, collectivism and solidarity. In addition, there have arguably developed more generalised feelings of insecurity and anxiety, revolving around questions of status, powerlessness, the seeming fragmentation and chaos of daily life and the disintegration of 'community'. Simultaneously, however, the benefits of economic growth and the 'pleasures' of privatised consumption, however unequally and unevenly distributed and grossly flaunted, have been significantly extended to growing numbers of the British public.

It is within such a context – allied to the dominant cultural (postmodern?) 'commonsense' of the 'entrepreneurial' pursuit of self-interest and the 'main chance', the immediate gratification of material and nonmaterial needs, and the unreserved benefits of universal commodification and 'market-embeddedness' – that the 'individual', albeit sometimes in the form of the increasingly alienated and disempowered self, has seemingly triumphed over the 'collective', the 'social'. Deregulated capitalism has apparently cast class and community into the dustbin of history.

This is not, however, the complete picture. In terms of both economy and society and politics and culture, complexities and contradictions have been at work to confound simple, one-dimensional pictures of uniformity and easy consensus. There exists intense public unease concerning the dismantling of the welfare state, growing inequality, a visibly mushrooming 'underclass', and the seeming decline of decency, fairness and responsibility in matters public and private. The miners' strike of the mid 1980s, the degree of public support for the miners both in that strike and in their more recent campaigns against pit closures, and the massive opposition to the poll tax illustrate the continued existence of social and class conflicts. The rise of 'new' social movements and struggles – among women, blacks and environmentalists – have drawn acute attention to the plights and struggles of 'others' beyond the 'traditional other' of the white, working-class male member of the labour movement. The manifest disintegration of the country's social fabric and infrastructure, and the perceived perils of pollution and profit-maximising 'short-termism', have occasioned renewed and quickened concerns with seemingly redundant notions of regulation, planning and 'community'.

In sum, whereas the initial and highly abstract sketch of social reality in contemporary Britain suggested the terminal decline of class and the 'social' and the 'final triumph' of the deregulated 'individual', the more detailed and considered picture would suggest a more complex and nuanced interpretation. Absolutely crucial to the latter would be the exploration of the continuing, shifting, complex, and by no means necessarily antagonistic engagements between class and gender, class and race, class and ethnicity, and the 'social' and the 'individual'.

The chapters in this book, written by two sociologists, two political scientists and two labour historians, simultaneously offer a multi-disciplinary based critique of the new anti-class revisionism, recognise the necessary complexities of the relations between class-consciousness and other kinds of identity, and consciously situate themselves within the determining context of social complexity and contradiction outlined above. The aim is not to preclude discussion by offering a blind defence of class, but rather to explore and expand relevant areas of dialogue and debate. The successful realisation of this aim involves a frank recognition of the weaknesses and limitations as well as the strengths and potential of class-based analysis. Above all, we make claims concerning the explanatory powers of class which are conditional and relative rather than unqualified and absolute. We do not argue in favour of the primacy of class as opposed, for example, to gender or ethnicity, in all contexts and periods in modern British history; or class as being 'universally the most important determinant of everything social'.[7] We do however strongly argue that class, with reference to both method of analysis and substantive findings and conclusions, retains a relevance, vitality and powerful causal influence which we reject at our peril.

Before moving to a description of the contents and structures of the individual chapters, it is first of all necessary to make clear to the reader our shared general definition and usage of the term social class, and also briefly to indicate specific points of difference.

Our usage of social class relies heavily upon the pioneering work of E.P. Thompson. All the contributors to this book share Thompson's emphases upon class: as a historical relationship which can, and does, change over time (as opposed to class as a fixed structure or category); as being located *both* in experience or underlying structure *and* consciousness; and as manifesting itself in similar or common interests, values and patterns of behaviour which are expressed in opposition to those of other social groups and classes. Thompson argued further that, while productive relations largely determine class experience, nevertheless class-consciousness is not circumscribed or totally 'given' by those very same relations. Rather, consciousness is defined as 'the way in which these experiences are handled in cultural terms: embodied in traditions, value-systems, ideas, and institutional forms'. What is being expressed, therefore, is an anti-reductionist view of class. We are invited to explore the complex interactions between the 'economic' and the 'cultural', class structure and class-consciousness; with the 'economic' setting limits and exerting pressures upon the 'cultural' (and the political and ideological levels) rather than totally determining their form and content. Thompson's materialist view of class is thus simultaneously fundamentally anchored in relations of production and fully cognisant of the influence of agency, of human intention, creativity and influence, within the political, economic, cultural and ideological aspects of life.

Class, indeed the whole of social life, thus represented for Thompson an ongoing dialectical engagement between agency and conditioning, consciousness and structure. The particular skills of the historian reside in engaging concept and evidence (the 'disciplined historical discourse of the proof') with specific reference to tracing and explaining processes of class 'making' and class 'breaking' over time; to teasing out the changing constituencies, appeals and manifestations of class consciousness; and to the empirical description and demonstration of the relative importance of economic, political, cultural and ideological factors in the processes of class and wider social formation and change.[8]

While taking as axiomatic Thompson's general definition and approach to the study of class, the contributors to this volume would generally agree that research undertaken and socio-political developments since the publication of *The Making of the English Working Class* suggest that class-consciousness be more fully engaged with other forms of identity such as gender, race, people and nation, than was the case during the 1960s and early 1970s.[9] Beyond shared agreement on this area of addition to Thompson's framework, distinctive emphases, indeed potential and actual differences of opinion, begin to emerge among our contributors. For example, the editor would argue (in accordance with Thompson's concrete historical practice) that class experience/structure be located not only in social production, but also in the 'economic' in its widest sense (to include, for example, the heavily gendered spheres of consumption and the household) and more explicitly in politics, culture and ideology. To argue in this way is, as observed by Adam Przeworski, to avoid the mistake of seeing only the 'economic' as objective and the 'political', 'cultural' and 'ideological' as necessarily subjective and 'superstructural'.[10] However my extended location of class structure might well, in the manner of Przeworski, be too wide, imprecise and pluralistic for the more classically minded Marxist tastes of two further contributors to this volume, Robert Looker and David Coates.

Similarly, the attempt of another contributor, Michael Savage, to demonstrate the *constitutive* powers of geographical place and the construction of networks across space to class structure and class-consciousness does not fit neatly into a more traditional Marxist model of class, with its emphasis upon the primacy of production. Finally, questions concerning the precise nature of the limits and pressures exerted by the 'economic' meet with no easy, uniform answer. Thus David Howell's chapter tends to underline the major importance of political traditions, leadership and political cultures to the complex mosaic of popular politics in late nineteenth-century Britain, with the 'economic' more as contextual factor rather than prime mover. By way of contrast, Fiona Devine highlights the continued centrality of class, as defined largely in terms of economic position and experience, to workers' political allegiances in contemporary Britain. But Devine is, in the manner of Thompson and Howell, also insistent that political actors and institutions exert considerable influences upon their own fortunes.

In sum, within the general context of a shared 'Thompsonian' perspective on class, the reader will encounter distinctive nuances and even contrasting points of view among the various contributors. These elements of diversity should be welcomed. The continued promise of the study of class does not lie in the prospect of dull uniformity and fixedness of knowledge and position.

Part One of the book addresses the issue of social class. The three chapters concerned centrally with this issue may be described briefly in the following way. In 'The "new structuralism": Class politics and class analysis', sociologist Fiona Devine offers a powerful and detailed critique of the fashionable view that workers' differential experiences in the recent past concerning matters of production and consumption (revolving around affluence, and the public or private nature of employment and the consumption of housing and transport) have usurped the influence of class in the determination of socio-political attitudes and behaviour. Devine's conclusions are threefold: that sectoral cleavages do not have a major influence upon workers' political alignments in contemporary Britain; that class remains the most important influence; and that Labour's poor electoral performance has issued primarily from political rather than socio-economic factors.

In 'Space, networks and class formation', sociologist Michael Savage further develops the anti-reductionist theme. Savage argues that the spatial dimensions of class formation have been unduly neglected in many accounts, including Thompson's, and that geographical places are active constituents in rather than passive backdrops to the construction of social identities. The ability to construct close formal and informal social networks both within and across a range of localities and regions constitutes, according to Savage, an important ingredient in the development of class-consciousness and the wider construction of alliances, political power and hegemony. Savage's astute insights and challenging conclusions will hopefully stimulate further research into the important area of class and space.

In 'Class and the "linguistic turn" in Chartist and post-Chartist historiography', the editor, a labour historian, seeks to advance our understanding of the languages and actions of class and radicalism among nineteenth-century English workers. On the basis of a 'reading' of the relevant secondary material and an extensive range of Chartist and post-Chartist radical literature, I further develop my previous criticisms of the views of exponents of the 'linguistic turn' within modern English history. In opposition to the 'populist' claims of the 'turners', I suggest that class was of primary importance to Chartist men and women, and that even in the mellowed climate of the mid-Victorian years class retained a presence, if much diminished in significance and diluted in content, among the labouring people.

My chapter is as much concerned with methodology as with substance. In terms of the former concern, and in marked contrast to the anti-representational, or non-referential usage of language adopted by many practitioners of the 'linguistic turn', I employ a 'realist' methodology and epistemology. This locates social reality both in intended consciousness, including language, and in a reality in part external to consciousness and in part taking shape and developing in ways unforeseen and unintended among historical subjects. Realism emphasises the inseparability and mutually dependent character of language and material forces, demonstrable levels of correspondence, however mediated, between the 'linguistic' and the 'social', and therefore the necessary social contextualisation of language. Also, as argued by Michel Foucault, the latter process involves careful attention to the ways in which language with claims to truth, the public interest and social consensus is in fact constructed to serve the partisan interests of particular individuals or groups, and is contested and 'classed'.[11] As a corollary, careful attention must also be paid to the consistencies and contradictions between saying and doing, and the intended and unintended consequences of thought and action.

The four chapters comprising Part Two – by political scientists Robert Looker and David Coates, and political scientist and labour historian David Howell – take as their central concern the continuing vitality and promise of British and 'classical' Marxism, in the face of critiques from the New Right, from liberal pluralism and from 'rational choice' theorists of the Left. The precise nature and agendas of these three essays will be outlined below; but it is relevant to note at this point that these essays also make important statements about class.

For example, in 'Roger Scruton and the New Left', David Coates convincingly shows, in manifest opposition to the claims of New Right philosopher Roger Scruton, that the British Marxist historians, E.P. Thompson, Christopher Hill and Perry Anderson share a sensitivity in their work to social complexity and nuance and have generally eschewed crude, reductionist and deterministic models of class. These historians, observes Coates, have also paid scrupulous attention to the importance of context, to the dangers of erecting generalisations upon insecure empirical foundations and to the pitfalls of anthropomorphically and teleologically endowing the working class with innate and universal revolutionary characteristics and missions.

In his 'Reading Alastair Reid: A future for labour history?', David Howell presents a careful examination and defence of E.P. Thompson's methodology and findings, as expressed particularly in the latter's seminal, if somewhat neglected article, 'Homage to Tom Maguire'. Howell also offers the reader a typically nuanced and complex reading of the relatively autonomous and constitutive and simultaneously materially constrained and shaped nature of working-class politics, leadership and consciousness in the late nineteenth century.

Finally, Robert Looker's 'The logic of social democracy' and 'Class struggle, capitalist democracy and rational choice', demonstrate in some detail both the historical and contemporary importance of the balance of class forces and class conflict to the choices made by late nineteenth- and twentieth-century socialists concerning the adoption of revolutionary or reformist tactics and strategies. Such choices and outcomes, claims Looker, cannot satisfactorily be explained with reference to inadequately contextualised notions of rational self- and collective-interest.

Part Two of the book takes as its central theme a consideration of various defences of, and challenges posed by, Marxism. As noted earlier, Devine, Savage and Kirk, notwithstanding their general commitment to E.P. Thompson's Marxist notion of class, are not essentially concerned with questions concerning the continued epistemological, methodological and substantive utility of Marxism within the humanities and social sciences. Such questions do, however, centrally inform the essays by Looker, Coates and Howell.

Before proceeding to a brief consideration of these chapters, it is important for the reader to be clear concerning the nature of the usage of the word 'Marxism' employed by our three contributors. The importance of this task becomes all the more evident when we consider that Marxism, in a similar yet far more pronounced manner than class, is often equated and dismissed in the public mind with the collapsed 'communist' regimes of eastern Europe or with general totalitarianism and dictatorship. These equations are the very antithesis of those held by Looker, Coates and Howell. These authors generally equate Marxism with the central tenets, categories and methods of analysis of the 'classical' Marxism of Marx and Engels (such as the centrality of exploitation in production and class conflict to capitalist societies) and, more specifically, with the strongly empirical, tough-minded, disciplined and socialist-humanist, democratic, generous and in many cases libertarian British Marxist intellectual tradition. Illustrative of the latter has been the work of E.P. Thompson, Christopher Hill, Raymond Williams, John Saville, Eric Hobsbawm, Victor Kiernan and Ralph Miliband.[12] Notwithstanding the proven failure of many of the general predictions of Marx and Engels to materialise, it is the insights, categories and methods of Marxism so defined, and not some generalised 'Marxism' in the abstract, which are claimed by our contributors to merit continued attention concerning theoretical and empirical investigation and development.

In accordance with these claims Robert Looker engages with the 'rational choice' and 'analytical' Marxisms of the distinguished social and political theorist, Adam Przeworski. Looker's central thesis is that, within the social-democratic tradition, the decision whether or not to participate in the electoral politics of capitalist democracies – to adopt the 'logic of electoralism' with its necessary consequences of multi-class alliances and reformist strategies – has historically revolved around wider and, in most instances, more important 'objective structures of choice' than the democratic 'rules of the game' highlighted by Przeworski. In the manner of classical Marxism, Looker offers the detailed and challenging argument that trends in class relations and class conflict, and structured relations between the bourgeois state and the capitalist economy have mattered most in shaping political choices.

David Coates and David Howell offer lucid and interesting critiques of what they consider to be the largely caricatured and inaccurate pictures of 'Marxism' drawn by, respectively, philosopher Roger Scruton and labour historian Alastair Reid. Coates argues that Scruton's portrayal of Marxism as a dogmatic, absolute, inflexible and patently false system of thought bears precious little resemblance to the open and scholarly practices and conditional and provisional hypotheses of the British Marxist historians. In similar fashion, David Howell challenges Reid's view of Marxism as constituting an unduly 'committed' and insufficiently sharp and precise tool of historical analysis. Howell fully acknowledges the manifold deficiencies of reductionist approaches to labour history, complete with their insensitivity to complexity and diversity. But at the same time he points to the deficiencies of Reid's 'agnostic pluralism' as set against the complex and structured practices of E.P. Thompson's Marxist historiography.

In conclusion, two further observations may be of interest to the reader. First, our intention to devote an essay to an exploration of the vital engagements between class and gender has unfortunately not been realised. By way of small consolation the reader may wish to be pointed in the direction of the excellent work currently being undertaken in the area of gender and labour history by the following: Eleanor Gordon; Dorothy Thompson; Ava Baron; Alice Kessler-Harris; Mari Jo Buhle and other historians in Britain and the USA.[13] Secondly, the essays presented in this volume will hopefully not only provide the reader with a sample of current Left thought on class and Marxism, but also make a contribution to the necessary revitalisation of constructive debate, curiosity and co-operation across the humanities and social sciences in Britain.

Notes

1. See for example, Rose, S.O. (1992 *Limited Livelihoods: Gender and Class in Nineteenth-Century England*, London: Routledge; Walby, S. (1986) *Patriarchy at Work: Patriarchal and Capitalist Relations in Employment*, Oxford: Polity; Neal, F. (March 1992) 'English–Irish conflict in the northeast of England', in Buckland, P. and Belchem, J. (eds) *The Irish in British Labour History*, Conference Proceedings in Irish Studies, 1, Institute of Irish Studies, University of Liverpool with Society for the Study of Labour History; Roediger, D. (1991) *The Wages of Whiteness: Race and the Making of the American Working Class*, London: Verso; Boyd, K. and McWilliam, R. (1995) 'Historical perspectives on class and culture', *Social History*, vol. 20, 1, pp. 93–100.

2. See, for example, Joyce, P. (1994) *Democratic Subjects: the Self and the Social in Nineteenth-Century England*, Cambridge: Cambridge University Press, Introduction. For critiques of subjectivism and idealism see Kirk, N. (1994) 'History, language, ideas and post-modernism: A materialist view', *Social History*, vol. 19, 2, pp. 221–40; Palmer, B.D. (1993) 'Critical theory, historical materialism and the ostensible end of marxism: The poverty of theory revisited', *International Review of Social History*, 38; McNall, S.G., Levine, R.F. and Fantasia, R. (1991) *Bringing Class Back In: Contemporary and Historical Perspectives*, Oxford: Westview Press.

3. Jacques, M. and Mulhern, F. (eds) (1981) *The Forward March of Labour Halted?*, London: Verso; McKibbin, R. (1991) *The Ideologies of Class: Social Relations in Britain 1880–1950*, Oxford: Oxford University Press; Stedman Jones, G. (1983) *Languages of Class: Studies in English Working Class History 1832–1982*, Cambridge: Cambridge University Press.

4. Benson, J. (1994) *The Rise of Consumer Society in Britain 1880–1980*, London: Longman, ch. 9.

5. Glen, R. (1984) *Urban Workers in the Early Industrial Revolution*, London: Croom Helm, ch. 1; Kirk, N. (1994) *Labour and Society in Britain and the USA*, Aldershot: Scolar Press, 2 vols, vol. 1, *Capitalism Custom and Protest 1780–1850*, Introduction.

6. Coates, David, 'Roger Scruton and the New Left', see p. 194 below.

7. Wright, E.O. (1993) 'Class analysis, history and emancipation', *New Left Review*, 202, pp. 27–8.

8. Thompson, E.P. (1968) *The Making of the English Working Class*, Harmondsworth: Penguin, Preface; Thompson, E.P. (1978) 'The poverty of theory', in his *The Poverty of Theory and Other Essays*, London: Merlin Press, p. 231; Savage, M. and Miles, A. (1994) *The Remaking of the British Working Class 1840–1940*, London: Routledge, ch. 1.

9. For examples of such engagements see Thompson, D. (1993) *Outsiders: Class Gender and Nation*, London: Verso; Lunn, K. (ed.) (1985) *Race and Labour in Twentieth Century Britain*, London: Frank Cass and Co.; Colley, L. (1992) *Britons: Forging the Nation 1707–1837*, London: Pimlico.

10. Kirk, N. (1994) *Labour and Society in Britain and the USA*, vol. 1, Aldershot: Scolar Press, p. 9.

11. Foucault's particular concern rested, of course, with discourses of power rather than with discourses of class. See, for example, Foucault, M. (1967) *Madness and Civilization*, London: Tavistock Publications; Foucault, M. (1973), *The Birth of the Clinic*, London: Tavistock Publications.

12. Kaye, H.J. (1984) *The British Marxist Historians: An Introductory Analysis*, Oxford: Polity Press; Kaye, H.J. (1992) *The Education of Desire: Marxists and the Writing of History*, London: Routledge.

13. An essay was in fact commissioned for this volume on the subject of class and gender, but it was not completed. For examples of such work see Gordon, E. (1991) *Women and the Labour Movement in Scotland 1850–1914*, Oxford: Clarendon Press; Thompson, D. (1986) *The Chartists: Popular Politics in the Industrial Revolution*, Aldershot: Wildwood House, ch. 7; Baron, A. (ed.) (1991) *Work Engendered: Toward a New History of American Labor*, Ithaca: Cornell University Press; Buhle, M.J. (1990) 'Gender and labor history', in Moody, J.C. and Harris, A.-Kessler (eds) *Perspectives on American Labor History: The Problems of Synthesis*, De Kalb: Northern Illinois University Press; Harris, A.-Kessler, 'A new agenda for American labor history: A gendered analysis and the question of class', in *Perspectives on American Labor History: The Problems of Synthesis*; Frank, D. (1994) *Purchasing Power: Consumer Organizing Gender and the Seattle Labor Movement 1919–1929*, Cambridge: Cambridge University Press; and the Spring/Summer 1993 issue (vol. 34) of *Labor History* which further explores the role of gender in US labour history.

PART ONE
Social Class

CHAPTER ONE

The 'new structuralism': Class politics and class analysis

Fiona Devine

Introduction

Predictions about the demise of class are nowhere more apparent than in the study of working-class politics. It has long been argued that class is a declining influence on the socio-political attitudes and behaviour of members of the working class and accounts for their weakening allegiance to the Labour Party. There have been different varieties of this thesis throughout the post-war period. In the 1950s and 1960s, for example, proponents of the embourgeoisement thesis explained three successive electoral defeats for the Labour Party with reference to the growing affluence of the working class.[1] Affluence fuelled individual consumer aspirations which led members of the working class to vote for whichever political party met their individual material interests. In the 1970s and 1980s, the class dealignment thesis became the popular explanation for the Labour Party's electoral misfortunes.[2] Increased social mobility, the growth of cross-class families, the decline in trade union membership and migration south had undermined working-class collectivism still further. Working-class voters considered their economic self-interests with reference to the political parties' stand on issues. The declining significance of class, therefore, witnessed dwindling working-class support for the Labour Party.

However, other commentators have been critical of the view that issues are now the all-important factor shaping political alignments.[3] Rather, class has been replaced by new structural cleavages – which divide voters into producers or consumers in the public or private sector of the economy – in shaping voting behaviour. More specifically, consumption cleavages have *fragmented* the working class as the more affluent private consumers of housing and transport see their interests as best represented by the Conservative Party, leaving only a dwindling minority of less affluent council tenants and state dependents supporting the Labour Party. These new cleavages, it is argued, have undermined working-class loyalty to the Labour Party and explain Labour's routing at the polls on numerous occasions since the Second World War. The *relative* significance of class, therefore, has declined as the importance of new structural cleavages has increased.

The chapter focuses on the 'new structuralism' as espoused by political scientists and sociologists.[4] Advocates of the sectoral cleavages thesis are not all of one mind and their contributions to the debate on class politics will be reviewed individually. The earliest exponents of the thesis in the late 1970s and early 1980s were Dunleavy, and Dunleavy and Husbands, whose arguments will be considered in some detail.[5] As we shall see, some rather telling theoretical and empirical criticisms were levelled against the 'new structuralism' thesis in the mid to late 1980s.[6] As a consequence, the thesis was widely dismissed as an explanation of declining working-class support for Labour in the 1980s. The early 1990s, however, has seen the publication of research on the impact of sectoral cleavages on party political allegiances and has resurrected the 'new structuralism' thesis as an account of Labour's misfortunes throughout the 1980s and into the 1990s. Attention will focus on the work of Edgell and Duke, and Saunders[7] who have interestingly converged in charting the decline of class politics, despite their different starting-points on the left and right of the political spectrum.

It will be argued that many of the criticisms levelled against the early versions of the sectoral cleavages thesis apply with equal force to the later exponents of the thesis. The 'new structuralism' remains theoretically flawed since proponents of the thesis have failed to show that sectoral cleavages are the source of collective identities which generate a sense of shared interests which have, in turn, been mobilised by the political parties. At the empirical level, the evidence suggests that class remains the primary structuring influence on political alignments and that sectoral cleavages (especially the private and public consumption of housing), while not insignificant, come a distant second as they have done in the past. This is not to suggest that all politics can be reduced to class and that the study of sectoral cleavages should be completely neglected. After all, the consumption of housing in particular and consumption in general is an important component of people's daily lives.[8] Rather than examine either the effects of class location or sectoral location, there is room to examine the influence of both factors on voting behaviour and, more importantly, to examine how they might interrelate to shape political attitudes and behaviour.

Nevertheless, it will be emphasised that the 'new structuralism' does not explain why some members of the working class did not support the Labour Party in the 1980s. Indeed, it will be noted that the claims regarding the demise of class and the increasing significance of sectoral cleavages by supporters of the 'new structuralism' have been moderated over time. The crucial point is that while consumption may be important in people's lives, it does not explain their political attitudes and behaviour at the national level at least. An alternative explanation of Labour's four successive electoral failures since the late 1970s is needed. Following Marshall et al. and Heath et al.,[9] it will be argued that political factors such as the voters' evaluation of their party's performance in government and opposition explain why the Labour Party continues to perform badly at the polls. This argument implies, of course, that Labour's chances of electoral success are not entirely out of the question as a result of post-war social changes, but rather that contingent political factors currently militate against electoral success.

Finally, contrary to the views of Pahl,[10] the persistence of class politics suggests that class analysis has a 'promising future'. The evidence suggests that it is still important to consider 'class-differentiated patterns of action' in modern Britain.[11] The nature of working-class support for the Labour Party in the late twentieth century, and the extent to which it may or may not be changing, is still an important issue on the research agenda of class analysis. Of course, the relationship between people's class situation and their political attitudes and behaviour is a complex one. Voters' political alignments cannot be simply 'read off' from their structural location and all politics reduced to class. The relationship between social structure and party politics can only be understood with reference to both sociological and political factors in the analysis of electoral behaviour. This task remains to be fulfilled by political scientists and sociologists in the field of class analysis.

Sectoral consumption cleavages

The earliest exponent of the 'new structuralism' was Patrick Dunleavy, who set out his argument regarding the growing importance of sectoral cleavages in a number of position papers and in his subsequent monograph *Urban Political Analysis*.[12] Drawing on the work of Castells[13] in the field of urban studies, Dunleavy[14] argued that research into urban politics should embrace 'the study of decision processes involved in areas of collective consumption' such as health, education, housing and transport. That is, sectoral cleavages in the spheres of production and consumption are often the source of social and political conflict in both the national and local arenas.

Dunleavy noted that since the Second World War, the development of the welfare state has seen the huge expansion of urban public services. Local government expenditure on services increased threefold between 1955 and 1975 while nearly a fifth (19 per cent) of all employees were public-sector workers. Dunleavy, however, was interested in the social and political consequences of this change and, more specifically, the implications 'in changing the structuration of electoral politics and the social basis of political alignments'.[15] He argued:

> The most important implication of the growth of the public services
> for the social structure has been the emergence of sectoral cleavages
> in consumption processes, by which we may understand social cleav-
> ages created by the existence of public and private (broadly speaking
> collective and individualised and often also service and commodity)
> modes of consumption. The relative importance of public (service)
> and private (commodity) forms of consumption seems to be the most
> important determinant of the salience of the social cleavage created
> by sectoral differentiation, and the extent to which it comes to serve
> as a focus of ideological structuration and party political alignments.
>   (Dunleavy, 1980a: p. 70)

He distinguished between two types of 'consumption processes'; namely,
those which are largely private, such as housing and transport, and those
which are largely publicly provided, such as education and health. He
argued that while the ownership of a home and a car is determined by
income and occupational class, these consumption locations are not simply correlates of class since 50 per cent of home owners and 53 per cent
of car owners are manual workers.[16] They have an independent effect on
voters' political alignments and indeed, the private and public provision
of housing and transport have become 'a central basis of party political
and electoral alignments'.[17]

Moreover, Dunleavy rejected socio-psychological explanations of
how class or consumption locations influence political attitudes and
behaviour since 'there are no very significant local social pressures influencing a process of individual-level value formation'.[18] Rather, he
argued, 'powerful (national) ideological structures are socially created
and sustained by dominant classes groups or institutions and strongly
influence individuals' and groups' perceptions of their interests *vis-à-vis*
state policies and the interests of other social groups'.[19] That is, ideological structures shape social interests which have become the source of
increasing conflict between the political parties in the post-war period.
From the late 1950s onwards, and especially in local politics, the
Conservative Party has become increasingly associated with owner occupation in suburban areas, while the Labour Party has committed itself to
public sector housing in urban areas. Dunleavy concluded that, 'housing
began to rival social grade as a predictor of political alignments' as voters
could be seen 'as aligned intrinsically towards the party most clearly
identified with the interests of their consumption location'.[20]

Thus, the relative importance of consumption location on voting
behaviour had grown at the expense of class. Conducting a log-linear
analysis of odds ratios to control the effects of different variables as well
as exploring the interactive effects between them, Dunleavy found that
managerial workers (class B using market research social class categories) were 4.12 times more likely to vote Conservative than unskilled

manual workers in 1974. However, home owners with two cars were 4.38 times more likely to vote Conservative than council tenants without cars. From this analysis, Dunleavy argued that 'the independent effect of consumption locations on voting appears to be comparable to, indeed slightly greater than, the effects of social grade'.[21] He also asserted that the increasing significance of consumption locations would have a different impact on the political parties:

> Given the relatively homogeneous consumption locations of higher non-manual grades and the highly fragmented consumption locations of routine non-manual and manual workers, the Labour Party suffers very large net losses of votes from consumption effects while the Conservatives gain extensive support in lower social grades. Sectoral consumption effects produced by state intervention in predominantly private consumption processes may thus tend to fragment the occupational base of Labour support and to politically 'disorganise' the manual working class.
>
> (Dunleavy, 1980a: p. 79)

Since the working class is the most fragmented in terms of sectoral consumption cleavages, it is the Labour Party that will suffer most from the growing significance of these new forms of structuration.

Turning his attention to predominately public consumption processes such as health and education, Dunleavy found that while the effects are less strong and the political impact much lower, sectoral consumption cleavages have led to ideological and political conflict. He noted, for example, the considerable political controversy over public and private sector education which dominated the education debate in the 1950s and 1960s, clouding the debate on educational reorganisation in favour of a comprehensive rather than a selective school system in the 1970s.[22] In sum, Dunleavy argued that the growing significance of consumption cleavages has led to 'sectoral consumption conflict' which has, in turn, influenced policy developments. He concluded:

> In predominantly private consumption processes, where there is a high degree of fragmentation between individualised and collective provision, sectoral conflicts have generated important lines of political cleavage cross-cutting those of occupational class.
>
> (Dunleavy, 1980a: p. 163)

Sectoral cleavages, therefore, have undermined the importance of class in predicting political alignments and voting behaviour. New politically relevant sectoral consumption cleavages have fragmented class interests and, consequently, have undermined class voting. It is the fragmentation of the working class in terms of consumption cleavages, according to Dunleavy, which best explains the electoral failures of the Labour Party in the 1980s as affluent working-class private consumers have voted Conservative to protect and enhance their sectional interests.

British democracy at the crossroads

Dunleavy extended this thesis of the waning of class and the growing significance of sectoral cleavages with an analysis of the 1983 general election. The empirical findings of a specially commissioned survey, conducted two weeks after the election, are to be found in *British Democracy at the Crossroads* published by Dunleavy and his LSE colleague, Christopher Husbands, in 1985. In the context of debate about class dealignment, they argued, 'When an existing line of political cleavages begins to be less important in structuring alignments, we should expect to find that some new fault line has emerged which has cut across the previous cleavage, fragmenting earlier lines of differentiation'. Furthermore, they argued, 'postwar British society has seen some very rapid socio-economic trends, whose timing and importance are commensurate with the observed patterns of class dealignment'.[23] In other words, Dunleavy and Husbands asserted that class has been usurped by sectoral cleavages as the major structuring influence on political alignments.

Dunleavy and Husbands argued that the growth of the State has had three major effects on social and political cleavages. First, in the sphere of production, it has created a 'fault line' between the invariably highly unionised public sector workforce interested in increasing their wage levels and expanding state services, and a less unionised private sector workforce who are concerned more with their tax burdens. This *production* sector cleavage has also become the source of party competition in that the Labour Party is associated with the former and the Conservative Party with the latter. Thus they noted that 'because the public–private employment cleavage cuts across the occupational class divide and because unionisation is also determined chiefly by sector, those new cleavages fragment the previous class–party linkage'.[24]

Secondly, the LSE team reiterated Dunleavy's argument regarding the growing importance of *consumption* sector cleavages. Indeed, in the 1980s, there has been a 'polarisation and politicisation' of private and public consumption patterns especially in housing and transport where the electorate is almost equally divided across the cleavage. Moreover, they predicted increasing conflict in the spheres of education and health in that, 'As the Conservative Party in the 1980s presses ahead with plans to encourage private provision in health care and education, so patterns of sectoral differentiation in voting might come into existence in these areas as well'.[25] Thirdly, they made brief mention of the increasing number of people dependent on state pensions and benefits and the ways in which the political parties have aligned themselves around different groups which are either dependent on or independent of the welfare state.

Dunleavy and Husbands highlighted the impact of the growing significance of production and consumption sector cleavages on social classes. As Figure 1.1 shows, the production sector cleavage fragments both the middle class (non-manual workers) and the working class (manual workers). However, the impact of the consumption sector cleavage is much greater on the working class than the middle class. The consumption patterns of the middle class are predominantly private, while the working class is more fragmented in terms of private and public consumption of housing, transport and so forth. Again, this fragmentation has important political implications for the Labour Party rather than the Conservative Party. That is, 'Over the post-war period, the increasing importance of sectional cleavages, implies that Labour has lost support amongst a large group of private sector manual workers and gained support only amongst the much smaller public sector non-manual group'.[26] These processes explain the growth of support for the Labour Party among public-sector non-manual workers in the 1970s, the growth of third-party voting in the 1980s and the decline in working-class support in 1979, as the Conservative Party shifted to the right.[27] The fragmentation of the working class in terms of consumption sector cleavages and the political exploitation of these cleavages by Thatcher in the 1980s and 1990s, account for Labour's continued electoral failures.

Dunleavy and Husbands extended their 'radical approach' by examining the influences of dominant ideologies and party competition on voters' political attitudes and behaviour. They identified the mass media as playing a crucial role in 'disseminating political information' by defining the facts from which views are derived. They also argued that the 'reception' of dominant ideological measures varies between locations: 'closed' locations insulate people from the mass media and as a consequence their interests are not well served by the dominant ideology; while 'open' locations are receptive to the mass media and the interests of this group are then represented in dominant ideological messages. People in different 'social locations' develop collective perceptions of how their interests are presented in policies and by parties and how they may conflict with other group interests and the party which represents them. As a result, people vote instrumentally in the interests of their social location.[28] It is through these processes, and not through local networks of personal relations, that interests are realised and become the source of collective action.

Turning to the empirical findings of the 1983 survey, Dunleavy and Husbands adopted a neo-Marxist definition of social class (in terms of the system of production and the distribution of power) and distinguished between manual workers, non-manual workers, controllers of labour and the employers/bourgeoisie. They found a strong association between class and voting in that 46 per cent of manual workers voted

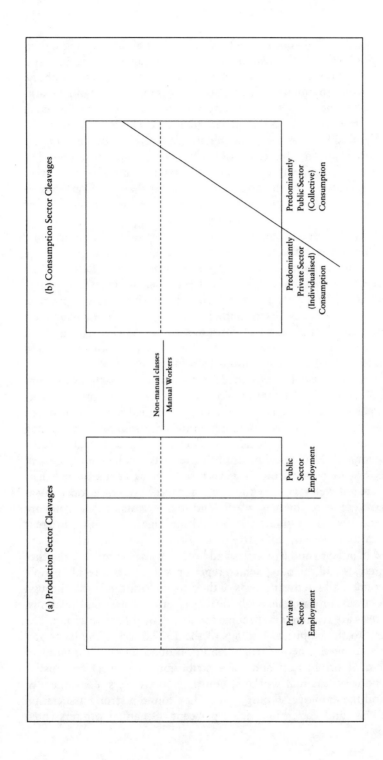

(a) Production Sector Cleavages

(b) Consumption Sector Cleavages

Non-manual classes
Manual Workers

Private
Sector
Employment

Public
Sector
Employment

Predominantly
Private Sector
(Individualised)
Consumption

Predominantly
Public Sector
(Collective)
Consumption

Source: Dunleavy and Husbands, *British Democracy at the Crossroads* (1985), Figure 1.4, p. 25.

Figure 1.1   The patterning of production and consumption sector cleavages

Labour in comparison to 28 per cent for the Conservatives; while only 14 per cent of employers/bourgeoisie voted Labour and 68 per cent voted for the Conservatives.[29] However, while acknowledging the relationship between class and voting they argued that different patterns emerge when the data are disaggregated in various ways. They argued, for example, that trade union membership which is three times higher among public-sector male workers than private-sector workers, has an effect on voting which is independent of class. Manual workers who were trade union members were more likely to vote Labour than non-union manual workers (46 per cent compared with 34 per cent). The Labour Party holds on to the support of trade unionists but loses support among non-members who divide almost equally between Labour, Conservative and Alliance (34 per cent, 34 per cent and 31 per cent respectively). The class basis of political alignments, therefore, is fragmented by trade union membership which is a proxy indicator of production sector cleavages.[30]

Turning to the effects of consumption cleavages on political alignments, Dunleavy and Husbands reiterated that they are not simply correlates or aspects of class. They argued:

> The sectoral approach stresses that class-consumption linkages have been overstated in the electoral literature. People's consumption locations are not influenced solely or simply by their class position. Rather, it is the combination of their class position and other social characteristics – such as their urban and regional environment, stage in the life-cycle, household position, the time period when they entered the housing market, ability to gain access to state subsidies – all of these other factors are also involved in how people consume goods and services. The basic reality of class-structured access to consumption is not in question. Yet neither are consumption positions simply corollaries of class.
>
> (Dunleavy and Husbands, 1985: p. 139)

They examined the cumulative effect of consumption by defining consumption locations according to five options: home ownership; access to a car; use of private medical care; use of an old people's home and past or present use of private schooling. Grouping respondents according to their use of these five consumption processes, they found that Conservative voting increased among manual workers as they consumed more items privately. As Table 1.1 shows, manual workers who consumed none of the items privately were more likely to vote Labour than Conservative (57 per cent compared with 21 per cent) while manual workers who privately consumed three or more items were less likely to vote Labour than Conservative (23 per cent compared with 40 per cent). In other words, there was a difference of 34 points in Labour voting between manual workers who did not consume any of the items privately and those who consumed three items or more.[31] Thus, the LSE team noted that, 'As integration into private consumption increases among manual workers, so the Labour vote ebbs away in almost exactly equal proportions to the Conservatives and Alliance'.[32] Once again, the political implications of the growth of sectoral consumption cleavages are clear. In the context of Thatcher's populist programme, they explain why Labour lost the 1979 and 1983 general elections.

Finally, Dunleavy and Husbands predicted that housing and transport locations would stabilise as more people became home owners and car owners. As the public/private cleavage disappears, so will the ideological and political cleavages as well. On the other hand, the shift towards private health care will see the emergence of a distinct public/private cleavage with a concomitant growth in ideological and political conflict. Although the Conservatives are pursuing private medical care, it will

Table 1.1   Voting in the 1983 general election by overall consumption sector and social class (in percentages)

Social class	Areas of private consumption	Labour	Conservative	Alliance	CON. LEAD over LAB.	N.
Manual workers	None	57	21	21	−36	112
	One	47	24	29	−23	99
	Two	38	36	26	−2	100
	Three or more	23	40	37	+17	30
Non-manual workers	None	37	47	16	+10	19
	One	21	50	29	+29	38
	Two	17	48	37	+31	103
	Three or more	10	51	39	+41	39
Controllers of labour	One or none	31	44	25	+13	36
	Two	17	54	30	+37	84
	Three or more	6	70	24	+64	66
Employers, etc.	Two	16	59	25	+43	32
	Three or more	0	88	12	+88	17

Source: Dunleavy and Husbands, *British Democracy at the Crossroads* (1985), Table 6.15, p. 142

probably be the Labour Party, as the defenders of the National Health Service (NHS), who will be the winners in the competition since the majority will still depend on the public provision of health care in the medium if not long term.[33]

Dunleavy's, and Dunleavy and Husbands's arguments have been set out in some detail with a particular purpose in mind. It should now be obvious that Dunleavy's thesis regarding the declining influence of class and the rising significance of sectoral cleavages on political attitudes and behaviour has changed over time. The 'new structuralism' thesis is somewhat inconsistent as a result. In his single-authored monograph, for example, Dunleavy confidently asserted that sectoral location has a stronger affect on voting than class position. This argument was also proposed in the opening theoretical chapters of his co-authored book with Husbands. In the subsequent discussion of the empirical findings, however, Dunleavy and Husbands's survey data showed that class was the major structuring influence on political alignments. While sectoral cleavages may have had an effect independent of class, they certainly did not explain voting behaviour as well as class did. It is at this juncture that the authors made the less ambitious claim that production and consumption cleavages, in 'combination' with class, best explain political attitudes and behaviour in the 1970s and 1980s. Thus, the disjuncture between theory and evidence was already apparent (albeit implicitly by the authors, given their shifting position) before critics of the thesis weighed in with their evaluation of the 'new structuralism'.

Critique

The 'new structuralism' has been the subject of a number of incisive criticisms by political scientists and sociologists alike. One of Dunleavy's earliest critics was Harrop who criticised the methodology and empirical findings from which Dunleavy derived his thesis. He was critical, for example, of Dunleavy's use of the crude middle-class/working-class dichotomy which he used in his early position papers rather than a more sophisticated continuous measure of social class. He also disapproved of the way in which Dunleavy failed to control for variables such as income and age, which might have affected his findings on the relationship between sectoral cleavages and voting patterns.[34]

More importantly, however, Harrop argued that Dunleavy's data could not and did not address his central claim regarding the *relative* decline of class and the growing importance of sectoral cleavages in shaping political alignments. Dunleavy had committed an ecological fallacy by discussing longitudinal issues from cross-sectional data. Harrop argued:

> Cross-sectional analysis cannot provide more than suggestive hypotheses for an understanding of social and political change. Indeed, Dunleavy's paper provides a clear illustration of the importance of the distinction between synchronic and diachronic analysis for if the greater Conservative propensity for home-owners and car-owners revealed by cross-analysis could be mechanically applied to the spread of home-ownership and car-ownership in the post war period, it would be doubtful whether the Labour Party would still exist at all, let alone a serious contender for political power.
>
> (Harrop, 1980: pp. 396–7)

Indeed, Harrop noted that the most rapid growth in home ownership occurred in the 1950s while the fastest growth in car ownership occurred in the early 1960s. Yet, there was little evidence of a decline in class voting in the period 1945–64. Subsequent evidence of a 'secular increase' in Conservative support among the working class had been partial. Approximately a quarter of the working class voted for the Conservative Party between 1964 and 1974, and there is little evidence to show that it has increased in the 1980s despite a high blip in 1979. It is on this basis that Harrop concluded that, 'The erosion of intense partisanship, increasing electoral volatility and the possible decline in class alignment . . . all require more sensitive longitudinal analysis than Dunleavy presents'.[35]

Somewhat later, Franklin and Page developed a wide-ranging theoretical and empirical critique of Dunleavy's thesis. They argued that, 'the way in which consumption cleavage theory is now being applied in the field of electoral studies forces us to accept with little justification a particular view of the relationship between objective interests and voter preferences which is incompatible with orthodox theories of party choice'.[36] While they did not rule out the idea that consumption cleavages might have social and political consequences, they were not impressed with the 'level of sophistication' of the 'new structuralism' thesis on a number of counts.

First, Franklin and Page highlighted the problem of cross-cutting consumption cleavages and its implication of predicting voting behaviour. Voters may be members of different consumption cleavages and move frequently between them, thereby straddling the simple public and private dichotomy on which Dunleavy so heavily relies. Analysing the 1979 British Election Study (BES), for example, they found that 13 per cent of respondents rented from a local authority (a public consumption location), while also owning a car (a private consumption location). A further 17 per cent of respondents owned their own homes, although they did not have cars.[37] A total of 30 per cent of the electorate, therefore, occupied positions across the public/private consumption divide. Given that these voters are open to cross-pressures, Franklin and Page raised the awkward question of how political scientists should identify the political consequences of these cross-pressures. As a consequence, they were also critical of the use of ideal types of respondent who consume either privately or publicly and the use of additive indexes of a range of consumption cleavages. While it may avoid the issue of cross-cutting cleavages, the approach is left, 'explaining the behaviour of a small subsection of the electorate which shrinks as the analysis becomes more sophisticated through the inclusion of more consumption sectors'.[38]

Secondly, Franklin and Page argued that Dunleavy does not explain 'how consumption cleavages may manifest themselves in political cleavages'. Indeed, he assumes that there is a link between stratification and political alignments as indicated in political conflict.[39] In other words, he reads off politics from sectoral cleavages in an overly determinist fashion while providing no empirical evidence on which to back up his case. There is very little evidence, for example, to show that consumption issues were or are highly salient to the electorate. In 1979, for example, only 6 per cent of respondents said that housing was the most important issue leading them to vote as they did.[40] Similarly, Dunleavy provided no evidence that sectoral cleavages are the basis of a group identity or shared interests which lead to an identification with one group and opposition to another. Dunleavy is very keen, they argued, to reject socialisation theory which underpins class politics but he fails to show the political basis for electoral choices.[41]

Franklin and Page also criticised Dunleavy's empirical findings arguing that, 'When applied as an explanation of electoral behaviour, consumption cleavage theory fails this test'.[42] Dunleavy's claim, for example, that home ownership and car ownership together have a greater effect on vote than class is 'highly misleading'. His findings on the close association of Conservative voting among home-owning households with two cars are not as significant as he suggests, since he does not acknowledge that there are relatively few households in such circumstances as compared with the number of middle-class individuals as a whole. Again, the finding only explains a tiny part of the electorate; his sectoral cleavages theory applies only to particular groups with certain characteristics, 'rather than on the extent to which voting behaviour as a whole is explained by those characteristics'.[43] The focus is on the effects of different consumption patterns rather than the extent to which they explain voting behaviour. Overall, Franklin and Page concluded that sectoral cleavages may shape political attitudes and behaviour and are worthy of study, but the thesis, 'can add only to the *quality* of an explanation, not to the *extent* of the phenomena that we can explain'.[44] Contrary to Dunleavy's claims, it certainly cannot account for Labour's electoral misfortunes in the 1980s.

Nor were sociologists slow to highlight the theoretical and empirical shortcomings of the 'new structuralism'. Franklin and Page's critique was subsequently echoed by Taylor-Gooby. First, Taylor-Gooby was highly critical of the way in which Dunleavy ignored the way people combine, for example, occupational with state pensions, and often do not have as much choice as Dunleavy assumed. He was also extremely critical of the use of additive indexes of consumption. He argued:

> An emphasis on sectoral location is not helpful unless the particular sector that the writer has in mind is specified and the choice has to be justified theoretically. The work of Dunleavy and others rests very much on particular sectors chosen through convenience of data, and the fact of cross-cutting access to the various sectors is ignored. Simply totting up a private service use score . . . is inappropriate. It does not explain why the effects of, for example, use of private medicine and housing should be cumulative. It would be just as rational to imagine cross-pressures resulting from use of some (out of a range of possible) market services with complex and variable political effects.
>
> (Taylor-Gooby, 1986: pp. 594–5)

There was absolutely no theoretical justification, in other words, for the use of additive indexes in the empirical analyses of the impact of consumption cleavages on party alignments.

Secondly, Taylor-Gooby also noted the failure to explain the processes by which sectoral location influences political behaviour. Like Franklin and Page, Taylor-Gooby suggested that Dunleavy's approach:

> does no more than demonstrate the existence of potential bases for political cleavage. It does not explain how these bases have become activated. To establish that some groups in the working class have interests associated with private housing and some do not, gives us no insight into the process whereby housing tenure emerges as a major political variable.
>
> (Taylor-Gooby, 1986: p. 595)

Once again, the unsophisticated theory of the connection between social structure and political action was found wanting. His rejection of socialisation theory and its substitution with a theory of ideology was deemed inadequate as an explanation of political mobilisation.

In an analysis of a national survey of public attitudes to welfare, Taylor-Gooby also found that the 'new structuralism' thesis fails the empirical test. He looked at judgments on particular issues in variables representing attitudes on the importance of private and public provision in health care, education and pensions and found that 'judgments on issues and social class correlate strongly with party support, in directions that correspond to declared party policies'.[45] In contrast, sectoral cleavages had only a modest influence on health and education issues (although they were important on pension issue judgments) leading Taylor-Gooby to conclude that the 'new structuralism' 'leaves many of the links between consumption sector and political consciousness, as measured by voting intention, unexplained'.[46] It was, he argued, a poor theory of political attitudes and behaviour in general and an inadequate explanation of declining working-class support for the Labour Party in particular.

Finally, in the context of debate about the increasingly spatial dimension of partisanship in the 1980s, Warde and his colleagues examined the effect on class and consumption in an analysis of 171 wards in 11 towns in the 1980 English local elections. Confirming Miller's earlier findings that class is increasingly influential at the constituency level, they found that class is the best predictor of local election results. That is, the class composition of a ward explains the 'statistical variance in local results' and, like Miller, they also found that the percentage of employers and managers living in a ward is the best measure of this effect.[47]

Turning to consumption cleavages, they found that housing tenure was the 'next most important predictor' of local election results. The percentage of council house tenure in a ward explained '40 per cent of the variance in the Labour vote, 43 per cent in the variance of the two-party vote, and 34 per cent of the variance in the Conservative vote' (the figures of socio-economic groups being 59 per cent, 65 per cent and 52 per cent respectively).[48] This finding is unsurprising, they argued, since classes are in a directly antagonistic relationship while home owners and council tenants are not. Consumption cleavages such as housing tenure are not necessarily the source of ideological and political conflict and mobilisation. That said, they argued that while class is the strongest determinant of local election results 'consumption measures were not unimportant and added strength' to the measure of the effects of class on voting. Consumption may be important in explaining political mobilisation which cannot be entirely reduced to class. In conclusion, they argued for:

> the need to go beyond a simple polarity between 'either class or consumption' explanations of voting. While priority continues to reside in class-based models of voting, it is vital to examine the complex relationship between class and consumption positions to fully account for voting. This might illustrate the significance of employers and managers, since they may be a good measure of the general social environment of a place.
>
> (Warde et al., 1988: p. 346)

Like previous commentators, then, Warde et al. emphasised that the study of consumption cleavages added to, rather than superseded, the analysis of class politics.

By the late 1980s, therefore, Dunleavy's somewhat ambitious claim that sectoral cleavages had superseded class as the main source of structuration in British politics, had been seriously undermined by critics across the social sciences. There were considerable difficulties with dividing the electorate into production and consumption cleavages. As Goldthorpe and Marshall noted most recently,[49] the boundary problems which have long troubled class analysis are even greater in relation to the 'new structuralism' thesis. Moreover, given that individuals and families move in and out of sectoral locations, sectoral locations are extremely fluid and lack the stability of social class. Against this background, it is doubtful whether sectoral cleavages could facilitate 'the formation of collective identities and a perceived commonality of interests' as found in relation to social classes.[50] They argued that there is little evidence to suggest that sectoral cleavages are able 'to exert an influence on partisanship that has anything like the generality or the overall strength of that of class'.[51] The 'new structuralism', therefore, does not explain Labour's successive failures at the polls since 1979. After a decade of debate, therefore, the emerging consensus was that the 'new structuralism' did not explain seemingly volatile political behaviour in the 1980s. The early 1990s, however, saw the publication of two major studies which refuelled the controversy regarding the influence of class and sectoral cleavages on voting behaviour. It is to the work of Edgell and Duke, and Saunders that we now turn.

Measuring Thatcherism

The early 1990s saw the publication of research findings broadly supportive (to a greater or lesser degree) of Dunleavy's 'new structuralism' thesis. Drawing on panel data from a survey conducted in two areas of Greater Manchester, collected in two stages in 1980–81 and 1983–84, Edgell and Duke produced a number of position papers throughout the 1980s.[52] The final results of the survey, corroborated with nationally representative survey data from the 1987 British Social Attitudes (BSA) survey and the 1987 British Election Study (BES), were finally published in *A Measure of Thatcherism: A Sociology of Britain* in 1991. The aim of the research was to provide a sociological account of 'the nature, extent and social implications of the post-1979 "cuts" in public expenditure and associated policy changes in Britain' with reference to 'sociological and political theories about class politics and social welfare'.[53]

In their early papers, Edgell and Duke extended Dunleavy's thesis to consider the changing nature of ideological and political conflicts and alignments in the 1980s as a result of public expenditure cuts by the Thatcher Government. They largely corroborated Dunleavy's evidence.

By classifying people according to whether they consumed a number of goods and services either publicly or privately (i.e. a cumulative measure) they found consumption cleavages had an important effect on political alignment in the 1979 general election. They noted that the working class was particularly fragmented by consumption cleavages such as housing, transport and health. On the basis of this evidence, the authors concurred with Dunleavy, in arguing 'that political party alignment is influenced more by overall consumption location than by social class'.[54] In contrast to Dunleavy however, they argued that 'it would be unwise to underestimate the relevance of social class', in that approval and disapproval of expenditure cuts is structured along class lines.[55] Indeed, subsequent analysis showed that class has a stronger impact on political attitudes to state expenditure and privatisation than sectoral cleavages.[56] Thus, Edgell and Duke were broadly supportive of Dunleavy's thesis although they did not hold that class could be wholly dismissed as irrelevant. Class was still important but internally fragmented by sectoral cleavages. The working class was especially fragmented by consumption cleavages. They called for accounts which take into consideration both the class and sectoral location of voters in accounting for attitudes towards privatisation.[57]

In their subsequent monograph, Duke and Edgell set out to investigate sectoral theory alongside class theory and to examine the relationship between them. In their opening review of the class dealignment debate, they cast a critical eye over the arguments of both proponents and opponents of the thesis. They were sceptical of the proposition of Crewe and others[58] that voters now decided to vote for a party on the basis of how they dealt with the issues in a general election. However, they were unconvinced of Heath et al.'s class schema and measure of relative class voting as indicative of the persistence of class politics.[59] As a consequence, they turned to Dunleavy and Husbands's 'alternative explanation' of class dealignment, emphasising that sectoral cleavages have replaced class as the major determinant of voting behaviour. Like Dunleavy and Husbands, their presentation of the argument is somewhat confused in that the sectoral cleavages thesis is employed as an alternative to class in one breath, while in another it is acknowledged that class is the crucial influence on party choice (although sectoral cleavages fragment classes). Summarising the key findings of Dunleavy and Husbands's sectoral analysis of the 1983 general election, for example, they concluded that 'the extent of class dealignment during the 1970s may have been overstated: class alignment was never total and certainly did not disappear altogether'.[60] In the context of public expenditure cuts in the 1980s, however, they emphasise that 'conflict and change in Britain in the 1980s cannot be fully understood without reference to the formation and politicisation of production and consumption sectoral divisions'.[61] Sectoral cleavages were of 'growing importance' in other words, in the 1980s, and the most appropriate way of 'measuring the effects of Thatcherism' over the decade in question.[62]

Like Dunleavy and Husbands, they found that the working class fragmented around the axis of public/private consumption and the middle class fragmented in terms of public/private production cleavages. Using an additive measure of consumption location and a neo-Marxist class schema (distinguishing between employers, petty bourgeois controllers and workers), they found a clear class gradient in the private and public consumption of goods and services such as housing, health and transport. All their employers in the 1983–84 GMS consumed totally or mostly privately as compared with the bourgeoisie at 81 per cent, controllers at 71 per cent and workers at 57 per cent. To put it the other way round, 34 per cent of workers' consumption was either mostly or totally public, declining to 21 per cent among controllers, 14 per cent among the bourgeoisie and 0 per cent among employers. These findings were endorsed in a secondary analysis of the 1987 BES.[63] Classes, they concluded, are increasingly fragmented by sectoral cleavages.

Against this background, Edgell and Duke examined the social basis of Thatcherism in the 1979, 1983 and 1987 elections drawing on GMS and BES data. As Tables 1.2 and 1.3 indicate, they found declining support for the Conservatives descending down the class structure, confirming the influence of class on vote. Subdividing the employee class by production sector, they found the sectoral effect on voting behaviour was more pronounced between 1979 and 1987. Non-Conservative voting among workers, for example, increased between 1979 and 1983. It was equally divided between private sector workers (52 per cent in 1979 and 61 per cent in 1983) and public sector workers (50 per cent in 1979 and 60 per cent in 1983). By 1987 the public sector vote was 6 per cent greater than the private sector vote, indicating the radicalisation of public sector professionals in the 1980s in the context of public expenditure cuts.[64]

More importantly, they found that the 'pattern of voting in relation to consumption sectoral location is the most distinct and consistent of all'. They found that Conservative and non-Conservative voting varied in relation to consumption cleavages, indicating that the higher the level of private consumption, the greater the incidence of Conservative Party voting. To put that another way around, they argued that non-Conservative voting was highest among the public consumers than private consumers. In 1979, they found that 61 per cent of totally private consuming households voted Conservative in comparison to 23 per cent of totally public consuming households. In 1983, these figures were 53 per cent and 17

Table 1.2 Voting in the 1979 and 1983 general elections by social class, household production sector and household consumption sector (1979 and 1983 data based on GMS1 and GMS2)

Sub-group	% vote 1979				% vote 1983			
	Con.	Lab.	Lib.	Non-Con.	Con.	Lab.	All.	Non-Con.
Social Class:								
Employer	67	16	0	16	64	14	7	21
Petty bourgeois	62	26	3	29	53	21	16	37
Controller	48	36	7	43	37	29	22	51
Worker	34	46	5	51	27	39	21	60
Household production sector:								
Controller private	45	35	8	43	37	28	19	47
Controller public	51	37	6	43	37	29	25	54
Worker private	32	47	5	52	26	41	20	61
Worker public	36	45	5	50	28	36	24	60
Household consumption sector:								
Totally private	61	19	11	30	53	22	14	36
Mostly private	45	39	6	45	36	28	23	51
Mostly public	37	43	5	48	27	41	18	59
Totally public	23	50	25	75	17	54	15	69

Source: Edgell and Duke, *A Measure of Thatcherism: A Sociology of Britain* (1991), Table 3.3, p. 65

Table 1.3   Voting in the 1987 general election by social class, household production sector and household consumption sector
(BES 1987)

Sub-group	% vote 1987			
	Con.	Lab.	All.	Non-Con.
Social class:				
Employer	60	12	15	27
Petty bourgeois	42	19	20	39
Controller	49	18	21	39
Worker	31	33	21	54
Household production sector:				
Controller private	52	15	20	35
Controller public	45	21	21	42
Worker private	32	32	19	51
Worker public	30	33	24	57
Household consumption sector:				
Totally private	59	10	18	28
Mostly private	42	21	23	44
Mostly public	27	40	18	58
Totally public	16	50	14	64

Source: Edgell and Duke, *A Measure of Thatcherism: A Sociology of Britain*
(1991), Table 3.4, p. 66

per cent respectively and in 1987 59 per cent and 16 per cent respectively.
To put it another way, non-Conservative voting among totally private
consuming households was 30 per cent in 1979, 36 per cent in 1983, and
28 per cent in 1987, while among totally public consuming households it
was 75 per cent, 69 per cent and 64 per cent.

In sum, Edgell and Duke concluded that the social basis of
Thatcherism was relatively narrow throughout the 1980s, being consistently confined to employers, the petty bourgeois and totally private consumption sector households. The social basis of the non-Conservative
vote, in contrast, was spread over more sub-groups of the electorate
including both private and public sector workers and mostly public and
totally public sector consumers. It was on this basis that they concluded:

> In sum, between 1979 and 1987, the highest and most consistent
> level of support for the Conservative Party was among employers
> and totally private consumption sector households, and the highest
> and most consistent non-Thatcher voters were workers and totally
> public consumption households. Thus, British politics remains
> markedly (social) class based but it has become increasingly sectoral
> in terms of production and consumption sectoral locations. We
> would anticipate that if the policy to privatise the production and
> consumption of goods and services is maintained the sectoral dimen-
> sion of politics in Britain in the 1990s is likely to be of increasing sig-
> nificance.
>
> (Edgell and Duke, 1991: p. 68)

Thus, while voting is still clearly influenced by class, sectoral cleavages
cross-cut class so that private consuming households are more likely to
vote Conservative than public consuming households. Class dealignment
is, they argued, 'a myth' but they went on to assert that 'our data also
suggest that sectoral factors are an important influence on the variation
in voting behaviour from one election to another, depending on particular historical circumstances'.[65]

Turning to attitudes to public spending, Edgell and Duke found patterning in terms of social class, consumption sector and partisanship.
While all groups disapproved of expenditure cuts by the second GMS,
the majority of totally public consuming households (83 per cent) disapproved, compared with just over half of totally private consuming households.[66] Similarly, nearly double the percentage of totally private
consuming households chose inflation as the top priority for the government, as against totally public consuming households (41 per cent compared with 24 per cent).[67] Differences were also found on the issues of
local government autonomy and trade union autonomy. The totally private consuming households, they argued, were more self-interested than
totally public consuming households.[68]

The variation in consumption and production sector effects on voting
and attitudes between 1979 and 1987, they argued, were due to the differential impact of public spending cuts on consumers and producers.
Public spending cuts increasingly affected consumers most reliant on
state services in the early 1980s, while public sector workers felt the
impact of cuts through unemployment later in the decade. Thus, while
the class patterning of the perceived impact of the cuts became more
marked over time, sectoral cleavages increased in importance over time
as well.[69] Moreover, the privatisation programme increased private sector employment and consumption, thereby increasing the Conservative
vote. They found, for example, that attitudes to privatisation varied with
sectoral location, private sector consumers favouring privatisation more
than public sector consumers.[70] Private sector consumers were also less

radical than public sector consumers. Social attitudes and political behaviour, therefore, were structured by both social class and sector.[71] In sum, Edgell and Duke found 'structured fragmentation' in that class structured, socio-political attitudes and behaviour and sectoral location fragmented the effect of class in Britain during the 1980s.[72]

Overall, therefore, Edgell and Duke use sectoral theory – with an emphasis on the increasing social and political significance of sectoral location on the structure of British society – to explain why the Labour Party did not enjoy the full support of the working class and lost three successive elections and the Conservatives won. That is, 'the greater the involvement of a household in private consumption, the more likely it was to vote for Thatcherism and vice versa'.[73] While there was a widely based opposition to Thatcherite policies, it was fragmented by sectoral cleavages and increasingly so over the 1980s. Edgell and Duke concluded:

> Overall, therefore, attitudinal and behavioural opposition to and, to a lesser extent, support for Thatcherism in Britain during the 1980s were characterised by structured fragmentation. That the support for Thatcherism, especially in Parliament, was less fragmented than the opposition is of great political significance. However, whatever the changing degree of fragmentation, both support and opposition are socially structured, notably, according to our data, by social class and sectoral cleavages.
>
> (Edgell and Duke, 1991: p. 223)

The opposition to Thatcherism was weakened, according to the authors, by internal divisions which were in turn exploited by Thatcherite policies and practices. Government policy deliberately and successfully wooed the more affluent (privately consuming) sections of the working class away from Labour in support of the Conservative Party.

Edgell and Duke's explanation of Conservative success and Labour failure throughout the 1980s is certainly a novel one. Again, however, there are a number of theoretical and empirical flaws in the research. Reference has already been made to their somewhat confusing theoretical discussion of the class dealignment debate. Like Dunleavy, there is evidence of an unstated shift in position, from arguing that sectoral cleavages have usurped class to their suggestion that class remains important as a structuring influence on voting behaviour although modified by sectoral location. Moreover, it is astonishing to note that no attempt was made to address the criticisms of the sectoral cleavages thesis which were levelled against Dunleavy in the mid 1980s and which appeared between their position papers in the early 1980s and their final research report in 1991 (if only to strengthen their theoretical case). As a consequence, they uncritically adopted Dunleavy's thesis and committed many of the errors previously identified by critics of the 'new structuralism'.

The empirical shortcomings of their research can be demonstrated by focusing on their analysis of voting behaviour alone. A number of points may be made. First, Harrop's call for a more sophisticated continuous measure of social class in his critique of Dunleavy's early research can be applied with equal force to Edgell and Duke's neo-Marxist class schema derived from Wright (where they distinguish between employers, the petty bourgeoisie, controllers and workers). In their discussion on the class dealignment debate, they criticised Heath et al.'s class schema for its 'restrictive definition of the working class that excludes routine white-collar workers and blue-collar foremen and technicians'. They stated this exclusion was 'regrettable' since, 'Arguably, these are strategic classes in a test of the class dealignment thesis, since their very marginality would lead one to expect that they are the classes most likely to change their vote.'[74] However, it is regrettable that they decided on such a loose, all-inclusive definition of the working class. While they found it necessary to make specific distinctions between employers, the petty bourgeoisie and controllers, it is then somewhat surprising that they lump a range of people – including white-collar and blue-collar employees – into an amorphous group called 'workers'. Their inadequate conceptualisation of class is not unimportant because it influences the findings and the interpretation of the findings they produce. It is highly likely, for example, that routine white-collar workers and foremen and technicians are more likely to consume privately than semi-skilled and unskilled blue-collar workers and appear in Edgell and Duke's analysis as privately consuming workers more inclined to the Conservatives than Labour.

Other analyses of the BES series however, suggest that routine white-collar workers and foremen and technicians have long been aligned to the Conservative and Liberal parties rather than the Labour Party.[75] The finding that privately consuming 'workers' have shifted from Labour to the Conservatives during the 1980s is highly doubtful. Despite their claims that their operationalisation of social class fits best with an analysis of sectoral cleavages, therefore, their evidence regarding the importance of the consumption sector divide within the working class is open to serious criticism.

Secondly, they do not support their argument regarding the growing importance of sectoral cleavages in the context of public expenditure cuts in the 1980s with genuinely longitudinal data. They draw on longitudinal panel data from their two Greater Manchester Surveys in 1980–81 and 1983–84 to substantiate the temporal dimension of their argument. They extend their arguments to the late 1980s by drawing on a secondary analysis of the 1987 BES and BSA data sets. That is, their panel data extends only between 1979 and 1983 but they do not compare like with like by moving as they do from an unrepresentative locality study (their major methodological preoccupation was to find two socially similar yet politically contrasting local authority wards) to a national representative cross-sectional survey. They found, for example, that non-Conservative voting was evenly divided between public and private sector workers between 1979 and 1983 (Tables 1.2 and 1.3). By 1987, the public sector vote was 6 per cent greater than the private sector vote. We do not know if this is a genuine change or a methodological artefact from using different data sets. At the very least, Edgell and Duke should have prefaced their remarks with some caveats about the difficulties of longitudinal analysis across different sources of data. Instead, their claims regarding the growing importance of sectoral cleavages and the causal processes at work, which might explain the association between sector and vote, are not firmly established and should be subject to critical scepticism.

Thirdly, they entirely fail to address the issues raised by Franklin and Page, and Taylor-Gooby regarding the difficulties of cross-cutting cleavages, focusing on small sub-samples or ideal-type voters, and the theoretical and empirical shortcomings of the use of additive indexes. They claim to have 'pioneered' the use of an additive index of overall household consumption location based on the public and private consumption of housing, transport and health. On this basis, they distinguished between totally private households (where all three services are consumed privately); mostly private households (where two services are consumed privately and one publicly); mostly public households (where two services are consumed publicly and one privately) and totally public households (where all three services are consumed publicly).[76] Here, it is interesting to note the small numbers associated with each consumption sector location in Edgell and Duke's sample. Totally private consuming households amounted to 7 per cent (n=61) of the GMS1 sample, 9 per cent (n=60) of the GMS2 sample and 8 per cent (n=121) of the two surveys which constituted their panel. Totally public consuming households amounted to 8 per cent (n=65) of the GMS1 sample, 6 per cent (n=41) of the GMS2 sample and 7 per cent (n=106) of the two surveys which constituted their panel. The 'extreme' (or ideal-type) positions in the consumption sector divide, therefore, were very small even in their small samples.

As a result, the majority of their sample were either predominately private consuming households or predominately public consuming households. Households consuming two services privately and one service publicly (mostly private) constituted 61 per cent (n=519) of the GMS1 survey and 63 per cent (n=400) of the GMS2 survey, amounting to 62 per cent (n=919) of their panel. Households consuming two services publicly and one service privately amounted to 25 per cent (n=210) of GMS1 and 21 per cent (n=133) in GMS2 constituting 23 per cent of their panel.[77]

The obvious question which comes to mind is whether the distinction here is in any way sociologically meaningful. Is the divide between such households (two private services/one public service versus two public services/one private service) mutually exclusive? The distinction between mostly private and mostly public households highlights the problem of cross-cutting cleavages and the fluidity of these cleavages. More importantly, is the distinction an adequate way of dividing voters into subgroups from which differences in their political behaviour are highlighted? Looked at from this angle, the 'new structuralism' thesis makes little sense as an explanation of Labour's electoral misfortunes in the 1980s.

Finally, with regard to voting, the analyses of the data which they report does not support the conclusions they reach regarding the fragmentation of the working class by sectoral cleavages. Like Dunleavy, they noted the 'differential class impact of the two types of consumption processes': namely, that production sector cleavages are 'pronounced' in the middle class while consumption sector cleavages are 'pronounced' in the working class.[78] In their analysis of voting behaviour in 1979, 1983 (from GMS1 and GMS2) and 1987 (from the BES) for example, they reproduced two-way tabulations on vote by social class, household production sector and household consumption sector separately. They note the impact of social class on voting behaviour. Examining household production sector, they highlight the differences between the two employee classes (controllers and workers). In a limited way, therefore, they conduct a three-way analysis of class, production sector and vote. However, with regard to consumption sector, the analysis is confined to exploring differences between totally private, mostly private, mostly public and totally public households; they do not explicitly examine the effects of class, consumption sector and vote. As a result, they are unable to substantiate the claim that totally private consuming and mostly private consuming households in the working class have become more inclined to the Conservative Party rather than the Labour Party during the 1980s. Again, their overall conclusion regarding 'structured fragmentation' is put into doubt.

The criticisms levelled against Edgell and Duke's research have focused, almost exclusively, on their findings on voting behaviour. The Greater Manchester Surveys embraced a wide range of topics including a study of central and local government relations, the social impact of Thatcherism, privatisation and so on which have not been commented upon here. Nevertheless, their analysis and explanation of voting behaviour derived from the GMS is fundamentally flawed. As Goldthorpe and Marshall[79] have also recently remarked, the conclusion on the importance of sectoral cleavages on voting behaviour 'does not follow in any

compelling way from the analyses they report, which are quite inadequate to the issues they address'. The 'new structuralism', in other words,
does not account for Labour's failure at the polls in the 1980s.

Property ownership and vote

The second recent proponent of the new structuralism is Saunders who
focused his attention on what he considered to be the most important
consumption cleavage: namely, housing tenure. Again, he wrote a number of position papers in the 1970s and 1980s,[80] while his survey findings
from three English towns (Burnley, Derby and Slough) were published in
A Nation of Home Owners in 1990.[81] Unlike Edgell and Duke, however,
Saunders was highly critical of Dunleavy's sectoral cleavages thesis, writing from a neo-Weberian position rather than the neo-Marxist perspective adopted by Edgell and Duke. Saunders is also increasingly associated
with the neo-liberal or New Right tradition in sociology.[82] Interestingly,
therefore, there has been a convergence from writers on the left and right
of the political spectrum in seriously considering the 'new structuralism'
as a plausible account of Labour's electoral losses in the 1980s.

As with Edgell and Duke's work, the focus of attention here is on
Saunders's findings regarding the relationship between housing tenure
and political attitudes and behaviour. Reviewing the debate on class
dealignment, he noted that the major question to be addressed is 'why
working-class people do not support the Labour Party as strongly as they
once did'.[83] Like Edgell and Duke, Saunders was critical of both proponents and opponents in the class dealignment debate attempt to address
this question. Like Edgell and Duke, he turned to Dunleavy's thesis
regarding the growing significance of sectoral cleavages to explain why
Labour Party support is especially confined to a smaller proportion of the
working class and, therefore, working-class support is increasingly fragmented. However, unlike Edgell and Duke, Saunders did not uncritically
endorse Dunleavy's arguments. On the contrary, he made a number of
highly critical remarks on the sectoral cleavages thesis. Two of his criticisms are pertinent for the issues at stake.

First, as earlier critics had noted (such as Franklin and Page),
Dunleavy's account of how consumption location shapes voting behaviour is seriously wanting. Saunders was sharply critical of Dunleavy's use
of instrumental Marxist theories of ideology. Referring to Dunleavy and
Husbands's account of the growing importance of the media, he argued,

> What all this means is that working-class home owners and car dri-
> vers are wrong footed by dominant ideologies, promulgated by the
> dominant class and expressed through dominant class institutions

such as the mass media. State intervention thus has the effect of disorganising the working class. . . . Newspapers and television perpet-
uate the myth that council tenants are subsidized while mortgage
payers are not, that only home owners pay rates, that public transport is a drain on the public purse while car drivers are heavily over-
taxed and so on. Not surprisingly, perhaps, Dunleavy provides not a
shred of evidence of all of this.

(Saunders, 1990a: p. 213)

Instead of viewing sectoral cleavages as ideological and political con-
structs, Saunders emphasised, instead, that they have an 'objective and
significant material base'. The private ownership of a home, for example,
requires much time and money so that political issues surrounding home
ownership are important to people.[84]

Secondly, like Taylor-Gooby, Saunders was critical of the use of additive measures to establish the relationship between consumption cleavages and voting. There is no theoretical justification for the use of
cumulative indexes, not least since Dunleavy rejects the political socialisation model of political behaviour. As has been noted with reference to
Edgell and Duke, they make little sociological sense either. In the context
of this discussion, Saunders was particularly keen to establish the importance of housing tenure over other consumption cleavages. That is, the
economic investment required to buy a house is somewhat greater than
to buy a car, and therefore, it is not unreasonable to expect that housing
tenure would have a greater impact on political attitudes and behaviour
than car ownership.[85] Saunders argued that 'additive indexation is
empiricist' in that it is sociological nonsense to assume that home ownership and car ownership are equivalent even if they are easy to analyse on
the computer. Rather, Saunders wanted to explore whether the growth
of home ownership among the working class over the twentieth century
has made its members more conservative and likely to vote for the
Conservative Party to protect and enhance their 'stake in the country'.

Overall, therefore, Saunders was far more critical of the 'new structuralism' thesis as espoused by Dunleavy than Edgell and Duke. He
explicitly discussed and embraced some of the theoretical criticisms levelled against the sectoral cleavages thesis in a manner almost entirely
opposite to Edgell and Duke (who barely engaged in the debate). Given
some of the damning criticisms against the sectoral cleavages thesis, it is
then somewhat surprising that Saunders still holds on to aspects of the
argument. Nevertheless, he noted that there have been few genuine
attempts to replicate Dunleavy's work. He employed his three towns' survey, therefore, to assess the adequacy of Dunleavy's sectoral cleavages thesis with particular reference to consumption and housing consumption.[86]

Turning now to Saunders's empirical findings, he found an association
between consumption location and political alignments. There was a sig-

nificant difference in Conservative voting between those who did not own a car and those who owned two or more (18 per cent and 41 per cent respectively). However, the effect disappeared once social class was controlled for, indicating that the association between car ownership and voting is a function of social class. Similar findings emerged in relation to private health insurance although a small association was found in relation to private pensions when class was held constant. The findings, therefore, cast doubt on the independent effect of consumption cleavages on class, not least since there were small numbers of working-class two-car owners or private pension holders in the sample.[87]

Despite his misgivings about their use, Saunders went on to test Dunleavy's theory directly by using an additive index to explore if the combined effects of consumption location are stronger than their individual effects. He found a close association between Labour voting and those who did not consume anything privately (81 per cent), and between Conservatives and Alliance voters and those who consumed three items or more (37 per cent and 40 per cent respectively: Table 1.4). The same pattern emerged when controlling for social class in relation to the working class, in that the association between private consumption and non-Labour voting persisted (see Table 1.5). While the overwhelming majority of working-class voters who did not consume anything privately voted Labour (87 per cent), this was less true of those consuming one item (67 per cent) and those consuming two items (54 per cent). Only

Table 1.4   The association between an index of privatised consumption (excluding housing) and voting intention (excluding non-votes)

Index score	Con.		Lab.		All.		Total	
	No.	%	No.	%	No.	%	No.	%
0	4	8	42	81	6	12	52	24
1	16	29	29	52	11	20	56	26
2	30	38	26	33	23	29	79	36
3+	12	37	8	23	13	40	33	15

N = 220
p< 0.01

Source: Saunders, A Nation of Home Owners (1990), Table 4.3, p. 225.

one respondent consumed more than three items so no percentage was available. Although Labour enjoyed majority support across these three groups, nevertheless, just under half of privately consuming working-class households placed their votes elsewhere.

When taking into account home ownership in an expanded five-way index, again Saunders found that those who rely on state support for services are predominately Labour (91 per cent). Labour support falls the more people consume privately. The association persists among the working class (only) when a control for class is introduced. He found that 90 per cent of working-class voters with a score of 0 voted Labour; 71 per cent of those with a score of 1, 58 per cent of those with a score of 2 and finally, 57 per cent of those with a score of 3 voted Labour. Again, while remaining the major source of alignment, support for Labour declined.[88]

On the basis of these findings, Saunders concluded 'that consumption location *may be* influencing voting behaviour among the working class but not among other groups'.[89] He went on to argue, 'if this is the case, then the electoral implications of continuing privatisation of consumption could be extremely significant, for as more working-class people aspire to achieve private provision of pensions, health insurance and so on, so support for the Labour Party would seem likely to ebb away'.[90] That said, Saunders did not believe that the findings fully confirm

Table 1.5   The association between an index of privatised consumption (including housing) and voting intention (excluding non-votes)

Index score	Voting intention							
	Con.		Lab.		All.		Total	
	No.	%	No.	%	No.	%	No.	%
0	1	3	32	91	2	6	35	16
1	8	23	21	60	6	17	35	16
2	11	26	18	43	13	31	42	19
3	31	42	24	32	19	26	74	34
4+	11	38	9	26	11	37	31	14

N = 216
p< 0.01

Source: Saunders, *A Nation of Home Owners* (1990), Table 4.4, p. 226.

Dunleavy's thesis. The association between consumption and vote only holds in the working class and he does not explain how the association works. There is the usual problem of dual causation: namely, whether those who consume privately tend to be Conservative in the first place rather than vice versa. Finally, Saunders added the caveat that the fragmentation of the working class by consumption cleavages may be an artefact of the methods – especially the choice of class schema – employed. He argued:

> We have seen that 'the working class' divides politically along a consumption cleavage. This *may be* because consumption has politically significant effects. It may, on the other hand, simply reflect the way 'the working class' has been defined. It is possible that a narrower and more restrictive definition would have reduced or eliminated the 'consumption effect' by reclassifying many of those who can afford private services into a higher class category. As always in sociology, the data are only as good as the concepts used to classify and interpret them. . . . there is always the possibility that the 'working class' with the cars and owner-occupied houses is actually in a very different class position from 'the working class' which ends up waiting for the bus on a municipal housing estate. It may be their patterns of consumption which make the difference in their voting, but it may also simply be that our class concept is insufficiently sensitive to the variations in their material life-chances.
>
> (Saunders, 1990a: pp. 227–8, emphasis in original)

Despite some statistical findings which appear to confirm Dunleavy's thesis, therefore, Saunders concluded by pointing to some of the methodological difficulties encountered in such an analysis which raises doubts about the sectoral cleavages thesis. On both theoretical and empirical grounds, he was reluctant to cede the case to Dunleavy. Interestingly, his caveat regarding the choice of class schema has already been seen as problematic in relation to Edgell and Duke's endorsement of the 'new structuralism'.

Turning more specifically to the issue of housing tenure and political alignment (Table 1.6) Saunders confirmed the long-established association between tenure and vote.[91] The majority of council tenants among his sample voted Labour (55 per cent in comparison with 29 per cent of mortgagees and 28 per cent of outright owners).[92] In controlling for class, however, the effect of tenure on vote was not as 'convincingly' established as Saunders had hoped, playing only a minor role in the working class. While 59 per cent of tenants voted Labour, nearly half (47 per cent) of working-class home owners voted Labour as well. He acknowledged therefore, that the 'results are not as compelling as might have been envisaged'. He went on to concede that:

This is partly because, while council tenants are overwhelmingly Labour, owner-occupiers, are divided across all parties, and it is partly because unskilled and (to a lesser extent) semi-skilled manual working-class households remain solidly supportive of the Labour Party even if they own a house.

(Saunders, 1990a: p. 233)

Thus, Saunders concluded that the small tenure effect 'is almost stifled by the class-based pattern of party allegiance'.[93]

Table 1.6   The relationship between housing tenure and voting intention, controlling for social class

| | Voting intention | | | | | | | | | |
| | Con. | | Lab. | | All. | | NV/DK | | Total | | Sig. |
	No.	%	No.	%	No.	%	No.	%	No.	%	level
Service class:											
Owner-occupiers	37	33	20	18	34	30	21	18	112	97	
Council tenants	1	25	3	75	0	0	0	0	4	3	n.a
Intermediate class:											
Owner-occupiers	36	31	24	21	32	27	25	21	117	81	
Council tenants	5	19	12	44	2	7	8	30	27	19	0.01
Working class:											
Owner-occupiers	20	16	60	47	19	15	29	23	128	58	
Council tenants	6	7	55	59	13	14	19	20	93	42	0.07

N = 481

Source: Saunders, *A Nation of Home Owners* (1990), Table 4.7, p. 233.

However, while Saunders acknowledged the dominance of social class, he insisted that the tenure effects on vote should not be ignored. He found for example, that council house purchase has favoured the Conservative Party. Irrespective of social class, council house purchasers were twice as likely to vote Conservative than non-buyers (35 per cent compared with 17 per cent). The two main political parties were also closely associated with the two major housing tenures, in that 96 per cent of council tenants believed the Labour Party supported their interests, while 97 per cent of home owners believed their interests were best represented by the Conservative Party.[94] In this respect, tenure divisions do have political significance. Overall, Saunders concluded that far from declining in significance, class is the major determinant of voting, although housing tenure modifies its influence. Thus, class is highly significant in shaping voting behaviour although he insists that 'tenure is also significant'.[95]

Saunders's findings on the effects of tenure on values were also inconclusive in that home owners supported state spending on some items but not on others. There was little clear evidence that working-class home owners were conservative and anti-collectivist. Tenants were more opposed to rate reductions and cuts in public expenditure generally than home owners. Only 12 per cent of tenants favoured lower rates as against 25 per cent of owners.[96] However, in relation to specific areas of state spending, there was no tenure effect. Over half of working-class tenants (61 per cent) and owners (53 per cent) were willing to pay more taxes for higher public expenditure on education. Similarly, 35 per cent of working-class tenants and 38 per cent of home owners opposed the right to contract out of NHS payments.[97] Working-class home owners, therefore, were not more conservative in their outlook than their renting counterparts.

Finally, with regard to home ownership and political mobilisation, Saunders argued that 'home owners do form a distinctive and crucial interest in the politics of housing at both local and national levels'.[98] Where local organisations exist, for example, he found than only 10 per cent of tenants belonged to one, compared with 51 per cent of owners (with no class effects). It seems that home ownership encourages and facilitates participation in local organisations representing home owners' interests.[99] At the national level, he found widespread support for mortgage interest tax relief although owner occupiers support it more than council tenants (79 per cent compared with 63 per cent).[100] Owner occupiers therefore, represent an important interest in local and national politics.

In conclusion, Saunders reiterated his interest as to whether the growth of home ownership and the decline of working-class Labour voting are related. He categorically rejected Dunleavy's sectoral cleavages thesis since it is 'susceptible to both theoretical critique and empirical disconfirmation'.[101] Rather, he supported a modified thesis of the significance of consumption cleavages on voting behaviour by focusing on housing tenure. There is an association between tenure and voting, he argued, 'because owners and tenants have different interests which can lead them to support different political parties and to develop different sets of political opinions and values'.[102] While Saunders acknowledged that class has a stronger effect on voting than tenure, he still asserted that this does not mean that the issue of housing tenure can be ignored and dismissed as politically irrelevant. He argued that the thesis of conservatism needs to be specified much more clearly particularly with regard to the intermediate class rather than working class. Finally, with respect to issues of political mobilisation, he argues that the most notable effects of the growth of home ownership will be in 'conflicts over housing-policy issues'. When owners are threatened, tenure is the basis of collective action in the political sphere.[103]

Saunders's work has been subject to much attention across a number of sub-fields of sociology and political science. An evaluation of research certainly cannot be attempted here but can be found in Savage and Warde[104] (in relation to urban studies) and Hamnett et al. (with regard to housing).[105] Again, attention will centre on Saunders's analysis of the relationship between housing tenure and vote. Has the growth of home ownership (i.e. one form of consumption) led to the formation of a new cleavage and the source of fragmentation within the working class? Have working-class home owners proved more willing to vote Conservative in the 1980s than has been the case in the past? Does it explain Labour's loss of working-class support in 1979, 1983, 1987 and beyond? Does this theory, in other words, stand up to theoretical and empirical scrutiny?

As has been noted earlier, Saunders was far from uncritical in his evaluation of Dunleavy's thesis. Unlike Edgell and Duke, he actually engaged in the controversy between proponents and opponents in the sectional cleavages debate. In this respect, his opening discussion on the theoretical and empirical issues at stake elevates his study over that of Edgell and Duke. Against the background of this informed and thoughtful discussion, for example, he is extremely cautious about the direct attempt (employing the same methods used by Dunleavy and subsequently by Edgell and Duke) to establish a link between consumption location and voting behaviour. He argues that consumption location may influence voting behaviour among the working class but he expresses misgivings over the findings on a number of methodological grounds: namely, the problematic use of additive indexes, the difficulties around dual causation and, finally, the definition of working class in the choice of class schema.

However, Saunders's research findings on housing tenure do not support his central thesis that the growth of home ownership has seen the parallel rise of working-class support for the Conservative Party. As was noted earlier, the effect of tenure on voting behaviour was not well established when controlling for class: in the working class, for example, home owners remain loyal to the Labour Party. It is class that patterns political allegiances first and foremost with the effect of tenure coming second. Thus, like Edgell and Duke, he is forced to modify his argument about the electoral significance of tenure. In his concluding comments he conceded:

> All studies support some sort of relationship between tenure and voting even when controlling for the effects of social class. That this is likely to be a *causal* relationship is indicated by evidence on voting

shifts among recent council house buyers. However, most evidence also suggests that tenure is only a secondary effect and that social class remains the primary basis of political cleavages. In the three towns survey, for example, multiple regression and log-linear modelling suggests that the association between class and voting virtually eclipses that between tenure and voting.

(Saunders, 1990a: pp. 261–2: emphasis in original)

As Goldthorpe and Marshall also noted, 'the weight of the empirical evidence' has forced adherents of the 'new structuralism' such as Saunders to step back from their earlier claims.[106]

Thus, Saunders's research on one particular mode of consumption – housing – has been beset with the same theoretical and empirical problems faced by proponents of the sectoral cleavages thesis. Home ownership, like other forms of private consumption, is closely interrelated with class location. It is for these reasons that housing tenure can be viewed as a 'proxy for the familiar class-vote linkage'.[107] Moreover, the problem of dual causation appears again, in that it is not clear how the association between housing tenure and vote actually operates. Do changes in housing tenure lead to a change in political attitudes and behaviour, or do certain political attitudes and behaviour influence the choice of housing? Longitudinal data suggests that the more Conservative-inclined council tenants took the opportunity to buy their houses in 1979 and 1983 and Labour-supporting households who purchased their properties have remained largely loyal to Labour.[108] As Heath et al. later went on to argue:

> But whatever the causal mechanisms involved, it is clear that the spread of owner-occupation within the working class cannot explain to any great extent why the Labour vote within the working class has crumbled. It is simply not the case that the old working class of tenants remained faithful to Labour while the new working class of home owners defected. The major factors which lost Labour votes in the working class, whatever they were, affected local authority tenants as well as home owners.
>
> (Heath et al., 1992: p. 108)

Thus, as Saunders himself found, the growth of home ownership and the division between owners and tenants in the working class does not account for the decline of working-class support for Labour in the 1980s. Working-class home owners and tenants alike remain strongly supportive of Labour. The spread of home ownership has not led to the social and political fragmentation of the working class in the 1980s. There must be other reasons for Labour's electoral misfortunes – which involves the loss of support across all classes and not just the working class – in the 1980s.

Explaining Labour's misfortunes

So far, we have seen that the 'new structuralism' thesis (the decline of class and the spread of sectoral cleavages) is neither adequate, nor plausible as an account of Labour's defeats at the polls throughout the 1980s. Sociological factors – such as the growth of affluent, private-consuming, home-owning households in the working class – do not explain Conservative Party success. Rather, political factors such as the Labour Party's performance in government and opposition, its programme and policies, sense of unity or disunity and so on, explain Labour's low level of support across *all* social class in the 1980s. This argument has been sustained by sociologists and political scientists from a number of quarters.[109]

One of the major adherents of this argument, for example, can be found in the work of Essex sociologists, Marshall and his colleagues, in *Social Class in Modern Britain* (1988). In a nationwide survey of social class (which was part of an international project on class and class consciousness), the Essex team found little support for the 'new structuralism' thesis; in contrast, they argued that 'class politics is far from exhausted'.[110] More than half (53 per cent) of those at the top of the service class (Class I) voted Conservative while 51 per cent of semi-skilled and unskilled workers voted Labour. Interestingly, they found the highest level of Labour voting (62 per cent) among skilled workers so often identified by Sunday newspapers as the affluent section of the working class which has left Labour for the Conservatives.[111] The difference in finding is an artefact of the different class schemata involved. The MRS 'C2' category which always throws up high levels of Conservative voting includes the self-employed who have long been the bedrock of Conservative Party support.[112]

Moreover, the Essex team also found class identification had an important effect on voting behaviour. It is important, for example, for the Labour vote. They found that 34 per cent of working-class respondents who identified with the middle class voted Conservative compared with only 19 per cent of those who assigned themselves to the working class. Putting it another way, over half (59 per cent) of working-class respondents assigning themselves to the working class voted Labour against 40 per cent of those who saw themselves as middle class.[113] These findings were reinforced in relation to attitudes to class in that Labour has a majority among those who believe that class conflict, for example, exists in Britain today. Thus, the evidence suggests that 'class identities exert a powerful influence on electoral choice'.[114]

Overall, Marshall and his colleagues concluded that class politics is not in abeyance; sectoral cleavages have not replaced class as the major influence on voting:

> The persistence of class identities, and their apparently undiminished effect on electoral preferences suggests that the lines of class cleavage that are highlighted by the present recession – between those employed in public sector and private sector enterprises, those self-sufficient on wages and welfare claimants, home owners and council tenants – are likely to prove no more an obstacle to the continuance of class based politics than were earlier forms of sectionalism among the electorate. The 'working class' has always been stratified according to industry, locality, grade and occupation, and was so long before the emergence of Labour as a political force. Yet this prevented neither the emergence of a specifically working-class party on the political stage nor the subsequent structuring of politics in Britain along class lines. The sources of recent fluctuations in this party's electoral fortunes must therefore be sought elsewhere.
>
> (Marshall et al. 1988: pp. 253–4)

The working class has always been a heterogeneous entity,[115] so 'new' sectoral cleavages fail to explain the recent electoral misfortunes of the Labour Party.

The Essex team were not, therefore, convinced of the political consequences of sectoral cleavages as identified by proponents of the 'new structuralism' thesis. The answers, they suggested, have to be sought elsewhere and they looked to political factors to explain Labour's electoral failures in the 1980s. That is, voters (be they working class or middle class) have become disillusioned with the Labour Party; believing there is little to distinguish between the political parties, that Labour is disunited rather than united, and that its policies and style are unpopular. Marshall and his colleagues concluded that it is organisational failures which explain why the Labour Party lost the support of working-class and middle-class voters in the 1980s. Labour's electoral failures should be explained with reference:

> to such factors as the unpopularity of much of Labour's electoral programme, and the party's lack of credibility during successive election campaigns, and rather less to the search for novel cleavages in the social structure which make either Thatcherism or the Liberal/SDP Alliance harbingers of entirely novel electoral arrangements.
>
> (Marshall et al. 1988: pp. 260–1)

This argument has been sustained by Heath and his colleagues in their analyses of the 1983, 1987 and 1992 British Election Studies (BES). In 1983, for example, they found that the working class was still politically distinctive. In an election in which the Labour Party received only 27 per cent of the vote, half (49 per cent) of the working class voted for the Labour Party with the rest of its support dividing between the Conservatives and the Alliance (30 per cent and 30 per cent respectively). Similarly, the parties were also distinctive in class terms in that the

Labour Party was a working-class party. Over half of its votes (55 per cent) came from the working class while a fifth (21 per cent) of its support came from routine non-manual workers.[116] Labour remained a class party in 1983 although it was a less successful class party than before.[117] There was a decline in overall support for Labour but there was no evidence of a decline in its relative class support. Labour's lowest level of electoral support derived from its unpopularity among voters, its previously poor performance in government, and disunity in the party alongside the development of the Alliance and the record of the Conservative Party in office. Voters, therefore, had little confidence in the Labour Party.

In their analysis of the 1987 general election, Heath and his colleagues went on to specify the political factors influencing Labour's continued misfortunes: they noted the failure of previous Labour administrations to satisfy their supporters, as was evident in 1970. Compounded by the extension of the franchise in the late 1960s, and the Liberal Party's decision to move from contesting only half the predominately middle-class constituency seats in the 1960s, to contest more working-class constituencies in the 1974 elections, Heath et al. found absolute and relative class voting did decline in the early 1970s. They argued:

> While there have been some important social changes over the past twenty-five years, political changes may have been even more important. Our period has seen the extension of the franchise, increased numbers of Liberal candidates, the formation (and more recently demise) of the SDP, changed tactical considerations, and changed ideological positions held by the Labour and Conservative parties. In all of these respects there are changed political circumstances facing the elector.
>
> (Heath et al., 1992: p. 211)

Finally, with reference to the 1992 election, Heath and his colleagues have argued that '**Political** factors remain the principal explanation of the scale of Labour's recent defeats' (emphasis in original).[118] That is to say, in the late 1970s and 1980s, the Labour Party lost the loyalty of a sizeable portion of the electorate who have since been loath to return to the party fold. Only 34 per cent of voters identified with the Labour Party compared with 42 per cent of Conservative identifiers in 1992. While the percentage of Labour Party identifiers recovered from the low point in 1983, it has still not surpassed the figure of 38 per cent obtained in 1979.[119] On this basis, Heath and his colleagues concluded:

> Given the spread of this drop in Labour loyalties, the loss cannot have been brought about by any long-term social process such as a change in the composition of the electorate. Rather, it is clear that Labour's political difficulties in the late 1970s and early 1980s (such as the 'winter of discontent', the protracted row about nuclear disarmament, and the split which led to the formation of the Social

Democratic Party from Labour's ranks) not only cost the party votes
in the short term but also broke the long-term bond for many voters
that formerly linked them to the party.

(Heath et al., 1994: pp. 297–8)

Voters who have switched (predominantly) from Labour to the Liberal
Democrats have been slow to return to Labour. Of the 42 per cent of
panel respondents who switched from Labour to the Alliance in 1983,
over a third (36 per cent) were still voting Liberal Democrat in 1992,
while 12 per cent had shifted their support to the Conservatives.[120]

In sum, Heath and his colleagues concluded that Labour has a enormous problem with the electorate's perception of its competence. The
electorate is not confident that Labour will achieve either its economic
aspirations or its social goals. There is a real problem of credibility, especially for a party which has now been out of office for over 14 years and
only spent six years in office in its longest spell.[121] The loss of support
from the late 1970s and early 1980s appears to be 'demonstrably severe
and long-lasting'. The authors concluded that Labour's chances of winning are not hopeless in terms of denying the Conservatives a majority at
the next election but, with the rise of the Liberal Democrats as a third
party doing so well in the south, the chances of winning an overall majority remain highly problematical. Whether these political factors are
highly contingent, ephemeral issues or have a long-lasting impact on
Labour's electoral fortunes remains, of course, to be seen.

Conclusion

It has been argued that, irrespective of the version on offer, the 'new
structuralism' thesis does not explain Labour's successive electoral
defeats and the seeming loss of support among working-class voters.
Class has not been usurped by 'new' sectoral locations which have fragmented the working class either socially or politically. The crucial point
is that there is little evidence to suggest that sectoral cleavages have
become the primary source of collective identity which have, in turn,
formed the basis of political mobilisation. It is social class which has been
the major influence on partisanship. This is not to suggest that sociologists and political scientists should ignore the issue of consumption; as
Saunders rightly noted, the consumption of goods and services such as
housing, health and transport, is to a greater or lesser degree, a very
important dimension of people's everyday lives. As yet, however, empirical findings indicate that sectoral cleavages do not have a major influence
on political alignments. Claims about the relative decline of social class
and the growing significance of sectoral cleavages, therefore, cannot be

sustained either theoretically or empirically. As Goldthorpe and Marshall recently argued:

> It is important to recognise here that the argument that political partisanship may be influenced, over and above the effects of class, by such factors as whether an individual is employed in the public or private sector of the economy, or is a home-owner or council tenant, is in itself, far from new and, in any event, creates no problem whatever for exponents of class analysis. For the latter have never supposed that class alone determines vote; and sources of differentiation in political orientations and action *within* class have always been of interest to them. Class analysis is only challenged in so far as it is maintained that sectoral cleavages have by now superseded those of class in providing the major structural basis of partisanship across the electorate as a whole.
> (Goldthorpe and Marshall, 1992: p. 392, emphasis in original)

There is room, then, for an analysis (as they say) of 'sources of differentiation in political orientations' in the study of mass political behaviour.

Nevertheless, the persistence of class politics also suggests that class analysis has a 'promising future'. As Goldthorpe and Marshall have argued, 'class differentiated patterns of action' remain important and worthy of consideration in modern Britain.[122] The nature of working-class support for the Labour Party in the late twentieth century is still an important issue on the research agenda of class analysis. Why, for example, have previously Labour voters been loath to return to the party in the early 1990s? How do they now view Labour's economic and social goals? What are the political attitudes and behaviour of young members of the working class who have known nothing but Conservative rule for the last 15 years? These issues need to be addressed by sociologists and political scientists alike. Contrary to the popular view, the study of social class remains an important vantage point from which to understand political attitudes and behaviour.

Notes

1. Abrams, M. and Rose, R. (1960) *Must Labour Lose?*, Harmondsworth: Penguin; Butler, D. and Rose R. (1960) *The British General Election of 1959*, London: Macmillan; Mogey, J.M. (1956) *Family and Neighbourhood: Two Studies in Oxford*, London: Oxford University Press; Young M. and Willmott P. (1957) *Family and Kinship in East London*, Harmondsworth: Penguin; Zweig, F. (1961) *The Worker in an Affluent Society*, London: Heinemann.
2. Franklin, M.N. (1985) *The Decline of Class Voting in Britain*, Oxford: Clarendon Press; Robertson, D. (1984) *Class and the British Electorate*, Oxford: Basil Blackwell; Sarlvik, B. and Crewe, I. (1983) *Decade of Dealignment*, Cambridge: Cambridge University Press.

3. Dunleavy, P. (1980a) *Urban Political Analysis*, London: Macmillan; Dunleavy, P. and Husbands, C. (1985) *British Democracy at the Crossroads*, London: Allen and Unwin.
4. The term 'new structuralism' is drawn from Goldthorpe, J.H. and Marshall, G. (1992), 'The promising future of class analysis: A response to recent critiques', *Sociology*, 26, pp. 381–400; Dunleavy, P. (1980a); Dunleavy, P. and Husbands, C. (1985); Edgell, S. and Duke, V. (1991) *A Measure of Thatcherism: A Sociology of Britain*, London: Harper Collins; Saunders, P. (1990a) *A Nation of Home Owners*, London: Unwin Hyman.
5. Dunleavy, P. (1979), 'The urban basis of political alignment: Social class, domestic property ownership and state intervention in consumption processes', *British Journal of Political Science*, 9, pp. 409–43; Dunleavy, P. (1980b), 'The political implications of sectoral cleavages and the growth of state employment': part 1, *Political Studies*, 28, pp. 364–83; Dunleavy, P. (1980c), 'The political implications of sectoral cleavages and the growth of state employment': part 2, *Political Studies*, 28, pp. 527–49; Dunleavy, P. and Husbands, C. (1985).
6. Harrop, M. (1980), 'The urban basis of political alignment: a comment', *British Journal of Political Science*, 10, pp. 388–402; Franklin, M.N. and Page, E. (1984), 'A critique of the consumption cleavage approach in British voting studies', *Political Studies*, 32, pp. 521–36; Taylor-Gooby, P. (1986), 'Consumption cleavages and welfare politics', *Political Studies*, 34, pp. 592–606; Warde, A., Savage, M., Longhurst, B. and Martin, A. (1988), 'Class, consumption and voting: an ecological analysis of wards and towns in the 1980 local elections in England', *Political Geography Quarterly*, 7, pp. 339–51.
7. Edgell, S. and Duke, V. (1991); Saunders, P. (1990a).
8. Warde, A. (1990), 'Introduction to the sociology of consumption', *Sociology*, 24, pp. 1–4.
9. Marshall, G., Rose, D., Newby, H. and Vogler, C. (1988) *Social Class in Modern Britain*, London: Hutchinson; Heath, A., Jowell, R. and Curtice, J. (1985) *How Britain Votes*, Oxford: Pergamon Press; Heath, A., Jowell, R., Curtice, J., Evans, G. Field, J., and Witherspoon, S. (1991) *Understanding Political Change*, Oxford: Pergamon Press; Heath A., Jowell, R. and Curtice, J. (eds) (1994) *Labour's Last Chance?*, Aldershot: Dartmouth.
10. Pahl, R.E. (1989), 'Is the emperor naked? Some comments on the adequacy of sociological theory in urban and regional research', *International Journal of Urban and Regional Research*, 13, pp. 709–20.
11. Goldthorpe, J.H. and Marshall, G. (1992) p. 393.
12. Dunleavy, P. (1979); Dunleavy, P. (1980b); Dunleavy, P. (1980c).
13. Castells, M. (1977) *The Urban Question*, London: Edward Arnold.
14. Dunleavy, P. (1980a), p. 2.
15. Ibid., p. 56.
16. Ibid., p. 71.
17. Ibid., pp. 71–2.
18. Ibid., p. 74.
19. Ibid., p. 74.
20. Ibid., p. 78.
21. Ibid., p. 79.

22. Ibid., pp. 86, 163.
23. Dunleavy, P. and Husbands, C. (1985), p. 21.
24. Ibid., p. 22.
25. Ibid., p. 24.
26. Ibid., p. 24.
27. Ibid., p. 25.
28. Ibid., p. 20.
29. Ibid., p. 123.
30. Ibid., pp. 131–2.
31. Ibid., pp. 141–2.
32. Ibid., p. 142.
33. Ibid., p. 144.
34. Harrop, M. (1980), pp. 390–1.
35. Ibid., p. 398.
36. Franklin, M.N. and Page, E. (1984), 'A critique of the consumption cleavage approach in British voting studies', *Political Studies*, 32, pp. 521–36; particularly p. 523.
37. Ibid., p. 525.
38. Ibid., p. 525.
39. Ibid., pp. 545–6.
40. Ibid., p. 527.
41. Ibid., p. 529.
42. Ibid., p. 529.
43. Ibid., p. 529.
44. Ibid., p. 533.
45. Taylor-Gooby, P. (1986), p. 602.
46. Ibid., p. 606.
47. Warde, A., et al. (1988), p. 343; Miller, W.L. (1978), 'Social class and party choice in England: A new analysis', *British Journal of Political Science*, 8, pp. 257–84.
48. Warde, A., et al. (1988), p. 345.
49. Goldthorpe, J.H. and Marshall, G. (1992), pp. 392–3.
50. Ibid., p. 393; Savage, M., Watt, P. and Arber, S. (1990), 'The consumption sector debate and housing mobility', *Sociology*, 24, pp. 97–117.
51. Goldthorpe, J.H. and Marshall, G. (1992), p. 392.
52. Duke, V. and Edgell, S. (1984) 'Public expenditure cuts in Britain and consumption sectoral cleavages', *International Journal of Urban and Regional Research*, 8, pp. 177–201; Duke, V. and Edgell, S. (1987), 'Attitudes to privatisation: The influence of class, sector and partisanship', *Quarterly Journal of Social Affairs*, 3, 4, pp. 253–84; Edgell, S. and Duke, V. (1982), 'Reactions to the public expenditure cuts: Occupational class and party realignment', *Sociology*, 16, pp. 431–9.
53. Edgell, S. and Duke, V. (1991) p. 18.
54. Duke, V. and Edgell, S. (1984) p. 195.
55. Ibid., p. 195.
56. Duke, V. and Edgell, S. (1987).
57. Ibid., p. 280.
58. Sarluk, B. and Crewe, I. (1983) *Decade of Dealignment*, Cambridge: Cambridge University Press; Franklin, M.N. (1985); Himmelweit, H.T., Humphreys, P. and Jaeger, M. (1985) *How Voters Decide*, Milton Keynes: Open University Press; McAllister, I. and Rose, R. (1984) *The*

Nationwide Competition for Votes: The 1983 British Election, London: Frances Pinter.

59. Edgell, S. and Duke V. (1991), p. 57.
60. Ibid., p. 61.
61. Ibid., p. 40.
62. Ibid., p. 45.
63. Ibid., pp. 44–5.
64. Edgell, S. and Duke V. (1991).
65. Ibid., p. 69.
66. Ibid., p. 73.
67. Ibid., p. 79.
68. Ibid., p. 84.
69. Ibid., p. 138.
70. Ibid., p. 172.
71. Ibid., pp. 212–13.
72. Ibid., p. 214.
73. Ibid., p. 217.
74. Ibid., p. 57.
75. Heath, A., et al. (1985; 1992).
76. Edgell, S. and Duke, V. (1991), p. 42.
77. Ibid., p. 241.
78. Ibid., p. 43.
79. Goldthorpe, J.H. and Marshall, G. (1992), p. 396.
80. Saunders, P. (1978), 'Domestic property and social class', *International Journal of Urban and Regional Research*, 2, pp. 233–51; Saunders, P. (1984), 'Beyond housing classes', *International Journal of Urban and Regional Research*, pp. 233–51.
81. Saunders, P. (1990a).
82. Saunders, P. (1990b) *Social Class and Stratification*, London: Tavistock.
83. Saunders, P. (1990a).
84. Ibid., p. 216.
85. Ibid., p. 216.
86. Ibid., p. 222.
87. Ibid., p. 224.
88. Ibid., p. 225.
89. Ibid., p. 225.
90. Ibid., p. 226; Saunders however, does not provide any evidence to suggest that working-class people aspire to achieve private pensions or health insurance, which is needed to sustain this argument. As Taylor-Gooby, P. (1986), also noted, people do not always have the choice as to whether they consume something publicly or privately, which must have some bearing on how these factors influence political behaviour.
91. Butler, D. and Stokes, D. (1969) *Political Change in Britain*, London: Macmillan.
92. Saunders, P. (1990a), p. 232.
93. Ibid., p. 233; Saunders found that home ownership had a major influence on the politics of members of Goldthorpe's intermediate class, ibid., p. 243. However, Goldthorpe, J.H. and Marshall, G. (1992), p. 396, have cast doubt over this finding. They are critical of Saunders's use of the collapsed intermediate class category rather than looking at the political behaviour of the individual classes. After all, the self-employed (who con-

stitute the intermediate class along with white-collar workers, technicians and supervisors) have a long history of voting for the Conservative Party, see Heath, A., et al. (1985).

94. Saunders, P. (1990a), pp. 234–5.
95. Ibid., pp. 238–9.
96. Ibid., p. 251.
97. Ibid., pp. 253–4.
98. Ibid., p. 255.
99. Ibid., p. 256.
100. Ibid., p. 259.
101. Ibid., p. 261.
102. Ibid., p. 261.
103. Ibid., p. 262.
104. Savage, M. and Warde, A. (1993) *Urban Sociology: Capitalism and Modernity*, Basingstoke: Macmillan.
105. Hamnett, C., McDowell, L. and Sawe, P. (1989) *The Changing Social Structure*, London: Sage.
106. Goldthorpe, J.H. and Marshall, G. (1992), p. 392.
107. Marshall, G., Rose, D., Newby, H. and Vogler, C. (1988), p. 252.
108. Heath A., Jowell, R. and Curtice, J. (1985).
109. Evans, G. (1993), 'The decline of class divisions in Britain?: Class and ideological preferences in the 1960s and 1980s', *British Journal of Sociology*, 44, pp. 449–71; Devine, F. (1992) *Affluent Workers Revisited: Privatism and the Working Class*, Edinburgh: Edinburgh University Press; Heath, A., et al. (1985; 1991; 1994); Marshall, G., et al. (1988); Weakliem, D. (1989), 'Class and party in Britain, 1964–1983', *Sociology*, 23, pp. 285–97.
110. Marshall, G., et al. (1988), p. 236.
111. Ibid., p. 236.
112. Goldthorpe, J.H. and Marshall, G. (1992), p. 396.
113. Marshall, G., et al. (1988), Table 9.12.
114. Ibid., p. 248.
115. Marshall, G. (1983), 'Some remarks on the study of working-class consciousness', *Politics and Society*, 12, pp. 263–301, reprinted in Rose, D. (ed.) (1988) *Social Stratification and Economic Change*, London: Hutchinson.
116. Heath, A., et al. (1985), pp. 21–2.
117. Ibid., p. 29.
118. Heath, A., et al. (1994) (eds), p. 285.
119. Ibid., p. 2.
120. Ibid., p. 288.
121. Ibid., p. 2.
122. Goldthorpe, J.H. and Marshall, G. (1992) p. 393.

CHAPTER TWO

Space, networks and class formation

Michael Savage

Since the 1950s the idea of social class has been widely used by social historians and sociologists – especially (but not exclusively) those of a Marxist or Marxisant hue – as a key concept for analysing social change.[1] However, in the past decade a new body of opinion, influenced by the rise of post-structuralist and anti-foundational currents in the social sciences and humanities,[2] holds that the concept of class is over-deterministic and reductionist, unable to handle the complexity of people's ways of thinking and acting in the past.[3] The result has been to place defenders of the class perspective in an apparently conservative camp, in which they appear forced to maintain fundamentalist assumptions about the social world which their newer opponents claim to be unsustainable in the light of new theoretical developments. Some defenders of the concept of class seem happy to be cast in such a role.[4] However others, such as myself, think that it is unhelpful just to defend old orthodoxies and that it is necessary to critically incorporate what is useful in newer currents of work, without abandoning all that is valuable in older perspectives. This chapter is therefore an attempt to defend the concept of class in historical analysis, while recognising real problems in its existing usages, and some thoughts as to how it can be developed.

I argue that, properly conceived, the 'class formation' approach remains of continuing relevance to historians and sociologists. However, it would be mistaken to assume that there are no problems in existing work. I agree with critics that the concept of class as it is used in older work has serious shortcomings, and my chapter is therefore designed to develop as well as to defend recent analyses of social class. My main argument is that existing accounts focus upon the temporal, rather than spatial, dimensions of class formation. This was largely due to the inspirational work of social historians such as E.P. Thompson which offered a dynamic and therefore historical view of class, compared to the rather static and structural views of class evident within some sociological approaches. However, as some social geographers have argued,[5] a proper recognition of the role of spatial processes allows a more sensitive concept of class formation to be deployed which avoids some of the historicist problems latent in older work.

In the first part of this chapter I consider the basic features of the 'class formation' perspective, indicating both its considerable strengths, as well as some of its weaknesses. The second part explores how the concept of class formation might be broadened to include a spatial dimension, and here I suggest that lessons can be learnt from recent developments in the social network analysis carried out by American sociologists. The third part considers how space and class formation has been treated by social historians, and points out that nearly all accounts emphasise the role of places as 'habitats' for social classes. I use historical examples from nineteenth-century Britain to suggest that while this is an important dimension it does not exhaust the relevance of spatial processes to the study of class formation. In the fourth section I argue that an emphasis on space as network can help aid our understanding of the dynamics of class relationships.

My general argument is that space needs to be seen as important in two different and possibly contradictory ways. First, particular places can become habitats for certain social groups so that these places become integrally linked into their 'habitus', their lifestyles, and so can be a base on which their collective identity is formed. Secondly, class formation can take place as social classes stretch across space by building networks which link members of that class together even though they are spatially dispersed. I suggest that there is a tension between these two distinct conceptions, which goes some way to explain why class formation can be difficult to sustain over long historical periods, especially for subordinate social classes.

Class formation and historical analysis

In recent years the concept of class formation has come to play a key role in historical analysis. This approach can be said to originate with Marx's historical inquiries, notably his studies of enclosure in England[6] and his account of the Eighteenth Brumaire in France.[7] This perspective was developed by Marxist historians such as Maurice Dobb, Rodney Hilton, Edward Thompson and Eric Hobsbawm,[8] who played a key role in directing interest in social class away from institutional labour history to the broader terrain of social history. In more recent times, the concept has been widely adopted by historical sociologists interested in exploring the relationship between class structure, class identity, and social and political action. In some hands this has led to specialist research on specific places and periods: such as Louise Tilly's[9] study of Milan at the end of the nineteenth century, or the work of Sewell or Aminzade[10] on France. In other hands it has led to comparative investigations of class formation in different countries[11] or different historical epochs.[12]

Central to this diverse body of work is the argument that social classes do not simply exist as inert objects, but are actively constructed historically, and shape historical change.[13] The early Marxist historians, many of them originally attached to the influential Communist Party Historians Group,[14] emphasised that classes both made and were made by history. This conception led them to view class as the product of agency (people act to make class matter), of historical specificity and of the need to see classes in relationship to other classes. In Thompson's much quoted words:

> class is a social and cultural formation (often finding institutional expression) which cannot be defined abstractly or in isolation, but only in terms of relationship with other classes; and ultimately the definition can only be made in the medium of time – that is action and reaction, change and conflict . . . class is not a thing, it is a happening.[15]

Let me try to unpack some of the strengths and weaknesses of this evocative approach to class. Its great strength is its sensitivity to the study of class and social relationships, and its determination to avoid reifying social relationships, not treating social groups and classes as if they were 'objects' in and of themselves. Thompson emphasised the contingency of class formation, and the need to examine the actual articulation of class by people in given historical settings:

> when we speak of a class we are thinking of a very loosely defined body of people who share the same categories of interests, social experiences, traditions, and value systems, who have a **disposition** to **behave** as a class, to define themselves in their own actions and in relation to other groups of people in class ways.[16]

This formulation of social class recognises its sensitivity to the complex interplay between structure and agency. It offers an alternative to what became the more standard sociological orthodoxy of distinguishing class structure from class consciousness and class formation, so that their relationship can be empirically explored. This latter approach to class, already evident in Marx's distinction between class-in-itself and class-for-itself, became standard in American and (especially) British social science: being enshrined in Lockwood's classic study of *The Blackcoated Worker*; in Ossowski's study of class consciousness; Goldthorpe and Lockwood's *Affluent Worker* studies; Goldthorpe's research on social mobility, and so forth.[17] Thompson's refusal to couch his own approach in these terms led to considerable criticism, especially in the 1970s during the heyday of structuralist Marxism, because it was claimed that he could not clearly distinguish the relevance of class structures for the construction of class consciousness.[18]

In longer-term perspective however, Thompson's dynamic view of class formation actually appears more in keeping with recent developments in social theory, and also seems to allow him to sidestep seemingly intractable problems in structural approaches to class.[19] For it has often been observed that structural theories of class, such as those of Poulantzas or Wright,[20] depend upon a notion of 'objective interests', in which people's interests are defined by virtue of the objective social structures in which they are located; with the result that these agents have no role in defining their interests.[21] The problem with this structuralist conception of class is that it has no viable theory of social action.[22] Within this formulation people act in class ways because it is rational for them to pursue the interests specified by their class location. Lockwood shows that this conception depends on theoretical assumptions which must view all social action as instrumental. People pursue their maximum self-interest as defined by their class position. In this case there are clear problems in explaining the types of non-instrumental action which appear all too commonly in social life. Furthermore, rational choice theorists argue that a 'free-rider problem' emerges, whereby instrumentally rational individuals will tend not to act collectively to pursue their general class interests, since this will entail individual costs without the guarantee of any resulting benefits.[23] A manual worker pursuing his or her maximum self-interest will not go on strike, since he or she will gain anyway if the strike is successful and will not have to expend any effort or lose any pay in the process. In other words, class-based collective action cannot be explained rationally!

In contrast to dilemmas such as these, Thompson was able to explore the cultural dimensions of class in ways which avoided such reductive assumptions, and was more sensitive to anthropological perspectives which recognised the contextual nature of rationality and belief systems. Particularly celebrated was Thompson's demonstration[24] that food riots in eighteenth-century Britain were not automatic responses to economic privation, but could only be understood in relation to a cultural framework of the 'moral economy'. Only where certain embedded assumptions about the proper handling of food shortages were violated by the authorities did collective protest result. Thompson also showed how working-class formation in Britain needed to be interpreted against a pre-existing cultural legacy, one which celebrated the liberties of the 'Free born Englishman'.[25] It can be argued therefore, that Thompson's approach seems more in keeping with the structurationist approach to social science recently popularised by Giddens.[26] Rather than attempting to isolate structure from agency, Giddens proposes that the two are inextricably intertwined, since structures – understood as sets of rules and resources – are drawn upon by agents, who in this process may transform or reproduce structures.[27]

Even from this brief account it can be seen that the great virtue of Thompson's approach was to develop the analysis of class as a historical subject, and indeed the Thompsonian influence on the development of social history and historical sociology in the 1960s and 1970s was profound. It is a project which remains a vital one to defend and develop. However, it would be foolish to assume that there are no problems with the class formation approach, and I now want to consider some of these. First, although the concept of class formation seems historically sensitive, its terminology continues to imply a certain evolutionary process – a sort of weak historicism. This may appear a surprising criticism given that Thompson appeared to offer a riposte to evolutionary approaches to social class which claimed that classes would develop at given times owing to long-term economic and social trends. Much of Thompson's ire was directed at functionalist sociologists who claimed that industrial societies produced class divisions as an inevitable or natural process: none the less, a certain weak historicism still pervaded Thompson's class formation perspective. Classes were still seen as the 'normal' social groupings of capitalist industrial society, and attention remained focused on the transition from feudal, agrarian social relations to capitalist industrial relations.[28] Although this process was conceived as a complex and drawn out one, none the less, there is a tendency to assume that once a class is 'made', its basic character is given. Thus Thompson argued that the period between 1780 and 1830 saw the 'making' of the English working class, and suggested that this making culminated in the Chartist movement of the later 1830s and 1840s. However, this left open the question as to how the subsequent decline of working-class radicalism could be explained, and why there was such a time lag between the making of the working class and the rise of the labour movement from the later nineteenth century. This issue was to pre-occupy British social historians for much of the 1970s and 1980s.[29] Certainly Eric Hobsbawm's early work continued to be centred on exploring the 'once-only' transition, the slow process by which workers with pre-industrial customs became manual workers who had learnt 'the rules of the game'.

Similarly, although Thompson himself was scathing towards writers who thought there was one 'proper' form of class formation, there remains a tendency to see class formation as a 'staged' process, leading from 'lower' (economic) to 'higher' (political) type of class formation, with some sort of a radical working class being the culmination of the class formation process. This can be seen in Katznelson and Zolberg's sophisticated approach to class formation which distinguishes between class as structure, as ways of life, dispositions and collective action.[30] As Katznelson himself recognises,[31] this continues to loosely draw upon a distinction between class-in-itself and class-for-itself. In fact it seems important to recognise that class formation is a more contingent and reversible process than these accounts suggest. Historiographical debate since Thompson and Hobsbawm has tried to deal with this by elaborating and extending the terminology of 'making'. In a particularly well-known article Gareth Stedman Jones argued that in the later Victorian period the working class was 'remade', away from the radical, artisanal class discussed by Thompson, and into a more passive, consumerist class which was to predominate afterwards.[32] However, if classes can be 'remade' in what sense is it useful to invoke the language of making, which implies a degree of fixity and permanence to the 'made' product? Does the remaking of a class mean a total remaking or rather a reworking?

More generally, the conceptual vocabulary of class formation itself needs improvement. In particular, it is important to examine not just the external conditions which may undermine class formation, but also to tease out some of the contradictions and tensions inherent within specific types of class formation, in order to show how it may actually have been difficult to sustain class mobilisation over the longer term. It is noteworthy that many of the historical arguments brought to bear on the decline of class conflict in the years after 1850 are remarkably unsubtle, and lack the historical sophistication which Thompson brought to bear on its 'making'. Thus Foster attributed the decline of working-class radicalism to the 'bribes' by which the ruling classes bought off the labour aristocracy, who subsequently abandoned radicalism.[33] Other historians simply point to the general social and economic improvement evident after mid century.[34] The decline of class formation has largely been attributed to the external conditions affecting classes rather than to any intrinsic features of class formation itself. This is something to which my account below suggests an alternative.

This points to another general problem, that the very concept of class formation seems evocative but vague.[35] Of course, as I have suggested above, this might be seen in some respects as a strength, since it manages to escape some of the problems in the structuralist approach to class, but the question remains: how do we know when a class is formed? Thompson gives no clear answer to this question, relying on detailed narratives of radical beliefs, revolutionary situations, and case studies of specific occupational 'experiences'. It is therefore quite possible to detect wishful thinking and a degree of working-class romanticism behind some of the socio-historical approaches to class.[36] This is one reason why in recent years Thompson's work can be reinterpreted as testimony to a populist, rather than a class-based radical tradition.[37] Since it is not clear how Thompson might distinguish the two, it is understandable that much the same evidence can be used for different ends. Given this ambiguity, the recent work of Stedman Jones and Joyce can be seen as an important attempt to take the issue of definition more seriously.[38] For both these writers classes can only be said to exist meaningfully when the terms are used in language and discourse. Now although this formulation carries its own problematic baggage (see Kirk, this volume), it does at least offer more distinct criteria for judging the existence of class than is possible within the rather loose framework offered by Thompson.

Finally, because the notion of class formation was designed to explore the historicity, or temporality, of class, it does not seem well disposed to explore the role of *space* in class formation. Thompson, notoriously, took examples of working-class radicalism willy-nilly from across England, building up his story of the making of an 'English' working class on the basis of these disparate local examples. Since Thompson, historians have been more circumspect and have tended to offer detailed case studies of specific towns and cities, even though these are often presented as offering more general implications. Indeed, in recent historiography it has become increasingly clear that the relationship between space and class is fundamental to the conceptualisation of class formation itself. Thus historians emphasising the persistence of aristocratic or 'gentlemanly' power in Britain have emphasised the imperial bases of their hegemony.[39] Others have shown how aristocratic influence was based in particular locations such as the south-east of England or in the West End of London.[40] Meanwhile, historians who are critical of the new orthodoxy which stresses aristocratic persistence, such as Gunn, Morris Davidoff and Hall or Koditschek[41] have emphasised the significance of the new middle classes by turning their attention to the new urban areas of Manchester, Leeds, Birmingham or Bradford. Thus, arguments about the social importance of the new middle classes is linked to claims about the relative importance of various cities in Victorian Britain. Furthermore, from the 1970s studies of the working class increasingly encompassed a local dimension, frequently being case studies of specific industrial areas which repudiated attempts to cover the entire nation, as was the case in E.P. Thompson's work (see the discussion in Savage).[42] Working-class formation has increasingly been explored in its local context. In short, the question of class formation in recent British historiography has increasingly become tied up with the questions of space, locality, territory, urbanism and empire. None the less, it is interesting to recognise that it is rare indeed for historians to explicitly bring out the spatial implications of their arguments (for an exception see Smith).[43]

I will suggest that the problems I have specified in the 'class formation' approach – its weak historicism; its problems in handling the 'break-up' as well as the 'rise' of class; its vagueness as to terms; and its inattention to space – can be remedied together. That is to say a greater awareness of the spatial dimension of class may give us a more precise way of thinking about class formation and may offer a way of sensitising us to the unmaking of class. This will indeed be the contention of this chapter. I begin by clarifying terms.

Conceptualising class formation

Let me first try to deal with the looseness of the term class formation. Most generally class formation can best be understood as the creation of classes as 'social collectivities'. This view owes something to the way in which Weberians explore the 'boundedness' of social groups, but its main claim suggests that classes do not just exist structurally, but need to exist in a sense which is socially meaningful to people themselves.[44] This is still rather vague: how do we know when a social collectivity exists? How collective do social collectivities need to be? And in what ways do social collectivities become involved in political action? Let me pursue this issue by considering some of the main theoretical approaches to the study of class formation.

One way of thinking about class formation is that developed by the American Marxist sociologist E.O. Wright. Wright suggests that class formation is the 'actual structure of social relations within a class' and he argues that these are determined as a result of structural class capacities and organisational class capacities.[45] The former are elements of capitalist society which allow workers to be unified, while the latter refers to organisational links which can be established. In the former case Wright points to two main forces which may unify the working class: through community processes and through economic processes which produce the 'collective worker' (notably through mass production). There are two problems here: first the emphasis is rather formalistic, in that it rests upon the delineation of formal sites in which individual class members may congregate. There is no necessary reason why workers in large factories might engage collectively with their colleagues, and indeed the evidence points rather towards the reverse (a point which Wright acknowledges). Secondly, it is possible to dispute the logic of Wright's account of communities and class formation. As the anthropologist A.P. Cohen has argued, communities actually create divisions between 'insiders' and 'outsiders', and while they might unite members of a class within one 'community', they may unite it against other working-class communities elsewhere.[46] Exactly the same point may be made about sites of mass production; they may actually create new types of intra-class division (between factories, or skilled trades) as much as overcome them. Further, Wright's distinction between structural and organisational class capacities entails distinguishing between the two sorts of phenomena (social relations from collective organisation and political mobilisation) which the concept of class formation might be supposed to illuminate.

The problem here, that of the relationship between social history and the 'political', is long-standing.[47] However, by simply claiming that there are two types of class formation, one concerned with social relations, the other with organisation, Wright simply reproduces this dualism by definitional fiat, without giving any conceptual indications of how the two might relate to each other.

A very similar problem arises in Lash and Urry's account of the way that social and cultural resources can be used to sustain collective action.[48] They suggest that organisational and discursive resources may be important in allowing the 'free rider' problem to be overcome, and collective mobilisation to be facilitated. However, like Wright, the distinction between these two resources disables any serious attempt to explore their interlinkage. Further, although their suggestion that discourses have an autonomous role in facilitating social action is attractive, yet it is also rather unclear why resulting forms of social identity should be seen in terms of class, rather than in terms of the discourse which is facilitating the collective action in question.[49] An interesting historical example of the problem which this might lead to is Epstein's claim that early nineteenth-century English radicals used the 'liberty cap' as a badge (a resource) to create a sense of unity and to identify themselves as a distinctly working-class (rather than middle-class) radical group.[50] Yet as Joyce rightly argues, this usage of the concept of class is entirely gratuitous, for there is no intrinsic reason why a badge should have a distinct class connotation.[51]

The approach to class formation offered by the sociologist John Goldthorpe also covers similar tracks.[52] Goldthorpe distinguishes between 'demographic' class formation and 'socio-political' class formation. He argues that classes are 'demographically' formed when they are self-recruiting. If a particular social class recruits extensively from other classes, then it is likely to be composed of heterogenous types of people, with the result that it is less likely to engage in collective action than if it is very largely self-recruited (see the discussion in Savage).[53] Even if there is a high rate of self-recruitment, Goldthorpe emphasises that it does not follow that collective action need ensue, since 'socio-political' class formation cannot be read off from demographic class formation alone. Political organisation and cultural mobilisation play an independent role.[54] Admittedly, having laid out this 'escape route', Goldthorpe does occasionally suggest that demographic class formation does explain some forms of political orientations and outlooks, for instance in his argument that the middle classes in contemporary Britain are politically divided because of the diversity of their backgrounds, while there is a much more 'mature' working-class culture based on the fact that most manual workers come from manual worker backgrounds.

The advantage of seeing class formation in Goldthorpe's demographic terms is that it can be measured and studied in more rigorous ways than are evident in other types of studies of class formation. The downside however, is that by distinguishing 'socio-political' class formation from 'demographic' class formation, Goldthorpe appears to concede at the outset that the implications of self-recruitment for other aspects of class formation are at best tangential. Indeed the processes relating self-recruitment to political mobilisation are by no means clear. Historians such as Stone have argued that the resilience of the English aristocracy, its ability to remain powerful and hegemonic, actually rested on the way it was open to outsiders.[55] This is a rather different logic to that presented by Goldthorpe who sees strong class formation as being based upon closure to outsiders.[56] On the other hand there is other evidence to support Goldthorpe's claims. Savage and Miles show that the growing political presence of the working class in late Victorian and Edwardian Britain did appear to take place at the same time that the working class became more demographically mature.[57] This is not the moment to pursue this matter. The important point is simply that the elaboration of the precise relationship between social mobility and class formation remains an open one which does not as yet yield a distinct approach to the subject. The main problem is clearly stated: existing accounts of class formation have found no plausible ways of relating class formation to collective action and political mobilisation.

At this point it is helpful to look at the issue of how social collectivities are formed from a different angle, by introducing a different body of sociological work – network theory.[58] Network analysts argue against the view that an individual's structural location at any one point in time has any intrinsic social significance. Rather, it is the networks in which people are embedded which explain how collectivities form as they chart how individuals are able to draw on contacts and mobilise resources. Only when social networks link people together can collective action occur. Network analysts have developed various techniques for exploring the types of contacts evident between people, examining how cliques and cores can be distinguished, and so forth. While this approach can be rather formalistic in that it is more interested in the existence of a measurable tie between two people rather than in its precise nature or quality, it contains valuable insights for us to reflect on.

The important point here is that network theorists have drawn attention to the different and possibly contradictory ways in which networks operate, and by this step have begun to show how we might think about class formation in more subtle ways than simply its existence or non-existence. Here I simplify network theory radically simply to distinguish two ways of thinking about networks. One way is to explore the density of networks (see Scott, 1991). Here interest resides in examining the extent to which a given group of individuals have contacts with each other. If a number of individuals all know each other then density is very high, and one might assume that it is easier for a sense of common identity to arise and hence for that group to become a 'social collectivity'. It is relatively easy to see how class formation might be seen in network terms as taking place when there are dense intra-class networks but weak or non-existent inter-class networks between individuals in different social classes.

However, another way of looking at class formation is possible. This is indebted to Granovetter's well-known study of how individuals find jobs, and in particular his recognition of the 'strength of weak ties'.[59] Granovetter means by this that those people who find it easiest to gain knowledge about job vacancies need not be those in small dense networks, but those who have a large number of contacts whom they know slightly but who might pass on information about job openings. Clearly the more people one knows, the more likely you are to get some sort of relevant information, whereas knowing a few people very well (having a dense network) may not be very helpful. The density of ties is not so relevant as their range. Thus, adopting Granovetter's reasoning, the British upper-class 'old boy network' works not by calling upon the help of a few close relatives or friends one knows very well, but by invoking the help, when necessary, of one of a large number of minor acquaintances, perhaps made at public school, university or in the gentleman's clubs.

This is a very suggestive opposition which offers an interesting way of thinking about the complex dynamics of class formation. Class formation has a dual dynamic. First it involves the construction of social networks of wide range, linking members of that class across different local sites – workplaces, residential neighbourhoods, leisure venues, and so forth. In these situations information can be passed on, organisations built, ideas pooled, mobilisation co-ordinated. This perspective is congruent with the historical sociologist Michael Mann's insistence that social class is based on 'extensive' ties, in contrast to the 'segmental' character of non-class social relations.[60] Secondly, class formation also involves the construction of dense ties which allows the forging of solidaristic and communal identities over time and in the absence of formal organisation. Here, classes can draw upon 'community', face-to-face relationships, which are conducive to social solidarity. The possible differences between these two types of ties has recently been examined by the historical sociologist Gould in his study of the Paris Commune.[61]

Gould argues that the Communards drew partly on dense neighbourhood networks, but also that they were able to collaborate at an inter-
neighbourhood level, because organisational activists were recruited
from different neighbourhood networks and were able to fuse separate
neighbourhood activities together. However, while in this case the two
networks reinforced each other it is equally possible for them to pull
against each other. The existence of dense ties of localism may work
against the construction of wider ranging ties, while an individual's
involvement in wide-ranging networks may preclude them from the
dense local world of the neighbourhood. These are empirical questions.
However, we do at least have a suggestion as to how the networks may
affect processes of class formation, and also how the spatial range of networks should be important focuses of inquiry.

Spatiality and class formation in British history

My argument is that the distinction between networks which are dense
and those with large ranges clarifies the contradictory ways in which
space is implicated in class formation. I proceed to develop this argument
by trying to indicate how this offers an improvement on the confusion
and ambiguity which is present in existing historical accounts of the role
of space in class formation. I have argued elsewhere (Savage, 1993) that
it is important to consider places not simply as sites in which class formation occurs, but as themselves constituents in class formation. Places are
not just passive backdrops to social process but are actively involved in
the constitution and construction of social identities. However, while this
view of space and class is helpful, it still remains rather vague and elusive.
In what precise ways is space involved in the construction of social identities? Isn't there a danger that space is given too much importance, in
ways suggested by geographers who talk of the problems of spatial
fetishism whereby space – understood here simply as a physical,
Euclidian entity – is held to cause social phenomena?[62]

Within existing historiography space has usually been handled in two
contrasting ways. Most commonly, the detailed study of a particular
place has been a methodological procedure. As I have argued elsewhere,[63] within this tradition places were mainly seen as 'case study
areas'.[64] A detailed study of a particular town or city allowed in-depth
research which, through the study of a geographically delimited area,
allowed complex connections between local economies, cultures, institutional frameworks and political movements to be explored. Support for
this 'case study' approach was evident as early as Briggs's[65] clarion call
for local studies of Chartism, but this approach reached a new level of

sophistication with John Foster's (1974) comparison of class-consciousness and social structure in three contrasting industrial towns: South Shields, Northampton and Oldham. Foster used case studies of these towns to show that revolutionary class-consciousness (which he claimed existed only in Oldham) was due not to extreme poverty, but to patterns of residential segregation and forms of political leadership. Although Foster's arguments have been empirically questioned and do not now carry conviction,[66] what remains interesting about his account is its methodology, its reliance on local case studies and the use of the comparative method.

Since Foster's day the use of local case studies has become even more widespread. In the 1970s a series of monographs on the labour aristocracy explicitly used local research on Edinburgh and Kentish London.[67] In the 1980s came a wave of studies on the labour movement in different localities[68] and also studies of the middle classes in various cities.[69] The proliferation of urban history, especially as manifested in the pages of the *Urban History Yearbook*, also popularised the local case study as a key research instrument. However, much of this work, while explicitly using local case studies, was not especially interested in how spatiality affected local social relations *per se*. The local was a methodological rather than a substantive focus. In fact space was usually allotted a rather insignificant role. Places were backdrops, or frames, in which the historian could trace certain processes of interest to him or her and they were not important in their own right (this argument is developed in Savage, 1993). However, in the course of the 1980s a number of historians and historical geographers began, sometimes haltingly, to develop a rather different approach to class and space. Here, the stress was not on a place as a case study area, where class formation might or might not occur, but on place as a constituent of class formation. Rather than place being a backdrop it was itself seen as playing a vital role in determining the extent, nature and form of class formation.

The central concept used in this tradition is the notion that places are important for class formation because they become the habitats of particular social groups. This notion implicitly draws upon the idea that the density of contacts within a given local arena are significant, and therefore draws upon one of the network concepts I have elaborated above. This 'habitat' view is actually a very old idea which has resurfaced, in one form or another, for over 150 years. Its earliest elaboration is found in the writings of Victorian social commentators who became concerned at the way that segregation allowed the social classes to live in different parts of the city, so becoming self-contained and – in the case of parts of the labouring poor – potentially dangerous and subversive groups. This concern is evident in Engels's account of Manchester and Salford in

1844, and the persistence of these concerns has been demonstrated by Stedman Jones's account of *Outcast London*, and more recently by Walkowitz's study of the *City of Dreadful Delight*.[70] In both these cases, the authors have shown how Victorian middle-class men were concerned that the changing social geography of London allowed greater separation of social groups with the result that social threats would be intensified.

In the course of the twentieth century this notion has been developed and refined, but has not, in its fundamentals, been significantly revised, and it remains the most common way for historians to examine how class formation is a spatial process. The Chicago School of urban sociology, the key influence on urban sociology from the early 1920s, developed this perspective by championing the idea of 'human ecology'. Here it was argued that just as plant species were located in their 'natural' habitats, so, within cities, different social groups tended to find their own habitats through a process of social segregation. As particular social groups established their own habitats, so distinct sub-cultures emerged. Although the theoretical framework of human ecology has been widely criticised,[71] the notion of social segregation remains central within urban history and geography (see the careful ruminations of Dennis, 1984).

Yet while the idea of place as habitat is commonplace it is also highly problematic. The fundamental question raised is how precisely social segregation is supposed to affect the social and political outlooks of various social groups. The most usual claim here is a version of Kerr and Siegel's arguments about the significance of the 'isolated mass'.[72] Kerr and Siegel argued that the strike proneness of coal miners was due to the fact that they lived in isolated groups, largely cut off from other social contacts, with little prospect of social or geographical mobility (see also Church et al., 1991; Gilbert, 1992).[73] Although subject to occasional attack,[74] the idea frequently resurfaces in one form or another. This is where the central ambiguity arises, known to us today as what might be termed 'Cannadine's dilemma'. In an influential article Cannadine suggested that social segregation had indeterminate implications for class-consciousness, and by implication, class conflict.[75] Cannadine's point was that social segregation could lead to class conflict as social classes, each in their own habitat, developed their own cultures with the result that they became antagonistic to each other. Equally, however, it might lead to class collaboration, since the separation of the classes might reduce contact and tension between them, drawing the working-class community inward, making them more concerned with status tensions within their own ranks. In short there is no obvious relationship between patterns of class identity, collective action, and segregation.

In so far as there is a 'conventional wisdom' on this point, it would appear to favour the idea that workers in self-enclosed communities, where dense social ties can easily be sustained, are better able to facilitate collective action than workers in large-scale urban areas where there is considerable population turnover, and a higher degree of anonymity and isolation. MacIntyre's study of 'Little Moscows' shows that in the inter-war years a militant political culture organised around the Communist Party could be created in a few isolated industrial villages, usually based around a single industry such as mining or textiles.[76] Such villages were very little different from any number of other settlements which saw very little Communist presence. MacIntyre shows how the isolation of these villages from the outside world allowed the Communist Party to come to prominence, constructing themselves as the local party of government by playing a key role in local affairs. In these situations the Communist Party was able to draw upon local loyalties and identification and present themselves as the natural party of local government.

By contrast, a number of historians have pointed to the weakness of the organised working class in large metropolitan areas where there tends to be high population turnover. Hobsbawm pointed out that early London trade unions identified with local areas rather than the city of London as a whole.[77] Savage and Miles have developed this argument by suggesting that Victorian cities in general proved to be difficult recruiting grounds for trade unions and left wing politics because of their weakly developed working-class neighbourhood structures.[78] Similarly Gould has shown that when it was possible for workers to unite on a wide-scale urban basis, as in the case of the Paris Commune, this was due to the way that different neighbourhood networks were allied to each other through the role of metropolitan associations and institutions.[79]

However, it would be too simple to think that working-class mobilisation is facilitated by the creation of small, dense communities rather than large urban conglomerations. There is contrary evidence which argues for the political passivity of working-class communities. Consider, for instance Robert Roberts's account of Edwardian Salford, which affirms its village-like character but also insists on how such isolation reduced militancy by lowering the horizons of its inhabitants.[80] In the terms introduced by Runciman, the reference groups of these workers are actually limited by being cut off, so making them less militant.[81] There is also evidence that class formation depends upon breaking localist ties and developing contacts over a wider scale. Consider Joyce's account of Victorian textile towns. Drawing upon Marshall's idea of the 'factory colony', Joyce argued that the typical pattern of urban growth was based not in large anonymous cities, but in self-contained factory colonies where workers lived in close proximity to their places of work and where employers could exert their influence over workers. Only with the break-down of the cohesiveness and isolation of such places – which Joyce sees as the product of mass transportation and the bicycle – did workers begin to question the existing order and engage in socialist politics. 'What was happening around the turn of the century was that the scope of people's lives grew larger, expanding as the towns and cities themselves grew larger. The old (i.e. paternalist) order had flowered in a culture marked by the concrete particular, the local view, and personal participation . . .'[82]

In fact Joyce may have correctly understood the role of the spatial dynamic while misunderstanding the chronology of worker militancy in Lancashire. For most of the Victorian period cotton workers were not especially deferential[83] and indeed were among the first group of industrial workers to see widespread unionisation.[84] It is however interesting to note that this unionisation involved breaking the specifically neighbourhood ties emphasised by Joyce. Unionisation was based on the creation of initially urban, and then Lancashire-wide allegiances, exemplified above all by the elaboration of trade union organisation at greater spatial scales. The development of wage lists for particular districts, which began in cotton weaving areas in the 1850s and cotton spinning areas slightly later, was an exemplification of this.[85] In short, class mobilisation was as much dependent upon the stretching of worker ties over broader spatial areas as the density of ties within neighbourhoods.

This same point arises in other cases. The South Wales mining districts were one of the most militant and combative in Britain. Their degree of support for the Labour Party and for Communist and left wing causes is well known.[86] Both Gilbert and MacIntyre relate this to the close local and community ties nourished there – the close relationship between pit and village, and the fact that absentee coal owners allowed an autonomous working-class culture to flourish.[87] Yet, as Cooke has argued, what is also striking about the South Wales case was the way in which the miners constructed an organisational infrastructure which linked different self-contained communities, especially through the South Wales Miners Federation, but also through the chapels.[88]

A final example is especially instructive. The changing nature of class relations on the railways from the end of the Victorian period represented, in microcosm, many of the broader changes taking place in British society at the time. For much of the period until the mid 1880s it had proved difficult to establish trade unions, largely due to the hostility of railway companies to the idea of collective bargaining and union representation.[89] The first major wave of railway unionisation took place alongside the growth of the 'new unionism' of the later 1880s. Union membership stabilised in the 1890s before rising again early in the twentieth century, and the industrial unrest on the railways in the years before the war forced employers to concede the unions' right to collective bargaining in 1909. In only a few years the railways shifted from being recognisably 'Victorian' in their labour relations, insisting on their sole right to deal with their workers, to being archetypes of the new bureaucratic employers who operated collective bargaining procedures. The railway workers themselves became bastions of the labour movement, playing a central role in national and local Labour Party politics, often providing the backbone of party organisations in those areas lacking unionised industries and Labour traditions.

Yet if workers on the railways played a central role in working-class formation, they hardly demonstrate the spatial characteristics of mining communities or other 'single-industry' areas. Outside the railway workshop towns such as Swindon or Crewe, railway workers were spatially scattered and could not form 'occupational communities'. Many travelled routinely in the course of their work, as engine drivers or guards, and a considerable number were moved by their employers to different parts of their network. The creation of railway unionism was itself dependent upon overcoming strong localist ties. As Bagwell recounts, in the 1860s and 1870s a major stumbling block to unionisation was the hostility between branches, and especially the reluctance of local branches to concentrate funds and administration in London. In 1874 a new centralising General Secretary took over at the head of the Amalgamated Society of Railway Servants. In response:

> Pontypool and Reading Branches refused to recognise his authority and were contemplating legal proceedings . . . Cambridge branch refused to remit any funds to Head Office, few branches confined their expenditure to the amounts allowed by the Society's rules and one hundred branches had not sent in their balance sheets from the previous year.[90]

Railway unionism depended upon being able to overcome such localism and create an institutional network allowing connections between places to be forged. The processes which facilitated this included the growing size of railway companies as they merged and the practice of railway companies to move their workers between stations or depots; but ultimately it depended upon the work of union activists, the development of institutional frameworks transcending particular places, and the cultural activities of the union; such as the creation of the newspaper, *Railway Review*, in 1873.

We can see therefore that the major problem with the notion of places as habitats is that dense ties do not in themselves appear to be enough to sustain class formation at the level of political mobilisation. It is therefore not surprising that Dennis could only emphasise the indeterminacy of the role of social segregation in his comprehensive survey of issues in urban historical geography.[91] It seems that the density of intra-class ties in an enclosed spatial area is not in itself enough to guarantee that class formation occurs. Rather, I have suggested that political mobilisation depends upon the creation of links between specific places. I now develop this point by considering how this argument might throw light on the general issue of class relationships.

Networks, class relations and power

I have argued that class formation depends critically not just upon the density of social networks but upon their range. Any long-ranging social networks depend upon a social, technical and cultural infrastructure which permits the maintenance of contacts beyond the 'face-to-face' level. However, as Dennis Smith has suggested in his book, *Conflict and Compromise: Class Formation in English Society 1830–1914*, different social classes have differing propensities to be able to establish such contacts, and class conflict partly takes place over the very constructing of such infrastructures. Smith distinguished between neighbourhood, 'face-to-face' networks; urban networks; and those at the level of the 'County'. Smith pointed out that these tended to be associated with particular social classes: the neighbourhood with the working class, the urban with the middle classes, and the county with the aristocracy; although he also emphasised that classes might try and mobilise at more than one of these spatial levels, and that the resulting resolutions might have important implications for social change. Smith's formulations suggest that social classes may be differently endowed with the ability to establish wide-ranging social networks, and that this fact may have considerable importance in explaining the general patterns of their class formation.

Before developing this point it is useful to clarify its importance through a brief digression. It has been argued by Anthony Giddens that a central feature of modern societies is the way that social relations are 'stretched' over time and space, with the result that it becomes possible to engage in interaction with people who are not actually present in a face-to-face setting.[92] Furthermore, it can be argued that it is those social groups which are able to stretch themselves between places, and who are able to draw upon institutional and technological means of establishing networks on wider spatial scales, who are more successful in establishing their social presence and in securing hegemony. Successful class formation involves the mobilisation of a dispersed, scattered population, and therefore it is those groups who are able to construct networks linking them to people in other, non-proximal places, who are best able to mobilise and organise to defend and advance their interests.

Giddens's point has interesting implications for considering the distinctive role of the British aristocracy in the nineteenth century.[93] The English landed classes were able to maintain their economic dominance until at least the 1870s.[94] The economic basis for this aristocratic endurance rested on rentier incomes, boosted by the enthusiasm of aristocrats to find new avenues for investment, such as in urban property development.[95] The commanding presence of the English aristocracy in social, political and cultural life endured, even as the agricultural depression from the 1870s and the rise of more specialised commercial interests began to erode their economic dominance.

This relatively cohesive class formation which the aristocracy were able to maintain was related to the sophisticated spatial networks which the landed and gentlemanly classes were able to draw upon. Particularly important here, as Davidoff has shown, is the way that etiquette and genteel conduct involved a complex spatial network (see more generally Elias).[96] The consolidation of the 'London season', which coincided with the sitting of Parliament, saw notables from different geographical areas brought together into a co-ordinated social network based on balls, formal visits and club activities. The dispersal of these dignitaries at other times of the year also allowed them to maintain contacts with the specific local power bases, and to engage fully in 'County' activities. Davidoff remarks, 'this seasonal migration . . . was a crucial factor in the continuing hold of these (aristocratic) groups over the leadership of a society undergoing such rapid change.'[97] She shows that as the century wore on the spatial network became more complex with different geographical locations playing a distinct role in the co-ordination of élite activities. Major country house parties away from London would be occasions to cement marriage alliances and appoint magistrates; the Scottish shooting season from 12 August would entail a significant migratory wave to the country houses of Scotland, and there were also important resort or spa towns which might also see further aristocratic congregation. Etiquette, it seems, was a ceremonial activity, a form of 'stretching' ritual behaviour over space and time by formalising the sorts of demeanour expected of nobles in particular forms of conviviality. Etiquette was taught and formalised in books, allowing it to be taken out of particular spatial confines and making it possible for members of the landed classes to know how to relate to each other in a great variety of settings.

The important feature, therefore, of 'gentlemanly' class formation was the extent to which its everyday routines of life and leisure enabled it to 'stretch' itself over space. Contrast this with the main forms of Victorian middle-class sociability. The middle classes were able to form cohesive networks in particular cities but were, by and large, unable to consolidate these at a national or even 'County' level.[98] This partly reflected the nature of British industrial growth, since specific industries tended to be located in distinct geographical areas which limited the extent to which merchants, industrialists and associated professionals needed to sustain business contacts on a broader scale. Instead the middle classes developed extensive civic networks, related to their crucial role in building, maintaining and ordering the new industrial and commercial towns. They helped construct an urban infrastructure of libraries, town halls, public parks, and so forth, which as Morris has shown, played a major role in the elaboration of an urban civic realm.[99] These helped to 'define' the city's identity while also providing it with a middle-class stamp. Rather than being a middle-class territory because of the numerical density of the middle classes – as the 'habitat' approach might have it – the crucial forces here were the symbolic and cultural activities of the middle classes who constructed their own hegemony through their role in defining a 'civic project'.

Morris has also explored the role of voluntary associations in middle-class sociability. Voluntary associations had begun to expand in the eighteenth century and proliferated in the nineteenth century around a remarkable range of charitable, religious, political and leisure pursuits. Morris points out that some of these voluntary associations (for instance the Bible and missionary societies) were branches of national associations and might therefore have played a role in articulating a local within a national consciousness.[100] However, a large number of voluntary associations were specifically local organisations, (many were key service providers such as the voluntary hospitals) or were only loosely co-ordinated beyond their specific urban milieux.

Morris argues that these voluntary associations were of critical importance in allowing a middle class otherwise divided by politics, occupation and religion to find common cause. They helped police gender divisions within the middle classes, since it was largely men who were involved in their affairs, with women being relegated to either a small number of specifically female organisations or to subordinate, servicing roles with the larger organisations (see generally Davidoff and Hall).[101] In short, middle-class networks were extremely well-designed to permit contacts at the urban level, but tended not to stretch beyond them.

The contrast with the working class is very important. For it can be argued that the working classes have historically been much more divided between different types of networks. As Eley points out in his reworking of Thompson's arguments, the working class played a crucial role in defining a public realm in early nineteenth-century Britain which allowed them to become key political actors.[102] This public realm was related to the construction of wide-ranging networks of migrant preachers and speakers, to the activities of early trade societies, to the practice of circulating chap-books, pamphlets and newspapers, and also to the considerable degree of spatial mobility exhibited by workers of the time. The case of Chartism reveals very interestingly the extent to which these wide-ranging networks were essential to the construction of a combative political movement (see generally Pickering).[103]

Chartism was distinctive first in having the means to publicise itself nationally through a remarkably sophisticated communication network, especially that based on the *Northern Star*. This paper was able to outdo its rivals and succeed in establishing itself as the 'voice' of Chartism by managing to surpass the local appeals of radical papers such as the *London Dispatch*, *Manchester and Salford Advertiser*, and *Birmingham Journal*. As D. Thompson has shown, the *Northern Star* rested on a truly remarkable network, by which the paper was circulated to agents in different towns and villages throughout the country, and then local beerhouses, subscribers and coffee house proprietors would pick up their copies.[104] By being a stamped, and hence legal paper, the *Northern Star* was able to draw on the most modern technologies allowing rapid spatial connections, notably the railway and Post Office distribution systems.

Secondly, and relatedly, leading Chartists were able to become national figures by going on speaking tours around the country. In this they followed in the footsteps of an established tramping tradition found, for instance, in Methodist and other religious groups, whereby leading figures would circulate around the country in order to preach. As D. Thompson shows, O'Connor's ability to become the unofficial Chartist leader followed his 1836 tour of Britain, when he spoke at Nottingham, Newcastle, Kilmarnock, Cannock, Leith, Edinburgh, Dundee, Dunfermline, Paisley, Halifax, Bradford, Hull, Burnley and Huddersfield. O'Connor was not alone, however, and the existence of the itinerant lecturer was a constant feature of the Chartist movement.[105]

Thirdly, Chartists were able to develop a series of political initiatives which enabled links to be made between people from different places. The most important of these were the national petitions, the Chartist convention of 1838 which had members from different localities, and then the more organised National Charter Association, with local branches, in the 1840s. These forms pioneered the regular, institutionalised forms of politics in which people in one area might know what was happening in another.

Of course Chartist networks were not perfect. They could not always co-ordinate their actions in different places. The failure of the Newport Rising in 1839 is a case in point. When 5 000 Chartists marched into Newport they appeared to hope that its seizure would be a sign to other Chartists to mobilise. In fact 20 000 other Chartists did not join them since they were still marching in the nearby hills, while Chartists elsewhere had no clear knowledge of what was intended.

Perhaps the most striking contrast with the aristocratic or middle-class networks discussed above is the fact that Chartist networks were mainly organised on a specifically institutional, political basis which made it difficult to sustain them if the movement met with political defeat, which is of course precisely what happened in 1848.[106] Further, as Driver points out in his study of the introduction of the New Poor Law, the period after the 1840s saw the considerable extension of central state networks:[107] but it is also important to point out that the wide-ranging Chartist and radical networks tended to be only weakly anchored in everyday cultural and social activities, in marked contrast to aristocratic practice, for example. Admittedly, in some areas Chartists did put down institutional roots in local social life (e.g. Epstein, 1982, on Nottingham),[108] but the fact that these initiatives were directly political always made it difficult to sustain them in times of political retreat. It was only in the years after 1850, and especially in the years after 1880 that large-scale, working-class networks began to be constructed in ways which more directly tapped a wide range of everyday practices and cultures. The development of Friendly Societies, Co-operative Societies and trade unions all led to the development of national organisations which were able to draw upon specific local activities and organisations.

Conclusion

Let me now draw the threads of my argument together. In the section 'Conceptualising class formation' of this chapter I showed that conceptional elaborations of the idea of class formation tended to distinguish 'socio-cultural' class formation from 'political' class formation without being able to establish clear links between them. In this chapter I suggest that this actually reflects the inherently 'Janus-headed' process of class formation. For class formation depends in some ways upon the creation of dense ties, while in other ways it needs the development of wide-ranging ties. It may be argued that the former is more important for the creation of distinctive class-based cultures and identities, while the latter is more important for organisational ties and political mobilisation. In this sense the use of network concepts and the recognition of the importance of space actually might clarify the reason for the distinctions used in existing work.

It should be clear from the above that the two types of class formation do not entail each other and indeed may in significant respects be in opposition to each other. This is particularly true, I have suggested, for the working class, where wide-ranging social ties are not constructed through everyday work or leisure-based interactions, as tended to be the case for the aristocracy. The hegemony of particular social classes rests to a large extent on their ability to be able to organise on broad spatial scales, and such is the nature of working-class labour markets, cultural and family life, that it tends to be difficult for them to 'compete' at this level. Among the working class the strength of the local face-to-face 'community' may work to the disadvantage of wider social ties, leading potentially to a cohesive social group but one which is weakly attached to its neighbours. On the other hand the construction of wide-ranging ties usually involves the elaboration of an organisational infrastructure, which may move the organisational activist away from the social and cultural world of his or her neighbour.

This perspective offers a new way of thinking about some familiar themes in labour and working-class history, for instance the possible divisions between activists and rank and file or between labour aristocrats and the rest of the working class and, indeed, between social and political history. Many debates about the working class have focused upon the politics, cultures and actions of specific categories of workers, defined either occupationally or by geographical area. However, by reformulating the issue to take the focus away from the culture and politics of specific categorical groups of workers, and placing it more on the types of social networks which workers in different times and places occupy, it is possible to allow questions to be posed without relying on an instrumental or reductionist approach to social explanation.

A further point is worth making here. The perspective outlined above may offer a new way of thinking about the significance of trade unions for working-class formation. Typically, the study of unions has been regarded as part of 'labour history', concerned with institutional practices which are remote from the social and cultural worlds of workers (see the discussion in Savage and Miles).[109] However, it may be argued that trade unions are important to the broader terrain of class formation, since historically they have been the major form which allowed the creation of wide-ranging ties (through regional and national union organisation, newspapers, etc.) alongside the dense ties in specific workplaces and communities. For this reason, it may well be correct to highlight the period at the end of the nineteenth century as being of particular importance for working-class formation.

However, this is not the point on which I wish to close. The main benefit of adopting a network perspective is that it allows us to move beyond ideas of classes being 'made' in some sort of definitive way. Rather, it places the emphasis on the fluid and dynamic nature of class formation in which two diverse processes constantly threaten to undercut the existence of classes as stable social collectivities. By doing this it can help to illuminate the very real ways in which class may matter historically in specific situations, as well as to recognise that classes are not things which necessarily have any pertinence to the analysis. It is therefore eminently possible to use the concept of class formation in ways which help explore the complexity of historical situations rather than reduce them to a neat formula.

Notes

1. Kaye, H. (1984) *The British Marxist Historians*, (overview), Oxford: Polity.
2. Dews, P. (1987) *The Logics of Disintegration*, London: Verso; Hunt, L. (ed.) (1990) *The New Cultural History*, Berkeley: University of California.
3. Reddy, W. (1984) *Money and Liberty in Western Europe*, Cambridge: Cambridge University Press; Furbank, P. (1985) *The Idea of Social Class*, Oxford: Oxford University Press; Hindess, B. (1987) *Politics and Class Analysis*, Oxford: Blackwell; Joyce, P. (1990) *Visions of The People*, Cambridge: Cambridge University Press.
4. Palmer, B. (1989) *Descent into Discourse: The Reification of Language in the Writing of Social History*, Philadelphia: Temple University Press; Wood, E. (1988) *The Retreat from Class: A New 'True' Socialism*, London: Verso.
5. Thrift, N. and Williams, P. (1987) *Space and Class*, London: Routledge; Dennis, R. (1984) *English Industrial Cities of the Nineteenth Century*, Cambridge: Cambridge University Press; Massey, D. (1984) *Spatial Divisions of Labour*, London: Methuen.
6. Marx, (1968) *Capital*, vol. 1, Harmondsworth: Penguin.
7. Marx, K. (1973) *Surveys from Exile*, Harmondsworth: Penguin.
8. Dobb, M. (1946) *The Transition from Feudalism to Capitalism*, London: Lawrence and Wishart; Hilton, R. (1971) *Bond Men Made Free*, London: Hutchinson; Thompson, E.P. (1963) *The Making of the English Working Class*, London: Gollancz; Hobsbawm, E. (1964) *Labouring Men*, London: Wiedenfeld and Nicholson.
9. Tilly, L. (1993) *Politics and Class in Milan 1881–1901*, New York: Oxford University Press.
10. Sewell, W.H. (1980) *Work and Revolution in France: The Languages of Labour from the Old Regime to 1848*, Cambridge: Cambridge University Press; Aminzade, R. (1981) *Class, Politics and Early Industrial Capitalism: A Study of Mid-Nineteenth Century Toulouse*, New York: Albany; Aminzade, R. (1993) *Ballots and Barricades: Class Formation and Republican Politics in France 1830–1871*, Princeton: Princeton University Press.
11. Katznelson, I. and Zolberg, A.R. (eds) (1986) *Working Class Formation*, Princeton: Princeton University Press.
12. Mann, M. (1986) *The Sources of Social Power, Vol. 1: A History of Power from The Beginning to 1760*, Cambridge: Cambridge University Press; Mann, M. (1993) *The Sources of Social Power, Vol. 2: The Rise of Classes and Nation States 1760–1914*, Cambridge: Cambridge University Press.

13. Abrams, P. (1980) *Historical Sociology*, Shepton Mallett: Open Books; Kaye, H.J. (1984) *The British Marxist Historians: An Introductory Analysis*, Oxford: Polity.
14. Schwarz, B. (1982) 'The "people" in history: The Communist Party Historians Group, 1946–56' in Centre for Contemporary Cultural Studies, *Making Histories: Studies in History Writing and Politics*, London: Hutchinson.
15. Thompson, E.P. (1965) 'The peculiarities of the English' in Miliband, R. and Saville, J. (eds) *The Socialist Register*, London: Merlin, p. 357.
16. Thompson, E.P. (1978) *The Poverty of Theory and Other Essays*, London: Merlin, p. 85.
17. Lockwood, D. (1958) *The Blackcoated Worker: A Study in Class Consciousness*, Oxford: Clarendon; Ossowski, S. (1963) *Class Structure in the Social Consciousness*, London: Routledge; Goldthorpe, J.H. and Lockwood, D. (1968/69) *The Affluent Worker in the Class Structure*, 3 vols, Cambridge: Cambridge University Press; Goldthorpe, J.H. (1980) *Social Mobility and the Class Structure in Modern Britain*, Oxford: Clarendon. Lockwood (1989) argues that the key moment in the development of this conventional approach to class was Lipset and Bendix's (1949) argument that once stripped of its historicist, teleological character, the study of the relationship between 'class structure' and 'class consciousness' could be conceived in ways that opened up the issue to empirical exploration.
18. Johnson, R. (1978) 'Edward Thompson, Eugene Genovese and socialist humanist history', *History Workshop Journal*, 6; Anderson, P. (1980) *Arguments within English Marxism*, London: Verso.
19. Abrams, P. (1980).
20. Poulantzas, N. (1973) *Political Power and Social Class*, London: Verso; Wright, E.O. (1979) *Class, Crisis and the State*, London: Verso.
21. Hindess, B. (1987) *Politics and Class Analysis*, Oxford: Blackwell.
22. Lockwood, D. (1988) 'The weakest link in the chain: Some remarks on the marxist theory of action' in Rose, D. (ed.) *Social Stratification and Economic Change*, London: Hutchinson.
23. Lash, S. and Urry, J. (1984) 'The new marxism of collective action', *Sociology*, vol. 18.
24. Thompson, E.P. (1971) 'The moral economy of the English crowd in the eighteenth century', *Past and Present*, 50.
25. Thompson, E.P. (1963).
26. Giddens, A. (1984) *The Constitution of Society*, Oxford: Polity.
27. Sewell, W. (1990) 'How classes are made: Critical reflections on E.P. Thompson's theory of working class formations' in Kaye, H. and McClelland, K. (eds) *E.P. Thompson: Critical Perspectives*, Oxford: Polity.
28. Kaye, H. (1984).
29. Hobsbawm, E. (1964); Foster, J. (1974) *Class Struggle and the Industrial Revolution*, London: Methuen; Gray, R. (1976) *The Labour Aristocracy in Victorian Edinburgh*, Oxford: Oxford University Press; Crossick, G. (1978) *An Artisan Elite in Victorian Society*, London: Croom Helm; Kirk, N. (1985) *The Growth of Working-Class Reformism in Mid-Victorian England*, London: Croom Helm; Savage, M. and Miles, A. (1994) *The Remaking of the British Working Class 1840–1940*, London: Routledge, ch. 1.

30. Katznelson, I. and Zolberg, A.R. (1986).
31. Katznelson, I. (1994) 'The bourgeois dimension: A provocation about institutions, politics and the future of labour history', *International Labor and Working-Class History*, Autumn, pp. 7–32.
32. Stedman Jones, G. (1974) 'The remaking of the English working class', *Journal of Social History*, 7, 4, Summer.
33. Foster, J. (1974).
34. Kirk, N. (1985), ch. 1.
35. Anderson, P. (1980).
36. See Calhoun, C. (1982) *The Question of Class Struggle*, Oxford: Blackwell, for a critique of Thompson which gains much of its force because of its ability to reinterpret what Thompson sees as class-based collective action as community-based politics.
37. Prothero, I. (1979) *John Gast*, Folkstone: Dawson; Reid, A. and Biagini, E. (1992) *Currents of Radicalism*, Cambridge: Cambridge University Press; Biagini, E. (1991) *Liberty, Retrenchment and Reform: Popular Liberalism in the Age of Gladstone*, Cambridge: Cambridge University Press.
38. Stedman Jones, G. (1983) *Languages of Class*, Cambridge: Cambridge University Press; Joyce, P. (1990).
39. Cain, P. and Hopkins, E. (1992) *British Imperialism 1600–1914*, London: Longman.
40. Rubinstein, W.D. (1981) *Men of Property*, London: Croom Helm; Atkins, P. (1990) 'The spatial configuration of class solidarity in London's west end', *Urban History Yearbook*, pp. 36–65.
41. Gunn, S. (1988) 'The failure of the Victorian middle class: A critique' in Wolff, J. and Seed, J. (eds) *The Culture of Capital*, Manchester: Manchester University Press; Morris, R.J. (1983) 'The middle classes and British towns and cities of the industrial revolution, 1780–1870' in Fraser, D. and Sutcliffe, A. (eds) *The Pursuit of Urban History*, London: Edward Arnold; Davidoff, L. and Hall, C. (1987) *Family Fortunes: Men and Women of the English Middle Class 1780–1850*, London: Hutchinson; Koditschek, T. (1990) *Class Formation and Urban and Industrial Society: Bradford 1750–1850*, Cambridge; Cambridge University Press.
42. Savage, M. (1993) 'Social class and urban history: Two paradigms', *Urban History*, 20, pp. 1, 61–77.
43. Gilbert, D. (1992) *Class, Community and Collective Action: Social Change in two British Coalfields, 1850–1926*, Oxford: Clarendon; Smith, D. (1982) *Conflict and Compromise: Class Formation in English Society 1830–1914*, London: Routledge.
44. This definition still raises complex issues. How are classes as social collectivities to be distinguished from other (non-class) collectivities? Elsewhere see Savage, M., Barlow, J., Dickens, P., and Fielding, A.J. (1992) *Property, Bureaucracy and Culture: Middle-Class Formation in Contemporary Britain*, London: Routledge. I have argued that the adoption of a critical realist account may offer one solution to this, since class collectivities can be defined when they draw upon exploitative social relationships. This raises further issues which cannot be discussed here however, but see the recent discussion in Butler and Savage (1995).
45. Wright, E.O. (1979) *Class, Crisis and the State*, London: Verso, p. 98; Wright, E.O. (1985) *Classes*, London: Verso.

46. Cohen, A.P. (1985) *Belonging*, Manchester: Manchester University Press.
47. Eley, G. and Nield, K. (1980) 'Why does social history ignore politics?', *Social History*, May, pp. 249–71; Stedman Jones, G. (1983); Katznelson, I. (1994).
48. Lash, S. and Urry, J. (1984).
49. To be fair to Lash and Urry, they are less concerned with the issue of class than with the general conditions allowing collective action itself.
50. Epstein, J. (1986) 'The cap of liberty', *Past and Present,* CXXII, February.
51. Joyce, P. (1990).
52. Goldthorpe, J.H. (1987) *Social Mobility and the Class Structure in Modern Britain*, Oxford: Clarendon.
53. Savage, M. (1994) 'Social mobility and class analysis: A new agenda for social history?', *Social History*, 19, 1, pp. 69–80.
54. Goldthorpe, J.H. and Marshall, G. (1992) 'The promising future of class analysis', *Sociology*, 26, pp. 384–5.
55. Stone, L. (1984) *An Open Elite?*, Oxford: Oxford University Press.
56. It might be argued that this is a confusing example, since Goldthorpe might accept that the English aristocracy was not demographically formed. However, if this were to be argued it would only strengthen the point that the cultural and political strength of classes seems difficult to link to the extent of their self-recruitment.
57. Savage, M. and Miles, A. (1994).
58. Scott, J. (1991) *Social Network Analysis*, London: Sage; Berkowitz, S.D. (1982) *An Introduction to Structural Analysis*, Toronto: Bellhaven.
59. Granovetter, M. (1974) *Getting a Job*, Cambridge, Mass.: Harvard University Press.
60. Mann, M. (1986); Mann, M. (1993).
61. Gould, R. (1991) 'Multiple networks and mobilisation in the Paris Commune', *American Sociological Review*, 56, pp. 716–29; Gould, R. (1992) 'Trade cohesion, class unity and urban insurrection: Artisanal activism in the Paris Commune', *American Journal of Sociology*, 98, pp. 721–54.
62. Duncan, S.S. (1989) 'What is locality?' in Peet, D. and Thrift, N. (eds) *New Models in Human Geography*, vol. 2, London: Unwin Hyman; Duncan, S.S. and Savage, M. (1989) 'Space, scale and locality', *Antipode*, 21, 3, pp. 179–206.
63. Savage, M. (1990) 'The rise of the Labour Party in local perspective', *Journal of Regional and Local Studies*, Summer, pp. 1–16; Savage, M. (1993).
64. Duncan, S.S. (1989); Duncan, S.S. and Savage, M. (1989).
65. Briggs, A. (1959) *Chartist Studies*, London: Macmillan.
66. Gadian, D. (1978) 'Class consciousness in Oldham and other north-western towns', *Historical Journal*, 21, pp. 161–72; Winstanley, M. (1993) 'Oldham radicalism, and the origins of popular liberalism', *Historical Journal*, 36, 3, pp. 619–44.
67. Gray, R. (1977) *The Labour Aristocracy in Victorian Edinburgh*, Oxford: Oxford University Press; Crossick, G. (1978).
68. Savage, M. (1987) *The Dynamics of Working Class Politics*, Cambridge: Cambridge University Press; Lancaster, B. (1987) *Radicalism, Co-operation and Socialism: Leicester Working-Class Politics 1860–1914*, Leicester: Leicester University Press; McKinlay, A. and Morris,

R.J. (1992) *The ILP on Clydeside*, Manchester: Manchester University Press.

69. Morris, R.J. (1990) *Class, Sect and Party: The Making of the British Middle Class, 1820–1850*, Manchester: Manchester University Press; Koditschek, T. (1990).

70. Stedman Jones, G. (1971) *Outcast London*, Harmondsworth: Penguin; Walkowitz, J. (1992) *City of Dreadful Delight: Narratives of Sexual Danger in late-Victorian London*, London: Virago.

71. Saunders, P. (1981) *Social Theory and the Urban Question*, London: Hutchinson; Smith, M.P. (1981) *The City and Social Theory*, Oxford: Blackwell.

72. Kerr, C. and Siegel, A. (1954) 'The inter-industry propensity to strike: An international comparison' in Kornhauser, A., Dubin, R. and Ross, A.M. (eds) *Industrial Conflict*, New York: McGraw Hill.

73. Church R., Outram, O. and Smith, D.N. (1991) 'The isolated mass revisited: Strikes in British coalmining', *Sociological Review*, 59, 1 pp. 55–87; Gilbert, D. (1992).

74. Edwards, P.K. (1988) 'Patterns of conflict and accommodation' in Gallie, D. (ed.) *Employment in Britain*, Oxford: Blackwell; Gilbert, D. (1992).

75. Cannadine, D. (1982) 'Residential differentiation in 19th century towns: From shapes on the ground to shapes in society' in Johnson, J. and Pooley, C.G. (eds) *The Structure of 19th Century Cities*, London: Macmillan.

76. MacIntyre, S. (1980) *Little Moscows: Communism and Working-Class Militancy in Inter-War Britain*, London: Croom Helm.

77. Hobsbawm, E. (1964).

78. Savage, M. and Miles, A. (1994).

79. Gould, R. (1993).

80. Roberts, R. (1971) *The Classic Slum*, Harmondsworth: Penguin.

81. Runciman, G. (1967) *Relative Deprivation and Social Justice*, London: Fontana.

82. Joyce, P. (1980) *Work, Society and Politics*, Brighton: Harvester, pp. 337–8.

83. Dutton, H. and King, J. (1982) *Ten Percent and No Surrender*, Cambridge: Cambridge University Press; Kirk, N. (1985); Savage, M. (1987).

84. Burgess, K. (1977) *The Origin of British Industrial Relations*, London: Croom Helm; White, J.L. (1978) *The Limits of Trade Union Militancy: The Lancashire Textile Workers 1910–1914*, Westport, Conn.: Greenwood.

85. Turner, H.A. (1959) *Trade Union Growth, Structure and Policy*, Manchester: Manchester University Press.

86. Gilbert, D. (1992).

87. MacIntyre, S. (1981); Gilbert, D. (1992).

88. Cooke, P. (1985) 'Class practices as regional markers' in Gregory, D. and Urry, J. (eds) *Social Relations and Spatial Structures*, Basingstoke: Macmillan.

89. Bagwell, P. (1963) *The Railwaymen*, London: Allen and Unwin.

90. Ibid., p. 75.

91. Dennis, R. (1984).

92. Giddens, A. (1984); Giddens, A. (1990) *The Consequences of Modernity*, Oxford: Polity.

93. Anderson, P. (1964) 'Origins of the present crisis', *New Left Review*, 23;
    Rubinstein, W.D. (1981); Cannadine, D. (1979) *Lords and Landlords:
    The Aristocracy and the Towns, 1774–1967*, Leicester: Leicester
    University Press; Cain, P. and Hopkins, E. (1992) *British Imperialism
    1600–1914*, London: Longmans.
94. Rubinstein, W.D. (1981); Thompson F.M.L. (1963) *English Landed
    Society in the Nineteenth Century*, London: Hutchinson.
95. Cannadine, D. (1979) *Lords and Landlords: The Aristocracy and the
    Towns 1774–1967*, Leicester: Leicester University Press.
96. Davidoff, L. (1973) *The Best Circles: Women and Society in Victorian
    England*, New York: Rowan and Littlefield; Elias, N. (1987) *The
    Civilising Process*, Oxford: Blackwell.
97. Davidoff, L. (1973), p. 21.
98. Morris, R.J. (1990); Koditschek, T. (1990); Smith, D. (1982); Gunn, S.
    (1988).
99. Morris, R.J. (1983).
100. Morris, R.J. (1991) 'Clubs, societies and associations' in Thompson,
    F.M.L. (ed.) *The Cambridge Social History of Britain 1780–1850*,
    Cambridge: Cambridge University Press.
101. Davidoff, L. and Hall, C. (1987) *Family Fortunes: Men and Women of the
    English Middle Classes 1780–1850*, London: Hutchinson.
102. Eley, G. (1990) 'Edward Thompson, social history and political culture:
    The making of a working-class public 1780–1850' in Kaye, H. and
    McClelland, K. (eds), *E.P. Thompson: Critical Perspectives*, Oxford:
    Polity.
103. Pickering, P. (1986) 'Class without words: symbolic communication and
    the Chartist movement', *Past and Present*, pp. 144–62.
104. Thompson, D. (1984) *The Chartists: Popular Politics in the Industrial
    Revolution*, London: Pantheon.
105. Thompson, D. (1984).
106. Saville, J. (1987) *1848: The British State and the Chartist Movement*,
    Cambridge: Cambridge University Press; Kirk, N. (1985).
107. Driver, F. (1992) *Power and Pauperism: The Workhouse System
    1834–1884*, Cambridge: Cambridge University Press.
108. Epstein, J. (1982).
109. Savage, M. and Miles, A. (1994).

CHAPTER THREE

Class and the 'linguistic turn' in Chartist and post-Chartist historiography

Neville Kirk

Overview

A theme running throughout this collection is that forms of class analysis are currently very much on the defensive in the humanities and social sciences. The importance, indeed adequacy, of social class as a useful means of social analysis and description has of course long been the subject of serious debate. Even in the predominantly radical 1960s E.P. Thompson's notion of class – as signifying a structured historical relationship, involving agency as well as conditioning, and manifesting itself in collective solidarity, struggle and conflict – met with a mixed reception within the British historical profession. Resorts to Weberian analysis, strands of positivism and various types of empirical evidence convinced divers critics that Thompson had exaggerated the process of class 'making' and its associated features of unity, mutuality and radicalism.[1]

Since the early 1970s, and especially during the years of Thatcher, Reagan and Major, criticisms of class have gathered, at least in academic circles in Britain, quickened and widened momentum and appeal. Indeed, it is not an exaggeration to suggest that class-based analysis now stands at a point of great crisis from which it might recover and grow in strength, or simply wither and die. Are the practitioners of class theory curious oddities, a minority of outmoded and beleaguered 'modernists', failing to come to terms with the new, shifting, flexible and individualised world of post-modernism? Or do they still have something of value to offer, even to dedicated followers of linguistic fashion in the western heartlands of 'choice, opportunity and classlessness'?[2]

This chapter will offer a negative answer to the first question and an affirmative response to the second. An attempt will be made to demonstrate the importance of class to workers during the Chartist period from the 1830s to the 1850s. In substantiating this claim the essay will take issue with recent linguistic emphases upon Chartist and post-Chartist attachments to 'populist', as opposed to class-based, identities.[3]

Before proceeding to an examination of Chartist languages it is, however, important for us briefly to consider the historiographical contexts in which recent debates concerning class have developed. Broadly speaking, criticisms of class, as articulated by historians of modern Britain, have been largely empirical, 'commonsensical' and 'traditional' in character. Explicit theorising has mainly been eschewed in favour of detailed empirical work which has highlighted the *differential*, as opposed to unified, character of the modern British working class with respect to both structure and consciousness. A long line of historians, running from A.E. Musson to Alastair Reid, has thus pointed to differences and divisions rooted in skill, income levels, relations at work, politics, culture and ideology, in opposition to claims of radical class-making and homogeneity.[4] In reply, practitioners of class analysis have denied attachment to static and completely homogeneous definitions of class.[5] In the decades before the 1980s historians of modern Britain did occasionally utilise Weberian and structural-functionalist categories in order to critique Marxist views of class: but, especially among home-grown historians of Britain, the focus upon class remained predominantly empirical in character. Indeed, there was often the cultivation of a deliberate and profound mistrust of theory, and especially theory emanating from beyond the shores of this island.[6]

Much of this 'traditionalism' persists in well-established and powerful British historical circles to the present day. However, of growing significance during the past decade or so has been the 'radical' resort to the linguistic constructions and deconstructive modes of post-structuralism and post-modernism, in order more sensitively to tackle current and historical questions relating to class, racial, and ethnic identities and meanings. This resort has been more pronounced among students of literature and culture than students of history, and more in evidence in France and America rather than Britain: but of its mounting general importance there can be no doubt.[7]

Concerns with the historical reconstruction of class-based, racial, ethnic and gender-specific forms of identity, in part by attention to subjectivity and language, are far less alien to practitioners of history (especially in the USA) than frequently claimed by post-modernists. Given the traditional neglect of 'the other' in much mainstream British historiography, increased attention to the identities and experiences of those people beyond the purview of white, middle-class males is to be warmly welcomed. An equally favourable reception is to be extended to those writers who, often following in the footsteps of Berlin, Gutman, Elizabeth-Fox and Eugene Genovese, Sivanandan, Rowbotham and Dorothy Thompson, have paid careful attention to the complex, shifting and nuanced relations between ethnicity and class, race and class, and gender and class.[8]

Simultaneously, however, some of the approaches to the study of language, subjectivity and identity invite a far more critical response. I am thinking at this point of works which have posited the (often absolute and fixed) supremacy of race, gender and ethnicity over class, and which have, in some instances, effectively denied the existence of social structure and interests beyond language and subjectivity.[9]

The construction of a comprehensive critique of such work lies beyond the scope of this essay. I have, however, adopted the closely related task of engaging with the 'revisionist' post-structuralist and post-modernist writings of Gareth Stedman Jones, Patrick Joyce and similarly minded scholars, which suggest that Chartist and post-Chartist languages and consciousness were more 'populist' than class-based in character. I have elsewhere offered some criticisms of the 'linguistic turns' offered by Joyce and Stedman Jones.[10] The purposes of this chapter are twofold: empirically to develop and strengthen such criticisms by means of reference to an extended and chronologically more extensive range of sources (especially those primary-based printed materials relating to the languages of the Chartists and post-Chartist radicals); and more sharply to specify my 'realist' theoretical critique of the subjectivist and idealist practices of Stedman Jones and Joyce. I will argue that, in effect, these two historians falsely conflate language and reality, and fail adequately to link saying and doing, consciousness and structure, and the intended, unintended and unrecognised aspects of life.

The chapter will proceed in the following manner. The reader will first be briefly introduced to the views of Stedman Jones and Joyce in relation to class. These views will then be situated within their wider theoretical frameworks of post-structuralism and post-modernism. The third, and most substantial, part of the essay will consider the strengths and weaknesses of their 'populist' perspectives in relation to Chartist and post-Chartist languages. The final part of the essay will suggest the continued utility and fruitfulness of a materialist framework of historical analysis which explores the dialectic between, on the one hand, consciousness and agency (embracing language) and on the other, conditioning and structure.

The question of class

As Dorothy Thompson has observed in her authoritative essay, 'Chartism and the historians' (1993):

> Until very recently few writers have questioned the definition of
> Chartism as a class movement. The nineteenth century was imbued
> with the concept of class, and all its earlier historians saw the social

divisions within British society as the main motivations of the Chartist movement. Some historians have questioned Frederick Engels's description of Chartism as 'the compact form of their (the proletarians') opposition to the bourgeoisie', but their objections until recently tended to stress the influence of middle-class thought and leadership on the movement's programme and policy rather than to dismiss the concept of class altogether. In recent times, how-ever, the very omnipresence of the word and the concept 'class' and its frequent use without precise definition has suggested to some writers that the term is of no value as a historical category.[11]

Working within a positivist framework which posits the existence of a 'true' or 'objective' reality 'out there', largely independent of its 'subjec-tive' (and not infrequently 'distorted') representations in language, ideas and other cultural forms, Norman McCord has, during the past ten years, been prominent among those 'traditional' British historians ques-tioning the precision, rigour, and indeed very adequacy, of the term social class.[12] In a review article written in 1985 McCord directed part of his fire against Gareth Stedman Jones's *Languages of Class* which had been published in 1983. It is accordingly highly ironic that a central essay in *Languages of Class*, 'Rethinking Chartism' (itself an expanded version of Stedman Jones's 1982 essay, 'The Language of Chartism'), adopted a Saussurean non-referential theory of language to suggest that Chartism, as defined by its 'public political' language, was not a class-based move-ment.[13]

In his essays Stedman Jones argued that the Chartists defined them-selves in the *Northern Star* and other printed radical sources as a politi-cally excluded and politically oppressed 'people', rather than as a working class exploited in production. In the opinion of Stedman Jones, the Chartists formed part of a long-established radical tradition, rooted in political and predominantly non-class-based theories of exploitation (revolving around exclusion from the franchise, excessive taxation, the power of 'Old Corruption' and so on); rather than being the constructors of a new class movement in which poverty and oppression were seen as issuing primarily from exploitation in production. While the Chartists could attack 'unfair' employers (who did not abide by the 'honourable' customs of paying 'fair' wages and deriving 'honest' profits from their businesses), they did not perceive any *necessary* (that is, structural) con-flict between workers and employers in production. 'Excessive' profits were condemned, and rent and interest were regarded as 'the product of no labour'; but, at least in his active, supervisory role, the capitalist did not rank alongside the usurer and landlord in radical demonology as 'parasitical'. In time-honoured radical fashion, the Chartists did detect exploitation in exchange. However, according to Stedman Jones, the capitalist as middleman was attacked more on account of his 'political beliefs and social attitudes' (being 'the willing complier in the tyrannical rule of property' and the supporter of the blatant 'class legislation' of the 1830s), than his economic role (being more slave to, rather than author of, the system of 'buying cheap and selling dear'). As members of the 'producing classes', 'honest' workers and employers were jointly arrayed against the machinations of the corrupt, parasitical and unrepresentative monopolists of political and (its consequent) economic power. Thus Stedman Jones (1983):

> What we have here ... is not a picture of two opposed classes thrown up by a new system of production, in which the role of the employer as manager and controller of the process is a crucial feature of its exploitative character, but rather *a harmonious world of production* inhabited by masters and men, degraded by the artificial imposition of a political system which sanctions and sustains the extraction of exorbitant interest payments to a purely parasitic class of capitalists who garrison every point of exchange. [emphasis added]

In direct opposition to the class-based 'social determinism' of Marx and Engels, in which, argues Stedman Jones, politics, language and ideology are essentially reflective of an anterior material reality of 'experience', he thus posits the primacy of language and politics in the construction of social reality and identity. The Chartist reality, and the driving force of the movement and its constituents' identities become politics and political languages. According to Stedman Jones, just as politico-linguistic factors (the inherited language of the 'people', the 'Great Betrayal' of 1832, and perceptions of the State as an evil and hostile force) underlay the rise and character of Chartism, so the movement's demise is to be located primarily not in economic and social factors (such as 'improvement' or the emergence of a 'labour aristocracy'), but in the increasing staleness and irrelevance of its language in the face of changed political realities (especially the mellowed nature of the State). Continuities, in the form of the determining influences of politics and the political language of the 'people', predominated, in Stedman Jones's view, over alleged discontinuities in socio-economic experience and the rise of class. Thus, 'despite the intensity of hostility to the "steam-producing class" in the Chartist period', the Chartists did not replace traditional radical analysis with a 'more class-conscious mode of thought', such as 'a class-based theory of exploitation of a social democratic or Marxist kind'. In the final analysis, Chartists remained convinced of the non-class-based 'political origin and determination of oppression'.[14]

A measure of Cambridge University's traditional strength in the field of the history of ideas, *Languages of Class* undoubtedly constituted a pioneering work in the 'linguistic turn' within English historiography.

Since its publication numerous authors have engaged with Stedman Jones's theoretical assumptions and empirical findings.[15] Apart from an essay entitled, 'The "Cockney" and the Nation' (in D. Feldman and G.S. Jones (eds), *Metropolis*), published in 1985, Stedman Jones has neither published further in the field of language and history nor responded to his critics.

It has been within this tantalising post-1985 context of Cambridge 'absence' or 'withdrawal' that the Manchester-based trio of Patrick Joyce, Anthony Easthope and, more recently, James Vernon has sought to demonstrate, with scrupulously correct regard for the complex identities of some, rather than all, 'Others' (feminist women and ethnic groups, but not 'phallocentric', 'authoritarian', 'bland', 'masterful' and 'desirous' realists and Marxists), its sublime linguistic credentials.[16] In the pages of *Past and Present, Social History* and in *Visions of the People* (Joyce: 1991), *British Post-Structuralism since 1968* (Easthope: 1991) and *Politics and the People* (Vernon: 1993), these three post-modernist writers have seriously questioned, 'the idea of a clear distinction between representation and the "real" ', fact and fiction, history and story-telling, and the realist view of the existence of an external social reality.[17]

At an empirical level explorations of popular politics and languages in nineteenth-century England have led both Joyce and Vernon to agreement with Stedman Jones: the dominant voice was that of the 'people' or 'populism' rather than class. Joyce does, unlike Stedman Jones, detect class, albeit at a secondary level. Vernon both elevates the language of the 'people' to central importance and contends that the political influence of the very same 'people' declined in the face of the development of an increasingly formalised, organised and manipulative system of representative democracy. From within the field of literature, Easthope's 'teasing' and 'playful' purposes have been to dissolve the distinctions between history and literature, and to teach historians and others the folly of pursuing 'objective' realist truths, and mastery of past, present and text. Certainty and cherished systems fall apart – subjectivity and relativity become the principles of study.[18]

It is too early to know whether the 'turn to language', especially in its anti-class form, will exert much influence among historians of modern Britain. In various history departments in the USA and in some American and European historical journals the post-modernist insistence upon the discursive construction of past and present (as opposed to their partially independent existence) has made considerable headway. However, there are signs that Marxist and other 'realist' positions, which embrace both language and being, are currently reviving in the USA.[19] In 'traditionalist' Britain both solidly empirical and materialist approaches to the study of history have sufficiently strong pedigrees to make Manchester's post-

modernist historians and literary luminaries feel unwanted and beleaguered. Within powerful parts of the British historical establishment a
sense of national pride is still taken in the dismissal of theory *tout court*.
Nevertheless, post-modernism's attentions to diversity, complexity and
relativity do hold a certain amount of appeal in an uncertain and atom-
ised world. In any event, given their leading roles in the 'turn to language', and their interesting and determined attempts to change the
character and aims of social history, the works of our selected scholars
merit considered and extended scrutiny.

Class, post-structuralism and post-modernism

The 'turns' of Stedman Jones, Joyce and Vernon against class cannot be
fully understood outside of the theoretical frameworks of post-structuralism and post-modernism. It is to a brief consideration of key features of these frameworks that we will now turn.

Throughout the humanities and social sciences the 'linguistic turn' has
been a central feature of post-structuralism – a body of ideas commonly,
if in some cases problematically, associated with Foucault, Derrida and
other French thinkers of the 1960s and 1970s. Post-structuralism frequently signals a reaction against the notion of structural determination,
against the view that structures matter most in the construction of social
reality. Many post-structuralists deny the existence of social reality independent of its articulation through thought and discourse, and proceed
to emphasise the fragmented, relative and mainly autonomous natures of
the various aspects of life. *Discourse*, *decentring* and *deconstruction* constitute key words in the post-structuralist dictionary.

As Anthony Easthope has informed us, in Britain post-structuralism
arose largely out of an engagement with Althusserian structuralism
(especially the latter's 'early' insistence upon theoretically conceived 'hidden' structures as the key determinants of 'experience' and social
thought), and as a result of a renewed interest in phenomenology and its
central concerns with agency and consciousness.[20] Stedman Jones's 'linguistic turn' was made in part-engagement with the work of Althusser.
This fact was illustrated in the effective rejection of material determination or 'social determinism' (even in 'the last instance') in *Languages of
Class* and the book's practical embrace of language, and more specifically political discourses, as primary agents in the construction of social
and personal reality. *Languages of Class* thus stands in marked contrast
to *Outcast London* (1971) and 'Class struggle and the industrial revolution' (1975), which had characterised Stedman Jones's earlier commitments to the 'determining role of the social'.[21]

Notwithstanding the many recent attempts to 'read' his 'post-modernist' discourse, Stedman Jones's endorsement of a Saussurean approach to the study of language properly belongs to the *post-structuralist* problematic noted above. In effect, we await the 'word' as to whether Stedman Jones views his specific post-structuralist concerns as being in harmony with the wider cultural project of post-modernism. By way of contrast, both Patrick Joyce and James Vernon have loudly proclaimed their adherence to, and the superior virtues of, post-modernism over 'modernism' and 'realism'. Simultaneously, however, neither Joyce nor Vernon offers a systematic definition of post-modernism. There are plentiful references to decentred subjects, deconstruction and discourse in their work: but detailed, internally consistent, rigorous and convincing expositions and defences of the terms post-modernism and modernism, and particularly their adequacy as descriptions of historical reality, are largely absent in the work of Joyce and Vernon.[22]

However, given the very frequency of the references to post-modernism by Joyce, Vernon and other supporters of the 'linguistic turn', its relationship to post-structuralism, and acute relevance to our discussion of class, it is important for us to essay a brief definition of the term.

As David Harvey has observed,[23] at the most general level modernism and post-modernism are claimed to be broad cultural movements spanning, respectively, the periods from c.1850–1950 and the late 1950s to the present day. Modernism is said to be identified with a number of features such as grand systems and modes of thought ('meta narratives' such as Marxism and Freudianism), social engineering ('Fordism'), certainty, closure, élitism and authoritarianism, high culture, absolute laws and truths, holism, homogeneity, synthesis, external reality, and unitary structures such as class. Modernism may thus be seen as the product of the Enlightenment, signifying freedom, liberty, equality and reason for some; terror uniformity, and individual entrapment within suffocating and 'totalising' systems for others. Post-modernism, with its attachments to scepticism, deconstruction, playfulness, contingency, decentring, life (or 'petite') histories, relativity, heterogeneity, individualism, pragmatism, hedonism, discursively constructed realities, the 'popular' (as manifested in culture and leisure), flexibility, choice and opportunity, and its opposition to 'total' and unitary systems and structures, stands in direct opposition to modernism.

As Harvey further observes, the extremely subjective, general, and often vague categories and characteristics of modernism and post-modernism, combined with contradictions within, and marked overlaps and continuities between, allegedly modernist and post-modernist periods of history and schools of thought, render precise and useful historical description and analysis very hazardous. For example, at the core of the

modernist/post-modernist problematic in the arts lies the shifting relationship between high art and mass culture (Andreas Huyssen). Within
the social sciences post-modernist emphases may be said to reside in multiple and changing meanings and subjectivities. It is not at all clear, therefore, that common meanings, definitions and problematics are on offer.
A further example consists of the fact that both 'flat' and 'Fordist' systems of management co-exist in John Major's 'post modernist' Britain
(the Prime Minister himself being a very 'unpost-modern' figure). In sum,
we may question the very adequacy of the terms of modernism and post-
modernism and the validity of a sharp rupture between modernist and
post-modernist periods of history.[24]

Notwithstanding such questioning, we should note at this point that
both Joyce and Vernon do embrace the notions of discourse, decentring
and deconstruction within their general post-modern framework. In this
embrace they display shared assumptions and aims with Stedman Jones.

In terms of discourse, all three historians have thus expressed mounting dissatisfaction with the view that social structures, such as class, exist
prior to, outside of, and thus beyond, their appropriation in language.
The latter, as the representative of thought and (at least for Joyce and
Vernon) signifying communication in its widest sense (both verbal and
non-verbal), is held to be of central importance to both the creation and
understanding of social reality. Thus Stedman Jones describes, in
Languages of Class, his movement away from 'any simple prejudgement
about the determining role of the "social" ' and towards an embrace of
language:

> In particular, I became increasingly critical of the prevalent treat-
> ment of the 'social' as something outside of, and logically . . . prior
> to its articulation through language. The title, Languages of Class,
> stresses this point: . . . that the term 'class' is a word embedded in
> language and should thus be analysed in its linguistic context . . .

This embrace has further moved Stedman Jones to treat class: 'as a discursive rather than as an ontological reality, the central effort being to
explain languages of class from the nature of politics rather than the
character of politics from the nature of class'.[25]

James Vernon agrees with Stedman Jones that it is language, and not
'some prior social structure', which 'creates the diverse, unstable, and
often contradictory identities of the decentred subject'. E.P. Thompson is
accordingly taken to task for allegedly employing a 'reflective' view of
language ('in which the language of politics is seen as reflecting, rather
than actively constituting, social experience'). Vernon also criticises
Thompson's supposed neglect of women, the issue of gender, and popular attachments to reactionary politics in The Making of the English
Working Class.[26] Joyce joins Stedman Jones, Vernon, and the post-mod-

ernist feminist, Joan Scott, in their various criticisms of the categories of 'experience', the 'social', and class 'structure' or 'interest'. In the introduction to *Visions of the People* Joyce thus argues that class is 'increasingly, and rightly, seen less as objective reality than as a social construct, created differently by different historical actors'. Two further propositions are put forward: that 'experience' is, *pace* E.P. Thompson, 'in fact not prior to and constitutive of language but is actively constituted by language'; and that class and other 'interests' are 'not somehow given in the economic condition of workers, but are constructed through the agency of identities'.[27]

Alongside this shared opposition to the notion of independent and objective class structure and class interest, there exists a common objection to the 'modernist' belief that the social world and individuals' lives are rooted, or 'centred', in a determining or 'essential' structure or presence. It is in this context that the issues of 'social' – and its corollary class – determinism become of crucial significance. In opposition to 'determinists' of a historical-materialist persuasion, Joyce, Vernon and Stedman Jones have come to reject the position that societies are centrally shaped by economic and social forces. Rather, in true post-structuralist and post-modernist fashion, societies are seen as consisting of largely autonomous discursive formations operating within their own spaces, patterns of articulation and chronologies. Furthermore, as class is (far too narrowly) identified by Stedman Jones, Joyce and Vernon with the 'social' (the languages of exploitation in production and 'expropriation of the expropriators' being the 'true' touchstones of class for Vernon and Joyce,[28] as well as Stedman Jones), so class is also logically and empirically afforded diminished influence upon people's lives.

Just as societies and class are decentred, so are individuals.[29] In place of the transcendent, sovereign and unified subject, standing at the very centre of the historical process, post-structuralism has identified the decentred human effect. Both empowered and disabled by language, and thus being agents as well as the passive bearers of discourse, individuals are possessed of multiple and shifting characteristics, relationships and experiences. Emphases upon diversity, complexity, relativity and bearer have come to contest the 'modernist' categories of unity, fixed centre and creator. The relatively stable and fixed class subject is accordingly decentred and deconstructed. Other forms of self-ascription – rooted in gender, nationhood, ethnicity and race – are brought into play. The construction of identity is correctly seen as a complex, and sometimes chaotic and contradictory matter. Notwithstanding their opposition to the 'essentialisms' at the heart of 'centring' and their endorsements of autonomy, our three historians depose 'social determinism' only to impose the determinism of politics and political discourses upon individuals and societies. We will later have occasion to revisit this essentialist contradiction.

Discursive and decentring themes are accompanied, most explicitly in the cases of Vernon and Joyce, by commitments to the deconstruction of Derrida. According to the latter, words and texts which provide us with indirect access to, and indeed construct reality, contain multiple meanings and interpretations. It follows, therefore, that there can be no single or absolute textual expression of truth about reality. Just as we begin to think that we are about to grasp the 'entire truth' about a supposedly unified object of enquiry, so we realise that other possible meanings, 'truths' or significations of the 'signifier' (the textual expression of reality) have necessarily slipped from our grasp. Seemingly unitary objects of investigation splinter into innumerable fragments of meaning. In the opinion of Derrida, the very 'facts' that reality is accessed and constituted by language and (following and developing the work of Saussure) that there is no absolute or essential connection between signifier and signified, means that the pursuit of truth (as expressed in words) is impossible; relativism thus assumes a position of paramount importance.

In the works of Joyce, Vernon and Stedman Jones notions of total relativism and absolute chaos in social life do not, however, prevail. Rather, *patterned* meanings and points of identity are seen to emerge in the course of social practice and within historical contexts. However, such discursive points of stability and identity are also subjected to disabling and fragmenting forces. For example, social classes do not assume 'centred' or unitary meanings, identities and common patterns of consciousness. Classes must be broken down to reveal various and often conflicting identities and meanings. One of the main results of deconstruction, as applied to labour history, has been to highlight gender-based differences and divisions within the working-class signifier, made evident especially in the work of Joan Scott; for Scott and others, pursuit of the working class, as a centred whole with a true meaning, is doomed to failure.[30]

Implications

The shared assumptions and tenets outlined above do not denote the absence of differences among our subjects. As I have shown elsewhere, significant differences – of focus, direction, influence, style, tone, temperament and of approach to language and ideas – exist between Joyce and Stedman Jones. It has been James Vernon, former student and current colleague of Patrick Joyce, who has most ardently championed postmodernism and most aggressively taken issue with defenders of empirical and holistic historiography.[31] But, in terms of the purposes of this essay, such differences matter far less than the shared assumptions and views outlined above.

Before moving to a consideration of the strengths and weaknesses of the anti-class perspectives of Joyce, Vernon and Stedman Jones, it is important briefly to recap, and to reveal the key implications of, their empirical and theoretical arguments.

We have observed that all three historians work upon the premise that class structures and class interests neither exist, nor have meaning outside of their discursive forms. This premise can be, and is, extended to apply to the nature of social reality itself. Opposition is then registered to the notion of 'centring', with particular reference to 'social determinism'. This opposition serves to reduce the influence of class – the latter being defined as a linguistic construction around the notion of 'social' exploitation. At this point questions concerning essentialism, autonomy and adequate definitions of class arise. Our subjects do not devote much attention to the first two questions; and, as we will later observe, the epistemological adequacy of their assumptions and formulations is more asserted than demonstrated. In terms of class, unitary views are rejected in favour of deconstruction and complexity. Relationships between fragmentary and unifying influences within classes, in specific contexts and over time, remain largely unexplored.

Empirical studies of (mainly) Victorian labouring people reveal to Stedman Jones, Joyce and Vernon that class identity mattered far less than non-class-based political languages revolving around the idea of 'the people'. We are informed that workers were far more desirous of claiming their traditional rights as 'Freeborn Englishmen'; and to a much lesser extent, as women[32] than in claiming exploitation and oppression at the workplace. It is further argued that this longstanding radical tradition, revolving around politics rather than class-based economics, enabled 'industrious' and 'respectable' Radicals successfully to cross class boundaries in order to embrace common political ideas. The latter opposed 'Old Corruption', and the exclusion of the 'people' from the franchise, and supported extensions of civil, religious and political liberties and rights, progress, reason, free trade, cheap government, low taxation and general reform.[33]

It is political and interclass-based continuity, in the form of this evergreen radical platform, which is highlighted by Joyce, and Stedman Jones's inspired 'Cambridge School' of historians.[34] In opposition to materialists, with their emphases upon class and 'discontinuity', the 'Cambridge School' contends that there were no sharp 'breaks' of consciousness and programme between Chartism and mid-Victorian Liberalism, and between late Victorian and early Edwardian Liberalism and the birth and 'rise' of the Labour Party. A conscious effort is thus made to reconstruct the centrality of Radicalism to England's political past and to debunk Marxist teleologies of class conflict and political discontinuity. The modern English working class has allegedly failed the linguistic test of class set by Stedman Jones and like-minded historians.

A critique of post-structuralist and post-modernist approaches

Strengths and weaknesses

The 'linguistic turn' has usefully reminded us of the importance of the 'cultural factor' – as expressed in language, ideas, values and norms – to the historical process. As E.P. Thompson, Raymond Williams, Herbert Gutman and more recently Lynn Hunt have demonstrated, history is more than structure, as expressed in material and other determinations of life. We also need to know about the various ways in which people, as conscious agents, have 'dealt with' (i.e. interpreted, modified and even changed) their structured conditions of existence.[35] Central to this dialectical interplay between agency and conditioning has been, and will continue to be, the study of language. The main theoretical value of the writings of Stedman Jones, Joyce and Vernon lies in the fact that they reinforce, rather than (as mistakenly claimed by the authors themselves) initiate, concerns with meaning and the socially constitutive role of language among historians of modern Britain.

Along with many anti-reductionist historical materialists (falsely lumped together as 'social determinists'), Stedman Jones, Joyce and Vernon thus argue that language and systems of discourse play *active*, as opposed to purely *passive* or 'reflective', (Vernon) roles in the construction of reality.[36] An empiricist/positivist view of reality – which assimilates social reality to nature and which posits an external reality to be studied and counted without due attention to the shaping characteristics of thought and language – has rightly been taken to task. Knowledge and interpretation/meaning are not automatically 'given' in reality/experience. As Stedman Jones has argued, it is not adequate to 'treat . . . language as a more or less immediate rendition of experience into words'. Also, to quote the realist philosopher, Roy Bhaskar, people are not 'passive sensors of given facts and recorders of their given conjunctions'.[37] It follows, therefore, that class-consciousness demands the same attention as class structure. The former cannot be seen as secondary to the latter, a 'mere' subjective derivation of 'objective' structure. Reductionism, as manifested in economic determinism of all hues, properly belongs to the dustbin of history.

In taking seriously the languages of 'ordinary people', Stedman Jones and Joyce have, much like ethnomethodologists, offered useful correctives to crude notions of 'false consciousness' and popular thought as being inherently 'distorted' or 'ideological'. Above all, perhaps, Althusserianism and some other forms of structuralism, with their forever hidden structures, and their all too hasty dismissals of the validity of the claims of popular 'consciousness' to the status of 'real'/'true' knowledge, have been exposed as deficient. To put the matter plainly, Joyce and Stedman Jones have said that historians of modern British society must take due cognisance of the thoughts and languages of people. This is a view to which I would subscribe. I would also add that Joyce's and Stedman Jones's empirical studies have enriched and broadened our understanding of people's languages in nineteenth-century Britain.

As against these undoubted strengths, the writings of our practitioners of the 'linguistic turn' do, however, suffer from a number of debilitating empirical and theoretical weaknesses. There is, for example, insufficient appreciation of the extent to which the Chartist movement was saturated by notions of class in relation not simply to economic affairs, but experiences as a whole; the degree to which class overshadowed other forms of identity; and the continued, if diluted, presence of class in post-Chartist popular movements. At the theoretical level there is, despite intentions to the contrary, the dissolution of social reality into language and the resulting (and unresolved) problems of idealism, subjectivism, and the epistemological inadequacy of their assumptions and procedures. In practice, links between language and social structure are not pursued; and language is taken at face value rather than examined critically and engaged with material and other structures. Finally, the presentation (and demolition) of a strawperson historical materialism on the part of our three historians blinds them as to the actual practices of historical materialism and its continued utility as a method of historical investigation.

Empirical defects

Popular languages and the question of class
In terms of the empirical material, it is first of all highly questionable as to whether it is necessary (or desirable) to resort to post-structuralist and post-modernist theories in order to reconstruct the languages of nineteenth-century workers. A number of historians, including Asa Briggs, E.P. and Dorothy Thompson, Iorwerth Prothero, Robbie Gray and Geoffrey Crossick, have excellently reconstructed nineteenth-century languages of class, the 'people', the 'producing' or 'useful' classes, and the multifaceted languages of Chartism and mid Victorian respectability. More to the point is the fact that these studies have paid due regard to the complexities, nuances and ambiguities of language and meaning; have

demonstrated scrupulous attention to context, linkages and change; have been conducted from within both materialist and non-materialist frameworks of analysis; and have been undertaken largely prior to, and uniformly outside of, the frameworks of post-structuralism and post-modernism. Similarly, these linguistic reconstructions challenge both the alleged novelty of the notion of 'populism' and the indispensability of post-modernism to the empirical investigation of language and identity.[38]

Secondly, a selective examination of Chartist and post-Chartist popular languages certainly reveals that class existed far more extensively and profoundly and mattered much more than Stedman Jones, Joyce and Vernon allow. For example, as extensively documented in my 1987 article, 'In defence of class' (*International Review of Social History*, vol. 32) leading Chartists in both the factory districts of Lancashire and Cheshire and in centres of 'artisan' production, such as Birmingham and London, articulated an unmistakable, if largely non-socialist, critique of exploitation in production. Growing out of practical experience rather than theoretical abstraction, this critique suggested that an 'unnatural' and oppressive capitalist system, based upon full-blown commodity production, profit maximisation, 'wage slavery', the subordination of labour to capital, and the replacement of the 'honourable' master by the 'dishonourable' capitalist 'tyrant' or 'steamlord', was becoming hegemonic within production. Workers were losing their independence, customary notions of reciprocity and fairness were being undermined, and the capitalist was consciously intent upon the exploitation and oppression of labour at work.

The Chartist leaders did identify 'exceptions', such as John Fielden, to the charge of capitalist oppression, and did often express the hope that employers would come to see the folly of their ways and treat workers in time-honoured 'honourable' fashion. Similarly, as noted by Stedman Jones, there was no general plan to take over the mills and factories and expropriate the expropriators: but the absence of a theory (of a Marxist kind) of necessary exploitation in production should not blind us to the actual extent of Chartist perceptions of exploitation in production. Although politics, via the achievement of universal manhood suffrage, continued to be seen as the ultimate means of working-class emancipation, notions of production-based oppression became increasingly common inside Chartism, alongside older notions of political and exchange-based exploitation. In sum, class was of manifest importance.[39]

'In defence of class' offered detailed evidence in support of the propositions advanced in the previous paragraph. The purpose of this chapter is not to rehearse this evidence in full. It is, however, important to present the reader with a representative sample of such evidence alongside material concerning class and other forms of identity more recently culled from Chartist journals and other contemporary publications.[40]

Peter Murray McDouall, Feargus O'Connor, James Leach, Bronterre O'Brien, Richard Pilling and numerous other Chartists identified the factory system as both the most advanced manifestation of industrial capitalism, and as being at the cutting edge of exploitation in production. 'I come to show you the system which has spread such ruinous changes around us', wrote McDouall, surgeon and delegate to the Chartist convention of 1839 for the Chartist stronghold of Ashton-under-Lyne. The *system* was, of course, the factory system, 'one of our most splendid systems of oppression'.[41] In the pages of his *Chartist and Republican Journal* McDouall detailed and thundered against the 'overwhelming evils' and 'REAL ROBBERIES' of the system as affecting workers: 'wage-slavery'; loss of the independence and control over work associated with the domestic system of industry; the disruption of the family economy; insecurity and misery; dependence upon the capitalist for employment; reduction to the status of a thing, an instrument of production; lack of 'due protection and full reward' for labour; subjection to the 'inhuman' imperatives of profit maximisation, cost cutting, merciless competition and the unregulated effects of the introduction of machinery and technological change; and the attempted subordination of labour to the absolute will of 'tyrannical capital'.[42]

Far from gaining in independence, the 'free' factory operative had experienced unprecedented degradation. The fining system, part of the despotic 'Rules of the Mill', symbolised labour's enslavement to capital. Thus McDouall:

> Should the weaver be found out of the area, he is fined, should he be found sitting down, he is fined, should he be found asleep, he is fined, in short, should the human being be found in any other position than that of rigid attention to the task before him, he is fined, the worker must be as constant in application, and as regular in movement and attention, as the metal itself. The worker must identify himself with the machine, and become a portion of the cast iron itself . . . No tyrant of a schoolmaster was ever more strict and severe than the factory master, and no system could be better adopted to break the spirit and degrade the independence of the human race, whether in a school or a mill.[43]

Contrary to the teachings of orthodox political economy, the accelerated growth of industrial capitalism had not enhanced the worker's freedom and equality in the market-place. Rather, the customary regulations of the 'industrial moral economy' – concerning 'fair' wages, 'honest' profits, 'just' prices and 'honourable' relations between journeymen and masters – were being obliterated in the names of 'freedom', 'liberalisation' and enhanced 'choice' and 'flexibility'.[44] McDouall pointedly entitled his articles on the factory system, 'The White Slaves of Great Britain' and exposed the 'cruel' and 'illusory' freedoms of ill-rewarded and unprotected labour. The freedom of the cotton spinner to change employers was thus, 'worth nothing if he cannot have the privilege of working when he pleases and gaining a sufficiency, and live by his labour'. 'To chain your body to the bloody footstool of the capitalist', continued McDouall, 'to say then that the mind is free, that you are a free labourer, is utter delusion'. He concluded that chattel slavery had more to offer than 'wage slavery':

> And if I were to have a choice between the two systems of slavery, that where I got all the physical benefits for mental ones, or that where I got a few imaginary ones and no bodily protection, I would not hesitate a moment which to choose; I would rather be the slave of the West Indies and possess all the physical benefits of real slavery, than be the white factory slave of England and possess all the hardships of an unreal freedom.[45]

This profoundly anti-capitalist, 'wage-slavery first' turn of mind would later be carried by notable Chartists to the United States, complete with far-reaching consequences for their attitudes towards the capitalist North, the slave South and the abolitionist cause.[46]

As the prime mover of, if simultaneously slave to, the system of 'buying cheap and selling dear', the factory master met with the full force of McDouall's wrath. The unceasing pursuit of profit, the defeat of workers' combinations, attachment to cash-based utilitarian values, self-interest, hypocrisy and lack of regard for workers' welfare were regarded by McDouall as the hallmarks of 'Manchester Man'.[47] Thus, the factory master was a 'heartless accumulator of gold', a slave to 'avarice and ambition'. In 'The Factory Master's Portrait', McDouall declaimed:

> Examine him, and you will find that his whole knowledge extends to the revolution of wheels; and although possessed of immense wealth, he knows nothing except the process of making cotton cloth or the most cunning way to drive a bargain. Every action of his life is measured by a foot-rule, and every thing he does is regulated by pounds, shillings and pence . . . He lives for no other purpose than to calculate, and the only end of his existence is to gain.[48]

Outward trappings of respectability and religiosity could not mask the factory owner's inhuman, calculative spirit:

> The civilized mill-owner, the christian, the church-builder, and the religious curate reasons thus; this little devil of a piecer is not my property, but his labour is: what use is his body except it be for the work it will do. I will make him work as long and as much as I can, and if I kill him, why another will supply his place. The raw material is as easy to be got as my cattle.[49]

McDouall's picture of the factory master as an uncaring and hypocritical utilitarian was shared by many other Chartists. According to O'Connor, the Anti-Corn Law League employers were motivated solely by consider-ations of self and profit, of 'how that living tomb can be worked with cheap labour'. James Leach, a leading Manchester Chartist, declared that the employers of the League were concerned only to 'amass princely for-tunes without any regard whatever for the well-being of their ill-used and toil-worn slaves'.[50] For O'Connor the free-trade employers preached freedom and independence, but practised slavery and dependence:

> Have they not, as masters and as magistrates, followed up, perse-cuted, tortured, and, in many instances banished from their homes, every individual who has taken an active part in exposing their dis-honesty and their ignorance? Have they not established the system of excommunication, by conspiring together, to banish from their employment every man who has taken an active part against them? . . . Do they not work your wives and daughters to death, while they compel you to walk the streets in idleness? Have not your wives petitioned them over and over again that their husbands may be allowed to share their toil, and have they not indignantly refused? Is it not a notorious fact that the stern virtue of your wives and daughters is the only guarantee you have for their protection? And yet with such fearful odds against the working classes, can the mind suggest a greater anomaly than the glorious opposition offered by the unprotected slaves to their all powerful oppressors?[51]

In their *Letters to the Manchester Chartists* and *Stubborn Facts from the Factories* (1844), McDouall and Leach lodged a number of damning indictments – 'grasping fines, grinding wages, and their inhuman factory regulations', the exploitation of women, the reduction of wages and increase in unemployment consequent upon the introduction of machin-ery, and their control over the law – against the master manufacturers.[52]

Bronterre O'Brien, a national leader, and Richard Pilling, an impor-tant figure in south Lancashire Chartism, agreed with O'Connor, McDouall and Leach. O'Brien saw the 'proprietors of steam and money' as 'the people's worst enemies'. Like O'Connor, O'Brien reserved special hatred for the master manufacturers and other supporters of Corn Law Repeal. These 'sham' Radicals rejected the Chartist demand that repeal should follow rather than precede the introduction of the Charter. Furthermore, they were, according to O'Brien, 'our sworn enemies' whose 'real' motivations lay in the reduction of workers' wages and liv-ing standards and the enhancement of their own 'tyranny'. The first issue of O'Brien's *Poor Man's Guardian and Repealer's Friend* observed in 1843 that:

> The Corn-law Repealers are, for the most part, money-mongers, great master-manufacturers, merchants, brokers, ship-owners,

bankers and all that description of gentry who flourish by *machinery*, *paper-money*, and *foreign trade* . . . Now, if there be a class of men in this world more hostile to the Rights of Industry than all others, it is this class of speculators, who flourish by *machinery*, *paper-money*, and *foreign trade*. By the unlimited use, or rather abuse, of *machinery*, they render the skill and labour of millions of industrious artisans almost valueless to them. By the abuse of *paper-credit* they purloin the fruits of honest industry from those who earned them . . . And by their system of *foreign trade* they . . . heap comforts and luxuries on the basest of the human race at home and abroad . . . whilst our own fellow-countrymen and countrywomen, including the producers themselves, are obliged to go without any participation in, or enjoyment of, the products of their own unrivalled skill and industry . . .

Now the class of men represented by the Anti-Corn Law party are mainly the authors and abettors of this desolating system. Everything that lowers wages and degrades the workman, finds in them a willing friend. It is their interest that the work people of both countries, [i.e. Great Britain and Ireland*] should be in the lowest bearable state of impotence and destitution . . . It is their interest that the industrious classes, generally, should be without house and land . . . in order that they may be more completely at the mercy of employers (*words in brackets added).[53]

Pilling testified at Lancaster Assizes in 1843 that, as a result of his involvement in wage struggles in south Lancashire, 'the masters combined all as one man against me, and neither me nor my children could get a day's employment'. 'The masters conspired to kill me', concluded Pilling, 'and I combined to keep myself alive'.[54]

The passion and depth of opposition to the 'tyranny' of master manufacturers can be gauged from the various collective and personal responses offered: 'Physical-force' political and industrial actions, as seen in Chartism and the general strikes of 1842; militant trade unionism in cotton and elsewhere; and resorts to moral outrage, 'riot' and 'turbulence', constituted manifestly challenging replies. The personal responses of our selected Chartists were equally defiant and militant. O'Connor, for example, declared that:

I have seen so much of this system; I have seen so much of the brutality of the purse-proud *liberal masters*, so much of the suffering of their slaves, both old and young, that I would cheerfully venture my life tomorrow to put an end to the damnable system, a system which if not stopped, will snap every tie by which society should be bound.[55]

In a lecture given in Manchester in 1843 Leach 'showed very clearly' that: the tyranny of the landlord on the one hand, and the grinding monopoly of the cotton lord on the other, was fast reducing the sons and daughters of England, to rags and wretchedness.

A year later Leach declared that the employers: 'wield a dominion and enforce a tyranny over the lives and the liberties of their fellow men, such as no government could for a moment attempt to enforce upon a nation without running the risk of a violent and terrible revolution'.[56]

A former handloom weaver forced into the mill, Pilling 'detested the factory system' and warned, 'it is a system, which, above all systems, will bring this country to ruin if it is not altered'.[57]

The sentiments described above demonstrate that Chartist perceptions of relations between employers and workers in production were, to say the least, far less favourable than claimed by Stedman Jones. Furthermore, as seen especially in the speeches and writings of O'Brien and O'Connor, Chartist attacks upon the 'steamlords' were often part of much wider indictments of large sections of the middle classes, both industrial and commercial.[58] As we will later observe in more detail, in the eyes of the Chartists many middle-class people had adopted 'dishonourable' and 'deceitful' economic and political habits; and were henceforth disqualified from membership of the 'useful' or 'producing' classes. Once again, concrete experiences, perceived to be interrelated rather than discrete, rather than refined academic abstraction, constituted the key to the development of Chartists' thoughts and actions. While it is not claimed that the views of our selected Chartists were representative of all strands of thought within the movement, it should be noted that O'Connor, O'Brien, McDouall and, to a lesser extent, Leach enjoyed great popularity well beyond the confines of the factory districts of Lancashire and Cheshire.

Sharp criticisms of the encroachment of 'dishonourable' capitalist practices upon the world of work were, furthermore, not confined to the factory areas. As Clive Behagg, David Goodway, Iorwerth Prothero, Adrian Randall and others have conclusively demonstrated,[59] structural economic change was, albeit unevenly, placing great strains upon the notion of harmonious 'producing' or 'productive' classes within the realm of workshop or 'artisan' production.

Thus Behagg argues that competitive production for a mass market altered the face of Birmingham's economy during the 1830s and 1840s. Faced with competition from factories, lacking the advantages of economies of scale, and increasingly dependent upon the credit and market facilities of the merchant or large-scale manufacturer, many of the smaller employers unilaterally resorted to 'dishonourable' practices: of wage cutting, increasing hours of labour, undermining apprenticeship systems, sweating and shedding labour. The customary notion of reciprocity between master and artisan was being supplanted by the rise of narrow self-interest and the cash nexus. Conflicts between labour and capital escalated and, contrary to the traditional wisdom, social and political movements in Birmingham increasingly fractured along class lines. Behagg can thus conclude that the notion of the 'productive classes' had become by the late 1830s 'a fairly hackneyed formula . . . because the class unity it implied was increasingly at odds with work-place reality'.[60]

Similar developments could be observed elsewhere. In London the widespread beating down of wages and trade defences, increased insecurity, unemployment, and dependency on the part of workers, and the accelerated pace of capitalist development underscored the capital's mounting class conflict and Chartist strength of the 1840s. As David Goodway observes, criticisms of capitalist employers' 'love or gain' and 'tyranny' grew. Some, such as a member of the Metropolitan Tailors' Protection Society, advocated 'a general union' of the members (women as well as men) of the individual trades and manhood suffrage in order to combat 'all tyranny'.[61]

We must remind ourselves that the pace and extent of structural economic change and proletarianisation did vary considerably both within and between trades. In some centres, such as Kentish London and parts of Edinburgh, where change was less rapid and threatening, the notion of an alliance of the 'producing classes' retained much of its strong appeal throughout the Chartist years.[62] Conversely, local and regional variations should not obscure three outstanding national facts: that accelerated capitalist transformation occasioned growing class conflicts within a variety of workplace settings; that criticisms of capitalist 'tyranny' in production and elsewhere united seemingly disparate artisans and factory operatives; and that general mistrust of the middle classes and a central emphasis upon political independence characterised Chartism. In such various ways did class display its considerable presence.

We have thus observed, contrary to the claim of Stedman Jones, that some Chartists did articulate a theory of class-based exploitation in production. This theory may have been primitive by the standards of the mature Marx of *Capital*: and the demands of our selected Chartists were more limited – calling for 'due protection, reward and acknowledgement'[63] for the worker – than Marx's call for socialist revolution. Moreover, Chartists such as McDouall and O'Connor did express an unduly rosy view of 'traditional' household and workshop production. As would become evident in the mid Victorian years, the elbow room afforded to the employers to 'mend their ways' provided a potential basis for improved relations at work and for the growth of more general working-class reformism.

Simultaneously, however, the various limitations of Chartist thought and action, as measured against Stedman Jones's 'true' Marxist standard of class, should not be exaggerated. The general unwillingness of employers, politicians and the State to meet popular demands for adequate recognition and reward moved workers, as seen in Chartism generally and in particular during the years 1838–39, 1842 and even 1848, to countenance very 'extreme' measures in order to achieve their 'reasonable' goals. Mainland Britain did not experience a revolutionary situation between the late 1830s and the late 1840s; but, as most recently described by John Saville,[64] many hundreds of thousands of moderate labouring men and women did resort to strikes and insurrectionary means in opposition to the general unfairness and intransigence of the 'system'. In themselves, demands for manhood suffrage, decent wages and so on were not necessarily 'limited' or 'reformist'. Such descriptions can only realistically be applied once demands have been situated within their full political, economic, social and cultural contexts; and the intended and unintended consequences of thought and action explored. Even in the post-Chartist period it is all too easy to underestimate the continued frequency and bitterness of industrial conflicts and evidence of more general class divisions within an overall context of growing social stability and bourgeois hegemony.[65]

Furthermore, in employing a narrow model of how the Chartists *should* have expressed themselves in order to pass the class 'test', Stedman Jones, as we have observed, effectively bypasses the actual, and considerable extent to which they *did* develop an experiential language and critique of exploitation in production. In effect 'is' is masked under 'ought'. As I noted in 'In defence of class' (p. 41), it is, moreover:

> extremely difficult to see how the Chartists could have moved 'in the direction of a class-based theory of exploitation of a social democratic or Marxist kind' when, at least in the years before 1848, Marx had not established the fundamentals of his theory of surplus value, and thus found the riddle of exploitation under conditions of commodity production.

Ironically, while sensitive to the 'limitations' of Chartism, Marx and Engels did recognise the movement's forceful critique of employer 'tyranny' and orthodox political economy. In *The Condition of the Working Class in England*, Engels thus wrote:

> Chartism is of an essentially social nature, a class movement. The 'Six Points' which for the Radical bourgeois are the beginning and end of the matter . . . are for the proletarian a mere means to further ends. 'Political power our means, social happiness our end', is now the clearly formulated war-cry of the Chartists.[66]

In their 'moral' critique of capitalist social relations, and their identification of a capitalist system, complete with underlying structural dynamic (of profit maximisation) and conscious agency (the desire to subjugate labour to capital's will), our selected Chartists did presage some of the key arguments in Marx's *Capital*.

Stedman Jones's restricted and decontextualised definition of class also leads him to overlook the manifest presence of class in extra-economic areas of life, in Chartist attitudes to politics and the middle classes, and in the attitudes of Chartist women. We will cite linguistic and other kinds of evidence in support of this extended presence of class.

Class: politics and the middle class

As I wrote in my article, 'In defence of class' (p. 39):

> Once we dispense with the notion of 'true' consciousness and agree with Edward Thompson's claims that 'Class eventuates as men and women *live* their productive relations, and as they *experience* their determinate situations, within "the *ensemble* of the social relations" ', and that 'No actual class formation is any truer or more real than any other, and class defines itself as, in fact, it eventuates', then we can more fruitfully explore the nature of Chartist consciousness within its own historical context, within its own meanings and points of reference, and in relation to the judgments of contemporaries and historians – without expecting a perfect fit between 'is' and 'ought'.

In keeping with these sentiments, we can also endorse Dorothy Thompson's view that: 'Chartism was pervaded by a sense of class – both a positive sense of identification and a negative hostility to superior classes – which was stronger than perhaps existed at any other point in the nineteenth century'.[67]

Thompson's writings on Chartism provide an outstanding account of the wide-ranging manifestations of class. In general terms the middle classes thus, 'certainly believed themselves to be superior in every way to the classes above and below them in morality, knowledge and understanding'. And: 'Class domination was not confined to the work-place. All aspects of social life – dwelling-places, shops, drinking-places, recreational and instructional institutions, churches and chapel seating – were segregated on class lines'. Most middle-class people saw workers as being 'without souls, minds, or culture', 'fierce', 'rough', 'undisciplined', lacking 'restraint', and easily led into 'riot and subversion'.[68]

As I have noted:

> The response of the Chartists was to attempt to build an alternative 'movement culture', free from the patronising and unwelcome attentions of both bourgeois and aristocrat. Concerns with personal dignity and independence . . . and, above all, with an unbending faith in the ability of workers to fashion their own destinies – these were the essential features of Chartism's alternative way of life.[69]

At times the words and emphases of the Chartists – upon universal manhood suffrage, the excluded 'people', and upon the importance of reason,
and peaceful, constitutional means – did, as argued by Stedman Jones,
have much in common with a past radical and broadly based tradition.
His adoption of a non-referential, largely autonomous, theory of language obscures the very considerable extent to which words, emphases,
political languages and so forth operated within, took their meanings
from, and shaped changing social contexts. Within these contexts there
existed questions of power, the balance of class and other social forces,
the role of politics and culture and what was considered to be tactically
and strategically possible and advantageous. Changed contexts could
and often did induce shifts in the meanings of language.[70]

Chartist languages and symbols thus often addressed and embraced
'physical-force' and sharply delineated class positions which were not at
all to the liking of middle-class constitutionalists and 'producers'. In not-
ing 'a serious lack of context' in Stedman Jones's work, Dorothy
Thompson provides a number of telling corrective examples. Thus:

> The Chartist appeal to the middle classes had the loaded pistols of
> huge crowds, torchlight meetings, millions of signatures and arming
> and drilling in communities in which the control of police and mag-
> istrates was minimal . . . behind the arguments for natural rights and
> natural justice lay the mass meeting and the threat of armed rising.
> Devyr specifically says, and was arrested . . . for saying so, that the
> alternative for the middle classes if the Charter was not achieved
> peacefully with their help, was the destruction of their families and
> the firing of their shops and factories . . . The appeal for manhood
> suffrage and an open, constantly-renewed parliament . . . may have
> been similar to the programme of the Association Movement, of
> Major Cartwright and of the London Corresponding Society. But
> the context in which it was proposed was very different. In still
> another context it was exactly the same programme which was put
> forward in 1791 by the United Irishmen and which led them directly
> into participation in the biggest rising against the British
> Government since the seventeenth century. This too was part of the
> context in which the Chartists put forward their arguments.

In terms of the semiotics of the movement:

> When the Chartists . . . toasted the memory of Robert Emmett . . .
> they were signalling admiration for some one who had been publicly
> hanged and decapitated for treason in the memory of most living
> people. The Cap of Liberty and the Tricolour signalled support for
> the early days of the French Revolution, and were to be seen regu-
> larly at Chartist rallies. When Feargus O'Connor dressed in a suit of
> fustian and submitted his name for election to the executive of the
> National Charter Association, he was making gestures towards egal-
> itarianism and democratic control which went far beyond anything
> in the political vocabulary of Hunt or Cobbett.[71]

Without wishing to reduce language to a specific context or constituency, we should insist upon the great extent to which the language of the 'excluded people' was not simply stretched (as suggested by Stedman Jones) but also *changed*, in class-based ways, by the 'Great Betrayal' of 1832 and the 'reforming' Whig measures of the 1830s. Middle-class Radicals were active in the early years of Chartism, there did develop local instances of successful cross-class political alliances, and during the 1840s some Chartist leaders, such as Vincent and Lowery, strongly supported a movement into Liberalism. Furthermore, in 1842 Joseph Sturge's Complete Suffrage Union did extend its middle-class hand of friendship to the principles, if not the name, of Chartism. However, such instances of inter-class co-operation paled into relative insignificance in the face of two outstanding facts of Chartism: its predominantly working-class character; and its central insistence from the late 1830s onwards upon its *political independence*. Thus, most of the movement's early middle-class friends turned against 'physical-force' Chartism in 1838 and 1839. In turning towards an alliance with the middle classes, Vincent and Lowery isolated themselves from mainstream Chartism.

During the 1840s O'Connor, the principal advocate of independence, was at the head of the movement. The Anti-Corn Law League failed to recognise the primacy of the demand for manhood suffrage and, as we have seen (and despite *some* instances of co-operation) forfeited mass Chartist support. Sturge's refusal to treat the Chartists as equals and to recognise the legitimacy of the name of the movement (in view of its contextualised violent implications) cost him dear.[72]

The insistence of mainstream Chartism upon political independence was steeped in the perceptions and actions of class. Thus Dorothy Thompson observes that Chartism's language 'at all levels was class language, the concepts of universal suffrage, the rights of man and of equality of citizenship were only held by the lower orders, the working class or classes'. Editor Edward Baines of Leeds, a reformer in 1832, but an opponent of Chartism, expressed a similar point of view in 1839:

> No man – not even the members of the Convention – pretend that Chartists are to be found (in numbers worth mentioning) in any class except the working class. All other classes of the people – the nobility, the gentry, the members of professions, the merchants, the manufacturers, the tradesmen and shopkeepers, and the farmers – are strenuously against Universal Suffrage.[73]

Thompson further underlines the class-based constituency of Chartism:

> The advocacy of suffrage extension to non-property-owners was, after 1832, almost entirely confined to politicians and political journalists who looked to a working-class constituency for support. Apart from the short and rather lonely excursion into complete

suffrage by Joseph Sturge and a few associates in 1842, the middle
and upper classes held firmly aloof. The Chartists did indeed appeal
on many occasions for support . . . to members of higher classes . . .
but support in the House of Commons even for hearing their
arguments never rose above 50 votes; on the single occasion when a
motion to implement the six points was presented it was defeated by
224 votes to 15, and only one Chartist MP was ever returned by a
post-1832 borough electorate. The hundreds of thousands who
signed the petition and turned out at their meetings and rallies were
overwhelmingly voteless men, women and young people.[74]

By no means all middle class people were perceived to be the Chartists'
natural enemies. Local shopkeepers, dependent upon working-class custom, and 'honourable' or 'good' employers (those 'who paid fair wages,
who negotiated with workers' organisations and who obeyed the laws
relating to the age and gender of employees') were included as part of the
'useful', 'producing' or even 'working' class or classes.[75] Similarly, even
in the face of the 'sham radicalism' of the 1830s, some Chartists continued to appeal to the reason and 'producerist' interests of sections of the
middle class. Parts of a placard, issued by the council of the Northern
Political Union in July 1839 and addressed 'To the Middle Classes of the
North of England', thus read:

> Gentlemen:– We address you in the language of brotherhood, proba-
> bly for the last time. Up to the very last moment you have shut your
> senses to reason: but now that the last moment for moral appeal has
> arrived, perhaps you will listen to this last appeal of the people . . .
>   Will the Aristocracy associate with you – will they endure an
> alliance by marriage with what they impudently denominate your
> base blood?
>   Do they not, in one word, despise and oppress you as much as
> they do the working men, the only difference being that you are able,
> and would appear *willing*, to bear the yoke, whilst we are unable,
> and thank God neither are we willing to bear it?
>   . . . even if you are content to remain quiescent slaves, you will be
> permitted to remain so no longer.
>   . . . If successful, the people will look on their fallen brothers and
> apostrophize their mangled remains thus: 'Well, you were sacrificed
> by the middle classes; they could have saved you but they would not;
> they assisted and encouraged the aristocracy to murder you! . . .
>   Praying that God, who endowed you with common sense and
> human feelings will free your mind from the prejudice and dispose
> you to do your duty in this terrible crisis,
>   We remain (if not, your own faults) your sincere friends . . .[76]

By the end of 1839 no such appeals were being made: calls for a general
stoppage of work (the Sacred Month); arming and drilling; widespread
rumours of insurrection and the Newport Rising of November; the mass
arrests of Chartist leaders (in some cases by those very same middle-class

reformers who had threatened violence in the tumultuous run up to the passage of the Great Reform Bill) severed inter-class ties. Patience had come to an end. In addition to an oppressive political system and exploitative employers, the vast majority of middle-class people had, in their indifference or hostility to the Chartist cause, come to be seen as enemies of the 'people'.

Confirmation had thus been given to the opinions of those Chartists who had earlier highlighted middle-class political betrayal, support for the New Poor Law and opposition to trade unionism and a reduction in the hours of factory labour. In his *National Reformer* of 1837, O'Brien had criticised the class-based political hypocrisies of a group of 'Pretend Radicals' meeting at a hotel in Blackfriars:

> If these radical-club men were honest, they would put extension of suffrage first, and urge the ballot and repeal of the corn-laws, only as useful and necessary consequences of general suffrage . . .
> I always suspected this club since a friend of mine, who is a member, once told me that the majority of them had a horror of universal suffrage. They are willing enough to get rid of kings, lords, and priests . . . but only talk of enfranchising the labourers, and that moment they look suspiciously on you, and affect to treat your opinions as either absurd or dangerous.

In his defence at Lancaster Assizes in 1843 O'Connor declared that, 'Since machinery and capital became represented in the House of Commons, the hostility between master and man has become greater and greater every year . . . '.[77]

By the early 1840s mainstream Chartism thus seriously questioned the sincere and genuine character of middle-class political, economic and socio-cultural overtures of friendship. While the Tories were seen as the 'open' enemy, generally united in their defences of inequality, tradition and oligarchy, the Whigs, including their more radical elements, were widely branded by the Chartists as 'a treacherous, deceitful, bad lot' whose commitment to political reform fell short of support for universal suffrage.[78] For their part, most middle-class people had come to associate the Charter with violent revolution and threats to the sanctity of property. For Macaulay, the Whig historian, universal suffrage was 'utterly incompatible with the very existence of civilisation'. To Karl Marx, universal suffrage was synonymous with working-class power:

> Universal suffrage is the equivalent of political power for the working classes of England, where the proletariat forms the large majority of the population, where . . . it has gained a clear consciousness of its position as a class . . . The carrying of Universal Suffrage in England would, therefore, be a far more socialistic measure than anything which has been honoured with that name on the

Continent. Its inevitable result, here, is the political supremacy of the working class.[79]

In such ways and to such an extent had the terms the 'people' and the 'producers' become closely identified with labouring people by the 1840s.

Chartist women and class

The labouring people embraced, of course, men and women. It is useful to remind ourselves that, despite male domination of the languages of Chartism, women's voices were not still.[80] As Thompson, Clark, Schwarzkopf, Jones and others have informed us, women's involvement in Chartism was predominantly class based in character. Women sought to protect their homes, families and communities – their primary points of attachment – from the ravages of capitalist industrialisation (overwork, poverty, ill health, exploitation, and male unemployment in the midst of waged work for women) and the oppression of the State (as seen, for example, in the disruptive effects of the New Poor Law and unprotected labour upon the customary unity and welfare of the family). Within Chartism there was more support for the enfranchisement of women (or at least unmarried and widowed women) than is often supposed.

Specifically feminist concerns do not appear to have had a substantial appeal among Chartist women and men. At the same time, it would be wrong rigidly to impose middle-class notions of domesticity, 'separate spheres' and the 'family wage' upon the working class during the Chartist period. Long and continuing traditions of work for women, both inside and outside the home, paid and unpaid, combined with the continued, if weakened, relatively flexible sexual division of labour associated with eighteenth-century household production, ensured that large numbers of working-class women had 'places' in the community as well as in the home. As a corollary, women had an established tradition of involvement in community- and household-based forms of protest.[81]

Within Chartism women thus fought for the contentment, well-being and security of their families and communities. In doing so they employed notions of class (Dorothy Thompson) and 'militant domesticity' (Anna Clark). The 'Address of the female political union of Newcastle upon Tyne to their fellow countrywomen', issued in February 1839, usefully illustrated the close connections between domestic- and class-based issues. Parts of the Address read:

> FELLOW-COUNTRYWOMEN, – We call upon you to join us and help our fathers, husbands, and brothers, to free themselves and us from political, physical, and mental bondage, and urge the following reasons as an answer to our enemies and an inducement to our friends.

We have been told that the province of woman is her home, and that the field of politics should be left to men; this we deny; the nature of things renders it impossible . . . Is it not true that the interests of our fathers, husbands, and brothers, ought to be ours? If they are oppressed and impoverished, do we not share those evils with them? We have read the records of the past, and our hearts have responded to the historian's praise of those women, who struggled against tyranny and urged their country-men to be free or die . . .

For years we have struggled to maintain our homes in comfort . . . Year after year has passed away, and even now our wishes have no prospect of being realised, our husbands are over wrought, our houses half furnished, our families ill-fed, and our children uneducated – the fear of want hangs over our heads; the scorn of the rich is pointed towards us; the brand of slavery is on our kindred, and we feel the degradation. We are a despised caste; our oppressors are not content with despising our feelings, but demand the control of our thoughts and wants . . . .

We have searched and found that the cause of these evils is the Government of the country being in the hands of a few of the upper and middle classes, while the working men who form the millions, the strength and wealth of the country, are left without the pale of the Constitution . . . to pass the people's Charter into a law and emancipate the white slaves of England. This is what the working men of England, Ireland, and Scotland, are struggling for, and we have banded ourselves together in union to assist them; and we call on all our fellow country-women to join us.

We tell the wealthy, the high and mighty ones of the land, our kindred shall be free.[82]

As seen in the 'Address', Chartists did not generally define class-based exploitation in purely production-based terms. Experience showed that politics and the 'social' could not be neatly compartmentalised, as if obeying the logic of a fine intellectual exercise. Women in particular experienced exploitation beyond the confines of paid work outside the home. It was Chartism's ability to tap community- and family-based, as well as workshop- and factory-based, and political grievances which resulted in its mass appeal.

The final word on Chartism, class and exploitation properly belongs to the leading authority on the movement, Dorothy Thompson. 'I find it difficult to believe', writes Thompson:

that anyone who has worked in the archives and has studied the published and unpublished language of the Chartists can fail to see that the idea that above all united them into a nation-wide movement was the belief that there was a profound unity of interest between working people of all kinds. The concept of universal suffrage – even in its all-male form . . . flies in the face of the view that the skilled feared the unskilled more than they feared the rich . . . If the divisions within the workforce were so great, it is difficult to see why so many skilled workmen were prepared to face imprisonment and even death alongside their unskilled brethren for the cause of general political emancipation. What is astonishing, in the light of later developments, is the extent to which the movement was able to incorporate people of different regional and ethnic origins, different genders and different occupations into a national campaign involving millions. The unifying factors were primarily a sense of class, a unifying leadership and a nationally distributed journal.[83]

Class: the post-Chartist period

As observed by a number of historians,[84] in the post-Chartist years this 'profound unity of interest' among workers was considerably weakened. Between the mid 1840s and the mid 1870s there occurred a pulling apart of formerly united groups, an accentuation of all manner of divisions within the working class (based on ethnicity, gender roles, 'respectability', skill and income), the decline of class-based political independence, and the growth of a more narrowly based and 'reformist' labour movement. As observed by Joyce and others, the mid Victorian period saw the powerful development of popular Liberalism, complete with its emphases upon progress and reason and its language of the 'people' or the 'masses' against the 'classes'. Furthermore, the very advances achieved by the collective institutions of the working class, such as co-ops, friendly societies and trade unions, and the personal gains made by labour leaders, combined with more favourable responses and initiatives on the part of the State and the political parties towards workers and organised labour, led to a mellowing of language.

Co-operators, for example, registered the dramatic financial and membership gains of their movement by speaking the languages of 'success', 'advancement' and the achievement of a 'stake' in British society. According to the Co-operator, the official organ of the movement during the 1860s, co-operation had enabled 'thousands of men' to attain that 'independence and contentedness of mind which is the happiest state the natural man can feel, having plenty of clothes and food and something to spare for the needy'. Within the male and craft/skill-dominated post-Chartist labour movement notions of 'separate spheres' and a 'women's place' hardened. There was also more extensive accommodation to the market mechanism and the everyday rhythms and structures of capitalism, and the adoption of more 'privatised' concerns and values than in the Chartist years. In effect, capitalism was increasingly being experienced as a relatively stable and secure system, to be 'lived with' (as opposed to totally incorporated into) rather than frontally challenged. Chartism, Owenism and other earlier schemes for a 'revolving of the whole system' came to be seen by labour activists as well-meaning but hopelessly utopian experiments, incapable of practical realisation: and languages of 'physical force' and general class conflict lost much of their earlier popularity. Co-operators and others spoke of social harmony and marching, as united 'communities' or 'productive' 'people', in 'the van of progress'. In these manifest ways did experience, and especially changed experience, demonstrate the full force of its presence upon language.[85]

However, this was not the total picture, as seen in terms of either social trends or the relationships between language and experience. For example, class may have diminished in importance in the post-Chartist years, but it most certainly did not expire. Especially at the workplace there occurred bitter, numerous and momentous industrial and class conflicts. Productive of countless acrimonious conflicts was the employers' continued insistence upon their absolute 'right' to 'manage their affairs'. During the mid Victorian period there continued to exist an abundance of 'unreasonable' and 'tyrannical' employers, both paternalist and non-paternalist in character, who stubbornly refused to recognise trade unions, however moderate the latter might have become. Trade union leaders did increasingly adopt the language of 'co-operation', 'restraint', 'responsibility' and the 'unity of interests' of labour and capital: but, in the face of 'unreasonable' employers, trade unionists' language could undergo dramatic changes. As Eleanor Gordon has argued in relation to the Scottish experience, language and ideas were multifaceted. Thus: 'The perception of an inherent conflict of interest between capital and labour permeated trade union discussions, and the awareness of the divide between the two classes was frequently articulated even by those union officials who advocated conciliation and co-operation if not class collaboration'.[86]

The actual behaviour of trade unionists was similarly many-sided. As Eric Hobsbawm declared in a memorable sentence in *Labouring Men* (p. 323): 'The labour aristocrat might wear a top-hat and think on business matters exactly like his employer, but when the pickets were out against the boss, he knew what to do.'

Beyond the workplace, politics, culture, leisure and ideologies were subjected to class-based influences. Liberalism, for example, was not a totally homogeneous and harmonious creed. Differences of opinion concerning the extent and nature of suffrage reform (household versus manhood); public intervention and regulation versus *laissez-faire*, and the further extension of democratic and egalitarian practices to political and social life, continued to reflect class divisions within both Liberalism and the wider framework of British politics. 'Respectability' could continue to carry connotations of class and conflict as well as privatised and socially soothing meanings. Beneath the rash of 'community-minded' projects in mid Victorian Britain (the opening of public libraries, parks and so on), there often lurked all manner of class- and gender-based fears and assumptions (ranging from 'pacification' of workers to concern with the further consolidation of complementary, if separate, public and private spheres).[87]

The continued, albeit diminished, influence of class holds a number of troublesome implications for Joyce, Stedman Jones, and members of the 'Cambridge School'. First, it becomes evident that the general passage from Chartism into Liberalism was less smooth, untroubled and harmonious than they suggest. Secondly, sharp political discontinuities characterised post-Chartist popular politics. As Thompson argues:

> in turning towards the Liberal Party after the end of Chartism the former Chartists were to a large extent abandoning the social programme which had been such an essential part of the movement, and reverting to the political questions alone, which had . . . always had the support of a considerable group in Parliament. It was the social content of Chartism which had made cooperation with this group impossible, and it was not until the revival of independent working-class politics towards the end of the nineteenth century that this submerged social programme again became a part of British politics.[88]

Thirdly, during the mid Victorian years the discourse of the 'people' encountered the language of class much more frequently than suggested by Joyce. Fourthly, rather than simply *identify* 'populism' or 'populisms', of a largely unitary character, Joyce could also have very usefully broken down, indeed deconstructed, these 'populisms' and *engaged* them, in specific contexts and over time, with class-based and other discourses. We would then be in a better position to observe and evaluate the complex interactions and relative importance of these discourses, and the relationship between language and the 'social' in mid Victorian Britain. In effect, Joyce sets up an over-simplified dichotomy between largely static languages of class and the 'people'. While usefully deepening and extending our understanding of the range of popular discourses at work, Joyce has nevertheless missed a golden opportunity to further develop that process of contextualised engagement between languages and social experience so central to the work of Crossick, Gray, Kirk and other historians of workers in mid Victorian Britain. Further research will hopefully further develop this contextualised agenda.

A final observation must be made concerning the relationship between language and the 'social'. Concrete examples have been offered in preceding paragraphs concerning the ways in which experience strongly influenced language: but this was not a one-way process, with language as the passive reflection of prior experience. Rather, while not exhausting the limits of reality, language did help to shape understanding and existence. Trade unionists, for example, consciously used the language of moderation and social harmony, highlighted the benefit features of their movement, and made strenuous efforts to translate words into action in an attempt to convince members of the public – and especially influential members of government and the Royal Commission on Trade Unions – that trade unionism should be afforded legal recognition and thus become an accepted part of the 'British way of life'.

As seen in the findings of the Royal Commission, this tactical and strategic use of language did help to define trade unionism in more acceptable ways to a largely unsympathetic middle-class public.[89] Strikes and 'outrages' were by no means erased from the 'public mind'; but they were increasingly seen as being untypical of the movement as a whole; although the discourses of moderation utilised by trade unionists were neither fully autonomous nor omnipotent. They gathered much of their practical force from the changed context in which they developed. The relaxation of earlier pressures upon capital accumulation, Britain's rise to a position of 'workshop of the world', the consolidation of bourgeois hegemony throughout British society and the decline of Chartism provided a determining context in which scope for class manoeuvre and concessions to workers greatly increased. Changed language constituted one factor among this wider range of influences reconstituting Victorian reality.

Theoretical defects

Our statement in favour of the limited powers and necessary contextualisation of language leads us to consider the main theoretical weaknesses of the 'linguistic turn'.

Idealism and subjectivism

Our first argument is that, despite intentions to the contrary, Vernon's, Joyce's and Stedman Jones's *practices* effectively dissolve reality into language, and result in an unconvincing idealist and subjectivist historiography. In *Languages of Class* (p. 6) Stedman Jones did not wish 'to imply that the analysis of language can provide an exhaustive account of Chartism'. 'It is not a question', continued Stedman Jones, 'of replacing a social interpretation by a linguistic interpretation, it is how the two relate, that must be rethought'. Similarly, in *Visions of the People* Joyce makes references to language and the social order, language and economic and social conditions and so on. And James Vernon has insisted in *Social History* that an emphasis upon the discursive construction of reality does not invalidate the investigation of socio-structural factors or 'the materiality of poverty or wealth'.

So far the charge of 'linguistic determinism' would appear to be misplaced; but matters do not end at this point. As we have noted throughout this chapter, our three historians also deny the very nature of the 'social' outside of and prior to its articulation by means of language, and the existence of class as an ontological, as opposed to a discursive, reality. In practice, we have seen that, in the eyes of Stedman Jones, the Chartist reality resided solely in a particular strand of the movement's decontextualised language. Joyce, while paying lip service to the importance of context, nevertheless fails to socially or discursively engage his 'populisms'; and further argues that notions of the economy, society and polity lack 'overarching coherence' and underlying structures beyond their linguistic constructions.[90]

In their absolute terror of being accused of 'reflective' or 'reductionist' approaches to history, all three authors abandon 'realist' assumptions and methodologies in favour of the 'conceptualisation of "the social" as a discursive construct'.[91] Any distinction between 'representational' and 'real' levels are collapsed; and reality becomes the narrow cul-de-sac of language and nothing more. Idealism and subjectivism come to prevail. 'Linguistic determinism' proves, after all, to be the most appropriate critical description of the 'linguistic turn'.

The conflation of reality and language has a number of damaging effects. At both the empirical and theoretical levels it becomes impossible to link, or engage, the 'social', the 'political' and the 'linguistic'. All we can engage are idealist discourses of politics, the economy and society. Discourses mysteriously emerge, circulate and command 'history', unencumbered by mundane 'modernist' or 'realist' considerations of materiality, power and inequality, and empirical controls. But opposition to 'social determinism' does not signal equality in the discursive universe; the languages of politics are asserted, rather than demonstrated, to exert hegemonic influence. Thus, whereas Althusser's theoretically constructed system was ultimately determined by the 'economic', Joyce's, Vernon's and Stedman Jones's idealist world is ironically 'determined' by political languages. 'Modernist' social history, with its categories of the 'real', 'experience', 'agency' and external reality is deposed. Political ideas, narratives and languages have been 'restored' to their 'traditional' thrones.

If the effects upon the study of social history as a whole are far-reaching and damaging, then the implications for any adequate study of class, are equally detrimental. In practice, the narrow equation of class with a particular linguistic construct means that an unsatisfactory fixed point of linguistic reference improperly takes precedence over the richness and complexity of class, both as a process and a relationship which changes over time. That vast space lying between, on the one hand, class structure and on the other, class-consciousness (involving language) and action is effectively denied historical investigation. The roles of individual agency, of institutions, of households and communities, of gender, ethnicity and race, and of the interplays between structural determinations and contingency and specific historical conjunctures in class formation and expression, are closed down. We are simply left with people as the agents and bearers of political discourse, and nothing more.

Further methodological and epistemological problems abound. There is, for example, the manifest tendency in the work of Joyce and Stedman Jones to take language at face value, uncritically to accept the maxim that people mean exactly what they say or communicate. There is precious little attempt to 'look behind' people's languages; to link saying and doing, to explore the intended and unintended effects of saying and doing; and to balance self-perception and self-presentation against the ways in which one is regarded and treated by others. Thus we have seen that, in the eyes of Stedman Jones, the Chartists meant only what they said: and for Patrick Joyce, John Bright's political reputation as 'the standard bearer of the people' is not set and measured against Bright's reputation in Rochdale as a tyrannical employer of labour.[92] Once again, we are presented with a very partial, and to some extent naive, view of reality.

Relativism, objectivity and truth

There is, furthermore, no sustained and convincing attempt made by Vernon, Stedman Jones or Joyce to demonstrate the epistemological adequacy of their discursive views of the world. In terms, for example, of the discourses of their historical subjects, there arise a number of important and largely unanswered questions. How, for example, do we evaluate the relative merits and purchases upon 'reality' of different and at times competing views of life, such as 'populist' and class based? More generally, how do we handle the claims of different kinds of knowledge, running from the 'commonsensical' to the 'socially-scientific', to validity and truth? Are such (in part) 'realist' questions to be admitted as valid by our practitioners of post-structuralism and post-modernism? Which procedures and criteria is the historian to set in place in order to evaluate the veridical nature of his/her subjects' concepts and views? Is an 'anti-representational', anti-realist methodology to be adopted, in which notions of referentiality, objectivity and truth are dismissed as outmoded 'modernist' fantasies, and in which subjective and shifting meanings are held to be of central importance?[93] As in so much post-modernist and post-structuralist work, do not descriptions of various discourses effectively replace analysis, evaluation (including moral judgment) and demonstrated (rather than assumed) causative priority, as the 'true' goals of historical work? Can the historian really afford to sit back, 'playfully' indulge himself or herself in the identification and choice of different discursive 'realities', and refuse to offer 'modernist' judgments upon past and present? Do historians' judgments necessarily involve, as argued by Easthope and Vernon, realist/modernist 'desires' to 'master' reality?[94]

Such questions lead, in turn, to wider, extremely difficult and much contested issues concerning historical truth, objectivity, representation and epistemological relativism. I would suggest, for example, that one does not have to subscribe to the absolute view of a single, true interpretation of the world in order to question, along with Terry Eagleton, poststructuralist and post-modernist epistemological relativism. The latter, clearly evident in the work of our three historians, maintains that identifiable discursive constructions carry equal validity and epistemological adequacy (even if ultimately dominated by discourses of the 'political'). In reply, I would suggest that, while such constructions may be equally valid to their authors, they might nevertheless not carry equal weight as forms of 'social-scientific' knowledge.

Traditionally, of course, historians and other scholars have resorted to the criteria of theoretical rigour and consistency and degrees of correspondence to the full complexities of the empirical evidence, in order to judge the claims of discursive and non-discursive, 'commonsensical' and more structured academic systems of knowledge, to accuracy and truth. The pursuit of historical objectivity and truth have, at least within a realist tradition, been regarded both as worthy goals and in character, provisional and open to revision (by means of 'paradigm shifts' and the quarrying of new evidence).

By way of contrast, anti-realists or anti-representationalists, including many post-modernists and post-structuralists and some pragmatists, contest the very idea that language and ideas are true, 'because they accurately represent, or correspond to, the way the world is itself' (Richard Rorty). In the eyes of anti-representationalists, subjectivity is all important; as subjective members of society, people are held to be incapable of 'stepping outside' their very subjectivity, of becoming 'God-like', in order to evaluate their world in dispassionate, objective ways. For the pragmatist Rorty there is thus no 'intrinsic nature of things', no past or present 'out there' as 'objective referent', but rather a variety of subjective realities.[95] For Easthope, history becomes a series of subjective textual realities, and the modernist divisions between fact and fiction, 'hard' history and 'soft' literature dissolve. The study of history becomes the study of texts and nothing more.[96]

As I have argued elsewhere, the writings of (especially) Vernon and Joyce, and (somewhat more ambiguously[97]) Stedman Jones, belong to the anti-representational school of thought. In their contributions to debate in *Social History* and in their other writings, Joyce and Vernon pull anti-realist, anti-representational faces and adopt 'macho' discursive and subjective postures. 'Modernist' (embracing Marxist and realist) historiography, rooted in holistic perspectives, detailed empirical research and (allegedly) unified subjects, is arrogantly dismissed as naive, bland

and passé. Joyce gives the strong impression that E.P. Thompson's 'historical discourse of the proof', residing in the dialogue between concept and evidence, belongs to an outmoded representational past. At no point, however, do Joyce and Vernon offer detailed, reasoned and cogent explications and defences of their anti-realist methodologies and epistemologies. Instead, we are arrogantly presented with fragments of seemingly self-evident, yet in fact incomplete and often confusing and unclear, postmodernist articles of faith. As previously indicated, in *Languages of Class* Stedman Jones does make a reasoned and strong case in favour of the constitutive role of language in social life. However, very little attention is directed by Stedman Jones to the epistemological adequacy of the idealist and anti-realist practices which result from his adoption of a non-referential approach to the study of language.

Conclusion: the virtues of realism

The general conclusion thus emerges that Vernon, Joyce and Stedman Jones effectively dissolve reality/being into the processes of thought and language, and do not offer a convincing defence of their anti-representational practices. Idealism is pervasive. Shifting languages and discourses circulate and sometimes overlap, but any real external (i.e. empirical) controls are conspicuous by their effective absence. Circularity and self-confirmation become the idealist norm. There is no way off this discursive merry-go-round apart from the option of making and breaking concepts against complex evidence, the 'real' task of social history: but the latter represents far too 'modernist', misguided and mundane a purpose for Joyce's and Vernon's post-modernist juggernaut.

A more precise conclusion to be offered is that, in conflating being and language, Joyce, Vernon and Stedman Jones fail to make the necessary distinction between, on the one hand, *existence* and, on the other, *interpretation*, *understanding* and *meaning*. These are two distinct, if interconnected, areas of life. Eagleton's criticisms of the 'inflation of discourse' in the post-structuralist thought of Laclau and Mouffe can usefully be applied to the work of our three historians. 'A way of *understanding* an object', observes Eagleton:

is simply projected into the object itself, in a familiar idealist move. In notably academicist style, the contemplative analysis of a practice suddenly reappears as its very essence. The category of discourse is inflated to the point where it imperializes the whole world, eliding the distinction between thought and material reality. The effect of this is to undercut the critique of ideology – for if ideas and material reality are given indissolubly together, there can be no question of asking where social ideas actually hail from. The new 'transcendental' hero is discourse itself, which is apparently prior to everything else . . . [98]

On a less abstract level, it is important to remind ourselves that historians have clearly demonstrated the existence of realities beyond discourse; of, for example, socio-economic, political and cultural systems and processes which have emerged, changed and declined. It has, furthermore, been shown that social forces and changes often take place 'behind people's backs', and in unintended and partly unrecognised ways. As brilliantly argued by Marxist social anthropologist, Maurice Bloch, there is, in opposition to the claims of our three historians, more to the construction and comprehension of social life than language alone. Language can exist alongside a variety of practical non-linguistic influences which relate to conceptualisation and doing. Scholars have convincingly pointed out that the presence of class structures, demographic trends and even concepts in social life is ultimately not dependent upon their registration in language. Language confers meaning and understanding upon realities which both embrace and extend beyond the kinds of popular languages and discourses examined by Joyce, Vernon and Stedman Jones.[99]

The validity of the notion of reality reaching beyond language has been usefully demonstrated by the critical-realist philosopher, Roy Bhaskar. While emphasising the interaction between agency and inherited structure in the creation of social life, Bhaskar convincingly argues that structures are not solely consciousness-dependent. Thus:

> while social structures are dependent upon the consciousness which the agents who reproduce or transform them have, they are not reducible to this consciousness. Social practices are concept-dependent; but, contrary to the hermeneutical tradition in social science, they are not exhausted by their conceptual aspect. They always have a material dimension.

Further, in contrast to 'subjective idealism', Bhaskar's philosophical realism 'stands for the idea that material objects exist independently of our perceiving them, and in the domain of the social sciences for the idea that the conceptual and the empirical do not jointly exhaust the real.'[100]

As a form of realism, historical materialism takes some hard knocks from Joyce, Stedman Jones and Vernon. Thus the charges of 'social determinism', of a 'reflective' or 'reductionist' approach to language, and of the presentation of unitary views of social phenomena such as class, are levelled against historical materialism.[101] Found guilty on all counts, historical materialism is deemed to have outlived its usefulness as a means of historical investigation: but this is a judgment which the concluding part of this essay wishes to oppose. In effect, our three historians, and especially Joyce and Vernon, construct a model of historical materialism which most contemporary historical materialists neither support nor practise. 'Vulgar' Marxists and Stalinists may well bear a strong likeness to the picture of Marxism drawn by Vernon and Joyce; but such Marxists have exerted marginal influence upon political and intellectual practices in this country. The leading exponents of historical and cultural materialism would not recognise themselves in the pictures drawn by the 'Cambridge School'.

For many years now E.P. Thompson, Eric Hobsbawm, David Montgomery, Eugene Genovese, Dorothy Thompson and many other historical materialists and/or 'social determinists' have thus rejected the notion that ideas, values, norms and languages can simply be reduced to, or be seen as passive reflections, expressions or effects of an economic base. Rather, in eschewing both liberal pluralism and reductionist Marxism, E.P. Thompson, Raymond Williams and others have explored the various ways in which the 'material' sets limits to, and exerts pressures upon, other forms of social activity, including language and consciousness: but a mechanistic base–superstructure model is most definitely rejected. Ideas and cultural processes are afforded spaces, patterns of articulation and influences upon the material and other practices; but they are not treated as being fully autonomous, totally free floating or non-referential. Rather, contextualisation, complexity, nuance and an exploration of *linkages* lie at the heart of Thompsonian practice. This is a far cry from 'social determinism'. Similarly, many of our 'determinists' have long appreciated and explored the importance of language in both moulding and being shaped by other aspects of social life. Montgomery, Marx, Engels, and Hobsbawm constitute classic examples of materialists who have opposed the presentation of unitary or undifferentiated views of class. These historians, along with Dorothy Thompson, Angela John, Herbert Gutman, Sivanandan and many others have offered sophisticated and complex examinations of the interplays between sources of fragmentation and unity, competition and co-operation, individualism and mutuality, and conflict and comradeship in working-class life.[102]

In effect, Joyce, Vernon and other members of the 'Cambridge School' have erected a false model of historical materialism and its assumptions and practices. Instead of attempting to demolish historical materialism, we should endeavour in our current and future work more fully to extend its complex and nuanced insights and methods, into examinations of the interactions of language, class, ideas, gender, race and ethnicity. In undertaking this project, we will be obliged to oppose reductionism, idealism and subjectivism and, much in the manner of Williams and E.P. Thompson, attempt to incorporate the study of language into a wider framework of reference which should embrace agency and structure, structure and historical conjuncture and contingency, similarity and difference, saying and doing, the conscious and the unconscious, and the willed and unwilled consequences of thought and action. In these various ways we can both reconstruct and advance the study of class in refreshing and demanding ways.

Notes

1. Thompson addressed such criticisms in the Postscript to the 1968 edition of *The Making of the English Working Class*, Harmondsworth: Penguin, pp. 924–34. See also Glen, R. (1984) 'Debate over the working class', in his *Urban Workers in the Early Industrial Revolution*, Beckenham: Croom Helm; Rule, J. (1986) *The Labouring Classes in Early Industrial England 1750–1850*, London: Longman, Conclusion.

2. For a brief survey of criticisms of class see Kirk, N. (1987) 'In defence of class: A critique of recent revisionist writing upon the nineteenth-century English working class', *International Review of Social History*, 32, especially pp. 2–3.

3. See especially, Stedman Jones, G. (1982) 'The language of Chartism', in Epstein, J. and Thompson, D. (eds) *The Chartist Experience: Studies in Working-Class Radicalism and Culture, 1830–1860*, London: Macmillan; and Stedman Jones, G. (1983) 'Rethinking Chartism', in his *Languages of Class: Studies in English Working-Class History, 1832–1982*, Cambridge: Cambridge University Press; Joyce, P. (1991) *Visions of the People: Industrial England and the Question of Class, 1848–1914*, Cambridge: Cambridge University Press, pp. 5–6, ch. 2; Vernon, J. (1993) *Politics and the People: A Study in English Political Culture 1815–1867*, Cambridge: Cambridge University Press, Introduction.

4. See for example, Musson, A.E. (1972) *British Trade Unions, 1800–1875*, London: Macmillan; Reid, A. (1985) 'The division of labour and politics in Britain, 1880–1920', in Mommsen, W. and Husung, H.-G. (eds), *The Development of Trade Unionism in Great Britain and Germany, 1880–1914*, London: Allen and Unwin.

5. See for example, Kirk, N. (1994) *Labour and Society in Britain and the USA*, Aldershot: Scolar Press, 2 vols, vol. 1, *Capitalism, Custom and Protest, 1780–1850*, pp. 3–12, vol. 2, *Challenge and Accommodation, 1850–1939*, pp. 167–72.

6. For the strengths and weaknesses of the pronounced empirical emphasis within British Marxist historiography see Johnson R., McLennan G., Schwarz B., and Sutton, D. (eds) (1982) *Making Histories: Studies in History-Writing and Politics*, London: Hutchinson, Part one; Gray, R. (1990) 'History, Marxism and theory', in Kaye, H. and McClelland, K. (eds), *E.P. Thompson: Critical Perspectives*, Cambridge: Polity Press.

7. Clark, A. (1992) 'The rhetoric of Chartist domesticity: gender, language and class in the 1830s and 1840s', *Journal of British Studies*, 31, January; Scott, J. (1988) *Gender and the Politics of History*, New York: Columbia University Press; Hall, C. (1992), *White, Male and Middle Class: Explorations in Feminism and History*, Cambridge: Polity Press; Easthope, A. (1991) *British Post-Structuralism since 1968*, London: Routledge.

8. See for example, the work of Gutman, H. and Berlin, I. (1987) *Power and Culture: Essays on the American Working Class*, New York: Pantheon; Genovese, E. (1976) *Roll Jordan Roll: The World the Slaves Made*, New York: Vintage; Thompson, D. (1993) 'Ireland and the Irish in English radicalism before 1850', in her *Outsiders: Class, Gender and Nation*, London: Verso; Genovese, E. (1988) *Within the Plantation Household: Black and White Women of the Old South*, Chapel Hill: University of North Carolina Press, especially ch. 4 and Epilogue; Sivanandan, A. (1990) *Communities of Resistance: Writings on Black Struggles for Socialism*, London: Verso; Rowbotham, S. (1977) *A New World for Women: Stella Browne, Socialist Feminist*, London: Pluto Press.

9. For statements in favour of the 'patriarchy first' approach see Walby, S. (1986) *Patriarchy at Work: Patriarchal and Capitalist Relations in Employment* and Rose, S.O. (1992) *Limited Livelihoods: Gender and Class in Nineteenth-Century England*, London: Routledge; for the complex interactions between race and class see Gilroy, P. (1987) *There Ain't No Black in the Union Jack: The Cultural Politics of Race and Nation*, London: Hutchinson, ch. 1. As seen below, the effective conflation of language and reality constitutes a core weakness in the work of Stedman Jones and Joyce. For an invaluable and refreshing study which does explore the links and tensions between the 'cultural' and the 'social', between meaning and socio-economic structure and context, see Walkowitz, J. (1992) *City of Dreadful Delight: Narratives of Sexual Danger in Late-Victorian London*, London: Virago.

10. Kirk, N. (1994) 'History, language, ideas and post-modernism: A materialist view', *Social History*, vol. 19, 2, May.

11. Thompson, D. (1993) *Outsiders: Class, Gender and Nation*, p. 21.

12. McCord, N. (1985) 'Adding a touch of class', *History*, 70, p. 230, October; McCord, N. (1991) *British History, 1815–1906*, Oxford: Oxford University Press, pp. 103–7.

13. McCord, Norman (1985); Stedman Jones, G. (1983), pp. 20–4, 94–6.

14. Stedman Jones, G. (1983) pp. 134–7, 153–8, 177; Stedman Jones, G. (1982), pp. 20, 30, 31, 51–2; Kirk, N. (1987), pp. 5–12.

15. Most recently, Mayfield, D. and Thorne, S. (1992) 'Social history and its discontents: Gareth Stedman Jones and the politics of language', *Social History*, vol. 17, 2, May; Lawrence, J. and Taylor, M. (1993) 'The poverty of protest: Gareth Stedman Jones and the politics of language – a reply', *Social History*, vol. 18, 1, January.

16. Joyce, P. (1991); Joyce, P. (1993) 'The imaginary discontents of social history: A note of response to Mayfield and Thorne, and Lawrence and Taylor', *Social History*, vol. 18, 1, January; Vernon, J. (1993), especially Introduction; Vernon, J. (1994) 'Who's afraid of the "linguistic turn"?: The politics of social history and its discontents', *Social History*, vol. 19, 1, January; Easthope, A. (1993) 'Romancing the stone: History-writing and rhetoric', *Social History*, vol. 18, 2, May.

17. See for example, Easthope, A. (1993), pp. 246–9; Joyce, P. (1991), pp. 9, 16; Joyce, P. (1993), p. 84; Joyce, P. (1991) 'History and post-modernism', *Past and Present*, 133, November, p. 208; Vernon, J. (1994), pp. 84–5.

18. See Joyce, P. (1991), pp. 5–6, 11, ch. 2; Easthope, A. (1991), ch. 8, Conclusion.

19. See for example, McNall, S., Levine, R. and Fantasia, R. (eds) (1991) *Bringing Class Back In: Contemporary and Historical Perspectives*, Oxford: Westview Press.

20. Easthope, A. (1991) *British Post-Structuralism since 1968*, pp. xii–xiv, 16–22. The British experience is, however, not necessarily typical of the post-structuralist experience as a whole. For example, and notwithstanding his claim to the contrary, there is substantial evidence to suggest that Foucault retained his allegiance to structuralism, albeit of a discursive kind rather than the general structuralism of his teacher, Louis Althusser. Like Althusser, Foucault downplayed the importance of agency in the historical process in the face of seemingly omnipotent structural forces. See the powerful and convincing essay by Freundlieb, D. (1994) 'Foucault's theory of discourse and human agency' in Jones, C. and Porter, R. (eds) *Reassessing Foucault: Power Medecine and the Body*, London: Routledge, especially pp. 166–8, 175.

21. Stedman Jones, G. (1983), p. 7.

22. See for example, the Introduction and n. 2, p. 355 in Vernon, J. (1993); Vernon, J. (1994), p. 88; Joyce, P. (1991) Introduction; Joyce's most recent work, (1994) 'The end of social history?', *Social History*, vol. 20, 1, January, and (1994) *Democratic Subjects: the Self and the Social in Nineteenth-Century England*, Cambridge: Cambridge University Press, appeared after the completion of the body of my text. It should however be noted that this work does contain a more detailed account of Joyce's post-modernist faith. However, major problems concerning lack of clarity, consistency and rigour remain. For example, (see pp. 11–12 of *Democratic Subjects* and pp. 89–90 of 'The end of social history?') the author maintains that cultural meanings (of a linguistic kind) simultaneously 'handle' and 'inevitably construct' reality. Therein lies an obvious contradiction. Reality cannot both be 'handled', presumably with an existence apart from cultural meanings, and at the same time be *totally constructed* by those very same meanings. To compound his confused and confusing definition, Joyce mistakenly enlists the support of Giddens in his conflation of language and reality. For a critique of Joyce's linguistic determinism and a statement in favour of realism – the view that reality both encompasses and exists beyond meaning-centred languages, to embrace saying and doing and the intended and unintended consequences of thought and action – see the final section of this chapter under the subheading 'Theoretical Defects'. See also the admirably clear and convincing 'practical realist' statement by Appleby, J., Hunt, L. and Jacob, M. (1994) *Telling the Truth about History*, London: W.W. Norton, pp. 230–1, ch. 7.

Notwithstanding his endorsement of post-modernist emphases upon the relative, elusive and partial nature of statements made about the world and the impossibility of the 'modernist' search for truth, Joyce embraces the notion of 'populism' as a 'centred collective subject', complete with an essential anti-class meaning or 'truth' which is largely unchanging in character. In practice, Joyce is insufficiently attentive to Derrida's deconstructive emphases upon the 'endless play' of the 'signifier', upon the multitude of meanings assumed by populism or class and the futility of the search for a single, immutable essence or truth. In loudly and impatiently pronouncing the 'truth' of his own findings and the assumed and massive superiority of his own method, as against the practices of 'modernist' social historians (any sense of intellectual engagement or debate between equals is conspicuous by its absence), Joyce could be seen to subvert the relativism of his own post-modernist general principles. After all, might not Michel Foucault have hypothetically incurred Joyce's full wrath by interpreting the latter's strident anti-class, anti-establishment and pro-populist stance as a calculated bid for power and fame within academia under the guise of a selfless search for truth? In sum, Joyce's absolute practices sit very uneasily alongside post-modernist injunctions to relativism, scepticism and recurrent irony. The 'saviour of history' might in consequence be well advised to attend to his own inconsistencies and contradictions before excommunicating 'sectarian' and 'sanctimonious' 'fundamentalists' such as Kirk and Palmer.

23. Harvey, D. (1991) *The Condition of Postmodernity: An Enquiry into the Origins of Cultural Change*, Oxford: Blackwell, pp. 7, 43.
24. Ibid., ch. 6; Huyssen, A. (1986) *After the Great Divide: Modernism, Mass Culture and Postmodernism*, London: Macmillan, ch. 10; Callinicos, A. (1989) *Against Postmodernism: A Marxist Critique*, Cambridge: Polity Press.
25. Stedman Jones, G. (1983) pp. 7–8. In *The Archaeology of Knowledge*, Michel Foucault argued that a discursive analysis revolves around 'the regular formation of objects that emerge only in discourse', and that discourses are 'practices that systematically form the objects of which they speak'. See Freundlieb, D. (1994), pp. 165–6.
26. Vernon, J. (1993), pp. 4–5.
27. Joyce, P. (1991), pp. 9, 16; Joyce, P. (1993), p. 84; Scott, J. (1991) 'The evidence of experience', *Critical Inquiry*, 17, Summer.
28. Joyce, P. (1991), pp. 3, 10–11, 95–6; Vernon, J. (1993), pp. 10, 325–6, 330.
29. Vernon, J. (1993), pp. 5, 6, 11, Conclusion; Riley, D. (1988) *'Am I That Name?; Feminism and the Category of 'Women' in History*, Basingstoke: Macmillan.
30. Scott, J. (1988); Scott, J. (1987) 'On language, gender and working-class history', *International Labor and Working-Class History*, 31, Spring, and the responses in ibid. by Palmer, Rabinbach and Stansell; Appleby, J., Hunt, L., Jacob, M., (1994), pp. 214–15.
31. See, for example, Vernon's grossly exaggerated criticisms of the allegedly 'totalising', 'authoritarian' and 'phallocentric' desires of 'modernist' realism, Vernon, J. (1994), p. 85; for the differences between Stedman Jones and Joyce see Kirk, N. (1994), pp. 231–2.
32. For the increasingly propertied and male-centred nature of formal nineteenth-century politics see Vernon, J. (1993), pp. 45–7, 327–8, 336–7.
33. Joyce, P. (1991) ch. 2. See also Biagini, E. and Reid, A. (1991) (eds), *Currents of Radicalism: Organised Labour and Party Politics in Britain 1850–1914*, Cambridge: Cambridge University Press; Lawrence, J. (1992) 'Popular radicalism and the socialist revival in Britain', *Journal of British Studies*, 31, April.
34. I have used the term 'Cambridge School' to refer to those historians, such as Alastair Reid, Eugenio Biagini, Jon Lawrence, Duncan Tanner and Steven Fielding (and embracing many of the tenets of Joyce and Vernon) who oppose class-based 'social determinism' and 'discontinuity', and

adhere to the notion of the primacy, and largely autonomous nature, of non-class-based political continuities in modern British history.

35.　For illuminating insights into the interactions between agency and conditioning see Gutman, H.G. (1976) *Work Culture and Society: Essays in American Working Class and Social History*, New York: Vintage Books, Introduction, ch. 1; Hunt, L. (ed.) (1989) *The New Cultural History*, London: University of California Press; Walkowitz, J. (1992).

36.　For the many non-reductionist ways in which the study of language has in fact informed the historical investigations of so-called determinists, see Palmer, B.D. (1990) *Descent into Discourse: The Reification of Language and the Writing of Social History*, Philadelphia: Temple University Press; Epstein, J.A. (1989) 'Understanding the cap of liberty: Symbolic practice and social conflict in early nineteenth-century England', *Past and Present*, 122, February; Belchem, J. (1981) 'Republicanism, popular constitutionalism and the radical platform in early nineteenth-century England', *Social History*, 6; Belchem, J. (1988) 'Radical language and ideology in early nineteenth-century England: The challenge of the platform', *Albion*, 20.

37.　Bhaskar, R. (1989) *Reclaiming Reality: A Critical Introduction to Contemporary Philosophy*, London: Verso, p. 51.

38.　Briggs, A. (1960) 'The language of "class" in early nineteenth-century England' in Briggs, A. and Saville, J. (eds) *Essays in Labour History*, vol. 1, London: Macmillan; Thompson, D. (ed.) (1971) *The Early Chartists*, London: Macmillan; Thompson, E.P. *The Making*, (1968 edn) ch. 16; Prothero, I.J. (1981) *Artisans and Politics in Early Nineteenth-Century London: John Gast and His Times*, London: Methuen; Gray, R. (1976) *The Labour Aristocracy in Victorian Edinburgh*, Oxford: Clarendon; Crossick, G. (1976) 'The labour aristocracy and its values: A study of mid-Victorian Kentish London', *Victorian Studies*, vol. 19, 3, March.

39.　Kirk, N. (1987) especially pp. 16–35; Weaver, S.A. (1987), *John Fielden and the Politics of Popular Radicalism 1832–1847*, Oxford: Clarendon.

40.　I have relied heavily upon Thompson, D. (1986) (ed.), *Chartism: Working-Class Politics in the Industrial Revolution: A twenty-two volume facsimile series reproducing contemporary documents of the Chartist movement in Britain, 1839–1848*, London, Garland Publishing Inc. Special reference has been made to vol. 1, *Chartist and Anti-Chartist Pamphlets*, and vol. 5, *Small Chartist Periodicals*.

41.　*McDouall's Chartist and Republican Journal*, vol. 3, 17, April 1841.

42.　Kirk, N. (1987), pp. 19–24.

43.　*McDouall's Chartist Journal and Trades' Advocate*, 28 August 1841.

44.　Kirk, N. (1987), p. 20.

45.　*McDouall's Chartist and Republican Journal*, 3 July 1841.

46.　Boston, R. (1971) *British Chartists in America 1839–1900*, Manchester: Manchester University Press, ch. 6.

47.　Kirk, N. (1987), pp. 27–8.

48.　*McDouall's Chartist Journal and Trades' Advocate*, 25 September 1841.

49.　*McDouall's Chartist and Republican Journal*, 26 June 1841.

50.　Leach, J. (1844) 'Stubborn facts from the factories by a Manchester operative', in *Chartist and Anti-Chartist Pamphlets*, London: John Ollivier, pp. 83–4.

51.　*The Trial of Feargus O'Connor, Esq., and Fifty-eight Others at Lancaster*, London, 1843, pp. vi–vii.

52. Leach, J. (1844), pp. 12–13, 23, 40–2, 46; McDouall, P.M. (n.d. 1842/3?) 'Letters to the Manchester Chartists', in *Chartist and Anti-Chartist Pamphlets*, pp. 6–12.

53. O'Brien, J.B. (ed.) (1843) 'Poor man's guardian and repealer's friend: A weekly journal of politics literature and moral science', in *Small Chartist Periodicals*, 1, pp. 1–2.

54. *The Trial of Feargus O'Connor, Esq.*, pp. 249, 255.

55. Ibid., p. viii.

56. O'Brien, J.B. (ed.) (1843) 10, p. 79; Leach, J. (1844) p. 40.

57. *The Trial of Feargus O'Connor, Esq.*, p. 249.

58. O'Brien, J.B. (ed.) (1843) 14; 'Bronterre's *National Reformer* in government law property religion and morals', in *Small Chartist Periodicals*, vol. 1, 11, 18 March 1837; Epstein, J. (1982) *The Lion of Freedom: Feargus O'Connor and the Chartist Movement*, London: Croom Helm, pp. 273–4.

59. Behagg, C. (1990) *Politics and Production in the Early Nineteenth Century*, London: Routledge; Goodway, D. (1982) *London Chartism 1838–1848*, Cambridge: Cambridge University Press; Prothero, I.J. (1981); Randall, A.J. (1991) *Before the Luddites: Custom Community and Machinery in the English Woollen Industry, 1776–1809*, Cambridge: Cambridge University Press.

60. Behagg, C. (1982) 'An alliance with the middle class: The Birmingham Political Union and early Chartism' in Epstein, J. and Thompson, D. (eds), p. 69.

61. Goodway, D. (1982), pp. 6–9; 'The life boat: A miscellany of politics and literature', in *Small Chartist Periodicals*, vol. 1, 1, 2 December 1843, p, 15.

62. Gray, R. (1976); Crossick, G. (1978) *An Artisan Elite in Victorian Society: Kentish London 1840–1880*, London: Croom Helm.

63. Kirk, N. (1987), pp. 31, 35–41.

64. Saville, J. (1987) *1848: The British State and the Chartist Movement*, Cambridge: Cambridge University Press.

65. Kirk, N. (1985) *The Growth of Working-Class Reformism in Mid-Victorian England*, London: Croom Helm, ch. 6.

66. Marx, K. and Engels, F. (1953) *On Britain*, Moscow: Foreign Languages Publishing House, p. 270.

67. Thompson, D (1993), p. 57.

68. Thompson, D. (1986) *The Chartists: Popular Politics in the Industrial Revolution*, Aldershot: Wildwood House Ltd, p. 245.

69. Kirk, N. (1987), p. 43.

70. For excellent insights into the contextualised power of language upon the development of law in Britain see Griffith, J.A.G. (1991) *The Politics of the Judiciary*, London: Fontana.

71. Thompson, D. (1987) 'The languages of class', *Society for the Study of Labour History Bulletin*, part 1, vol. 52, April, p. 55.

72. For mainstream Chartism's central emphasis upon political independence see Kirk, N. (1985), pp. 62–4; Epstein, J. (1982), pp. 263–71, 290; Thompson, D. (1993), p. 57.

73. Thompson, D. (1987), p. 57; Baines, E. (1839) 'The designs of the Chartists and their probable consequences', *Leeds Mercury*, 3 August 1839, p. 6, in *Chartist and Anti-Chartist Pamphlets*.

74. Thompson, D. (1993), p. 29.
75. Ibid., p. 37.
76. Reprinted in Thompson, D. (1971 edn), pp. 131–4.
77. 'Bronterre's *National Reformer* in government law property religion and morals', in *Small Chartist Periodicals*, London, vol. 1, 6, 11 February 1837; *The Trial of Feargus O'Connor*, p. vii.
78. Kirk, N. (1985), p. 64.
79. Thompson, D. (1993), p. 26.
80. For women's involvement in Chartism see Thompson, D. (1986), ch. 7; Schwarzkopf, J. (1991) *Women in the Chartist Movement*, London: Macmillan; Clark, A. (1992); Jones, D. (1983) 'Women and Chartism', *History*, 68, I.
81. See for example, Thompson, E.P. (1991) *Customs in Common*, London: The Merlin Press, pp. 305–36; Thomis, M.I. and Grimmett, J. (1982) *Women in Protest 1800–1850*, London: Croom Helm; Bohstedt, J. (1988) 'Gender, household and community politics: Women in English riots, 1790–1810', *Past and Present*, 120, August; Thompson, D. (1976) 'Women and nineteenth-century radical politics: A lost dimension' in Mitchell, J. and Oakley, A. (eds), *The Rights and Wrongs of Women*, Harmondsworth: Penguin; Hall, C. (1990) 'The tale of Samuel and Jemima: gender and working-class culture in nineteenth-century England' in Kaye, H.J. and McClelland, K. (eds) *E.P. Thompson: Critical Perspectives*, Cambridge: Polity Press.
82. Thompson, D. (1971) (ed.), pp. 128–30.
83. Thompson, D. (1993), p. 36.
84. See for example, Kirk, N. (1985), chs 1, 4 and 5.
85. Ibid., pp. 151–68; McClelland, K. (1989) 'Some thoughts on masculinity and the "representative artisan" in Britain, 1850–1880', *Gender and History*, 2, 1, Summer; McClelland, K. (1987) 'Time to work, time to live: Some aspects of work and the re-formation of class in Britain, 1850–1880' in Joyce, P. (ed.) *The Historical Meanings of Work*, Cambridge: Cambridge University Press; Gordon, E. (1991) *Women and the Labour Movement in Scotland 1850–1914*, Oxford: Clarendon Press, pp. 73–101, ch. 3; Rose, S. (1988) 'Gender antagonism and class conflict: Exclusionary strategies of male trade unionists in nineteenth-century Britain', *Social History*, 13; Seccombe, W. (1986), 'Patriarchy stabilized: The construction of the male breadwinner wage norm in nineteenth-century Britain', *Social History*, 11.
86. Gordon, E. (1991), p. 62; Kirk, N. (1985), ch. 6; *National Association for the Promotion of Social Science: Report of the Committee on Trades' Societies and Strikes: 1860* (1968 reprint) New York: Augustus M. Kelly.
87. Kirk, N. (1985), pp. 161–5, ch. 5; Taylor, P.F. (1991) 'Popular politics and labour-capital relations in Bolton, 1825–1850', D. Phil., University of Lancaster, especially introduction and ch. 3; Koditschek, T. (1990) *Class Formation and Urban-Industrial Society: Bradford 1750–1850*, Cambridge: Cambridge University Press, ch. 18; Schwarzkopf, J. (1991), ch. 8. In their important 'revisionist' edited collection, entitled *Currents of Radicalism: Popular Radicalism, Organised Labour and Party Politics in Britain 1850–1914*, Cambridge: Cambridge University Press (1991) Alastair Reid and Eugenio Biagini underestimate the tensions within Victorian Liberalism.

88. Thompson, D. (1993), p. 57; Tiller, K. (1982) 'Late Chartism: Halifax 1847–58' in Epstein, J. and Thompson, D. (eds), pp. 337–41.
89. See for example, Kirk, N. (1985), pp. 272–6.
90. See for example, Stedman Jones, G. (1983), pp. 7–8, 17–24, 95; Joyce, P. (1991), p. 208. Likewise, Vernon's statement (Vernon, J. (1994), p. 96) that, 'I am not arguing that society or the real do not exist' stands in glaring contradiction to his anti-realist diatribes and his belief that, 'we can have *no* knowledge' (my italics) of the real/social 'outside discourse'.
91. See, for example, Joyce, P. (1993), pp. 82–4.
92. Joyce, P. (1991), ch. 2. Contrast with the views of Cole, J. (1990) *Rochdale Revisited: A Town and its People*, vol. 2, Littleborough: George Kelsall, pp. 37, 41–4.
93. For a statement in favour of anti-representationalism see Rorty, R. (1991) *Objectivity, Relativism and Truth: Philosophical Papers*, vol. 1, Cambridge: Cambridge University Press, especially Introduction.
94. Easthope, A. (1993), pp. 246–7; Vernon, J. (1994), p. 85.
95. For representational and anti-representational approaches to issues of truth, correspondence and subjectivity see respectively, Thompson, E.P. (1978) *The Poverty of Theory and Other Essays*, London: Merlin, pp. 231–42 and Norris, C. (1992) *Uncritical Theory: Postmodernism Intellectuals and the Gulf War*, London: Lawrence and Wishart, chs 1 and 3; Rorty, R. (1992) 'We anti-representationalists', *Radical Philosophy*, 60, Spring, especially pp. 41–2, and Ankersmit, F.A. (1990) 'Reply to Professor Zagorin', *History and Theory*, 29, p. 281. See also Bevir, M. (1994) 'Objectivity in history', *History and Theory*, 33, 3, pp. 328–44.
96. Easthope, A. (1993), pp. 238, 247–9.
97. For such representational ambiguities, existing within a framework of overall commitment to the primacy of political discourse, see Stedman Jones, G. (1989) 'The "Cockney" and the nation' in Feldman, D. and Stedman Jones, G. (eds), *Metropolis London: Histories and Representations since 1800*, especially p. 275.
98. Eagleton, T. (1991) *Ideology: An Introduction*, London: Verso, p. 219.
99. Bloch thus maintains that, 'We should see linguistic phenomena as a *part* of culture, most of which is non-linguistic': Bloch, M. (1991) 'Language, anthropology and cognitive science', *Man*, new series, 26, June, p. 192.
100. Bhaskar, R. (1989) *Reclaiming Reality: A Critical Introduction to Contemporary Philosophy*, London: Verso, pp. 4, 190. See also Appleby, J., Hunt, L., Jacob, M. (1994) for a convincing statement in favour of practical realism. For example:

> That something exists as an image of something's being in the mind does not in the least diminish its external existence or its knowability through the medium of language. That it could be in both places, out there and in here where words reside, seems only to verify the objective nature of everything from buildings to time. They are knowable, usable things separate from the linguistic expressions used to describe them, yet capable of being 'captured' in the mind by words that point back out toward the thing itself (p. 250).

101. Joyce and Vernon, in particular, fail to appreciate the anti-reductionist practices of a realist historical materialism, as exemplified by the work of

E.P. Thompson and Christopher Hill. Joyce and Vernon mistakenly view all realist epistemologies and methodologies as *necessarily* reductionist, as, by their very natures, inattentive to the constitutive powers of language. See, for example, Vernon, J. (1994), pp. 84–5; Vernon, J. (1993), Introduction: Joyce, P. (1991) 'History and post-modernism', pp. 208–9; Joyce, P. (1993) 'The Imaginary Discontents', p. 83.

102. See, for example, Thompson, E.P. (1968) preface; Thompson, E.P. (1979), 'The poverty of theory'; Anderson, P. (1980) *Arguments Within English Marxism*, London: Verso, ch. 2; Williams, R. (1978) *Marxism and Literature*, Oxford: Oxford University Press, 2, 'Cultural Theory'; Gutman, H. and Berlin, I. (1987); Hobsbawm, E.J. (1984) *Worlds of Labour: Further Studies in the History of Labour* chs 10–13; Thompson, D. (1986); Montgomery, D. (1987) *The Fall of the House of Labor: The Workplace, the State and American Labor Activism 1865–1925*, Cambridge: Cambridge University Press, Introduction.

PART TWO
Marxism

CHAPTER FOUR

The logic of social democracy: Adam Przeworski's historical theses

Robert Looker

The contemporary crisis of social democracy

Recent decades have been times of profound crisis and questioning on the Left. The 'projects for socialism' which occupied centre stage for most of the past century have collapsed or crumbled away. Most spectacularly visible in the case of the supposed 'actually existing socialisms' in the Soviet block in the East, it is no less evident in the case of the so-called '3rd World socialisms' of the South from China to Nicaragua. In the West, where socialist and working-class politics have been dominated for much of the twentieth century by the struggle between Communists and Social Democrats, the spectacular discrediting and disintegration of both the USSR and Euro-communism might have been expected to result in ideological advance and greatly augmented mass support for reformist parties. In fact, social democracy also exhibits unmistakable signs of decay, whether measured in terms of strategic vision, electoral support or managerial competence.[1]

This is no temporary backlash against the entire Left, unfairly 'tarred with the same brush' as communism. Rather it is the latest phase in a longer-term spiral of decline in the aspirations in which social democrats have articulated their socialism. What was once proudly envisaged as a distinctive project for a new social order, and which more recently was proclaimed as a strategy for radical reform and regeneration within capitalism, has latterly become a mere rhetoric of abstract 'values'. Many years ago, Georg Lukacs observed that 'economic fatalism and the reformation of socialism through ethics are intimately connected'.[2] He could hardly have anticipated the degeneration even in socialist rhetoric which we are witnessing today as traditional social democratic themes of 'society', 'equality' and 'social justice' are superseded by a neo-liberal language of 'the individual', 'opportunity' and 'enterprise'. It comes as no surprise therefore, in Britain in 1995, to find the last echoes of the project for a socialist alternative to capitalism being redefined out of existence by the Labour Party to make way for a hymn of praise to 'the enterprise of the market and the rigour of competition'.

The post-mortems held on the collapse of communism have been vigorous affairs, and participants have not been slow to root their explanations in the historical trajectory of Soviet and Comintern politics from Lenin and the Bolsheviks onwards. By contrast, there has been little attempt on the Left to situate the recent experience and present the atrophied state of social democracy within the context of its historical development as a political tradition. Within the social democratic parties, disputes between the 'modernisers' and 'traditionalists' focus on the current situation and its implications for future strategy, to the virtual exclusion of any engagement with the historical experiences that have led them to their present position. 'Modernisers', of course, generally subscribe to a fashionable post-modernism which reduces all such issues to the status of a non-problem.[3] Reformists on the Left show a somewhat greater sensitivity to the problematic legacy of their history, but their actual analyses remind one of people whistling to keep up their spirits – either denying the existence of present difficulties or explaining them away as the paradoxical outcome of past successes.[4]

In truth, serious discussions of the historical development of the social democratic tradition have been pretty thin on the ground in recent years. If we look for narratives on a grand scale, we have to go back to Julius Braunthal's two-volume study – a work whose theoretical assumptions were buried behind the text rather than explicitly tested out in it.[5] There have been a quantity of national case studies, of course – the Labour Party in Britain has been particularly well served in this respect[6] – but insights into the historical logic and dynamics of particular parties are restricted by the lack of any systematically comparative dimension. Contrariwise, what comparative studies there are have been of limited historical and analytical value, concentrating in the main on cataloguing current policies and institutions.[7]

In the past decade, Adam Przeworski's *Capitalism and Social Democracy*[8] was one of the very few studies seeking to engage with social democracy in a manner which combines historical, comparative and analytical modes of discourse. Though limited by its essay format, its programmatic intent was wide ranging and highly ambitious, addressing core problems and dilemmas confronting socialist theory and practice. At one level, the focus of the work was historical-practical: Przeworski was responding to 'the urgent need to draw lessons from the history of the socialist movement' (*Capitalism*, p. 1) by providing a coherent historical overview of the trajectory of social democracy and unpacking its logic and implications for socialist practice. Beyond this, there was a wider theoretical and analytical agenda of constructing a new paradigm for Marxist social theory utilising the theoretical and methodological insights of the school of 'analytical Marxism' (AM) and more particularly the game theoretic models used by 'rational choice Marxism' (RCM).

Capitalism and social democracy – the core theses

In essence, Przeworski's work operates at three distinct but interconnected levels of analysis: historical; analytical and practical-political. Firstly, he aims to provide an account of the historical trajectory of social democracy within western capitalism; secondly, to use the AM and RCM methods to unpack the underlying developmental 'logic' of the tradition; and thirdly to evaluate its strengths and weaknesses as a viable strategy for the Left. We will begin, therefore, by disentangling the three strands of Przeworski's analysis.

The historical trajectory of social democracy – the logic of electoralism?

Przeworski's core thesis is deceptively simple. He approaches the social democratic tradition, not as some more or less settled body of theory, but as an historically evolving set of political practices which are fundamentally shaped and explained in terms of an initial choice to participate in the electoral politics of capitalist democratic states. Parties making this choice necessarily find themselves embroiled in what we may term 'the logic of electoralism'. Once involved in electoral politics, even socialist leaderships are impelled by the logic of their situation to follow a path which leads to multiclass alliance politics, reformist strategies, and the abandonment of any commitment to socialism or even the defence of specifically working-class interests within capitalism. Electoralism is thus not simply one facet of social democracy but its core and original characteristic, from which virtually all of the other features associated with the tradition – reformism etc. – are largely consequential and derivative.

Przeworski sees the 'logic of electoralism' as involving a sequence of three sets of choices which socialist parties are everywhere obliged to confront. These are: whether to participate in bourgeois democracy; whether to base electoral strategy on appealing solely to working-class support or to seek instead a wider and multiclass base; and whether to pursue socialism by reformist or revolutionary strategies. As each choice is made, the next choice presents itself for decision. If the first choice is to participate, then the logic of the situation makes opting for multiclass alliances and reformism the strategically rational option for social democrats to select. Przeworski sees this sequence of choices as explaining the historical trajectory of social democracy from the final decades of the nineteenth century to the present day.

Expressed this baldly, the thesis is hardly novel. Many analyses of social democracy have portrayed electoralism both as a defining characteristic of its ideology and as a major explanatory variable of its practice.[9] We may acknowledge the elegant simplicity of Przeworski's formulas and the ingenuity with which he elaborates them, but this hardly substantiates his larger claims for the analysis. Indeed it is a moot point as to whether the analysis can be said to offer a historically adequate explanation as distinct from a re-description of the processes. In order to see how Przeworski addresses such questions, we need to examine more closely the explanatory framework within which the 'logic of electoralism' is unpacked.

Social democracy, voluntarism and rational choice Marxism

Przeworski's study does not simply seek to chart the changes in social democratic theory and practice over the past century. It also seeks to explain its trajectory in terms of what we might call the developmental 'logic of the tradition'. His point of departure here is debate within Marxism over the relative priority of structure and agency in explaining human action:

> Neither 'ideological domination' nor repression is sufficient to account for the manner in which workers organise and act under capitalism. The working class has been neither a perpetual dupe nor a passive victim: workers did organize in unions and in most countries as political parties; these organizations have had political projects of their own; they chose strategies and pursued them to victory as well as defeats. Even if itself molded by capitalist relations, the working class has been an active force in transforming capitalism. We will never understand the resilience of capitalism unless we seek the explanation in the interests and in the action of workers themselves.
>
> (*Capitalism*, p. 3)

At first sight, Przeworski's position appears to be that explanations of the dialectics of structure and agency in historical analysis need to give adequate weight to the rationality of actors. Choices of political strategy are best understood as involving reasonable people pursuing their interests and responding intelligently to the constraints and opportunities of their situation. In the specific instance of social democracy, the logic of its tradition is the historically cumulative product of rational political choices made by socialists in the face of what the 'structure of choices' established by the social order of capitalism. In arguing this, he is also clearly targeting for criticism structuralist reductionisms, whether Althusserian or otherwise, which treat social democracy as a mechanism for the ideological incorporation of the working class into the values and assumptions of industrial capitalism and explain political practices as mere subordinate ideological reflexes of the structural constraints of the system.[10] Equally unacceptable are the purely voluntaristic accounts, characteristic of certain kinds of empiricist historiography, where political practice is explained by reference to the beliefs and values of actors which are then taken as 'givens' not in need of further explanation.

Expressed thus, Przeworski's position appears to offer much that is appealing for Marxists of an ecumenical persuasion. His commitment to the view that historical actors are neither cultural dupes nor passive victims of circumstances but rational beings who, in Marx's famous phrase, 'make their own history' is one that is bound to elicit a sympathetic response from such an audience. His rejection of both the extremes of structuralism and voluntarism will likewise strike a chord with any historian of Marxism who has grappled with the procrustean constrictions that the former imposes on, and the vacuous judgmentalism which the latter often substitutes for, historical analysis. Nor is there anything obviously defective about a broad framework of analysis which seeks to account for the historical trajectory of social democracy in terms of an historical interplay between the constraints and opportunities presented by capitalist democracy and rational choices made by socialists in the face of them.

There is more to Przeworski's argument than this however. Underpinning his approach is a very particular account of the structural constraints of the capitalist system, of the rationality of historical agents, and of the way they make choices in relationship to the structural conditions. It is here that Przeworski's commitments to AM and RCM prove central. Nor are these narrowly conceived points of methodological interpretation. The enterprise of which Przeworski's volume formed a part was much wider and ambitious. In the words of the general preface of the series[11] in which it appeared, this and related works 'exemplify a new paradigm in the study of Marxist social theory', one which aims to 'develop the theory pioneered by Marx, in the light of intervening history, and with the tools of non-Marxist social science and philosophy' in order to free Marxism 'from the increasingly discredited methods and presuppositions which are still widely regarded as essential to it . . .'. Clearly large issues are at stake in accepting or rejecting this approach.

Przeworski's version of AM and RCM will be examined more closely in the next chapter. Here, I wish to concentrate on how he handles the substantive historical question of unpacking the logic of the social democratic tradition. Here parties and leaders – and Przeworski's account is preoccupied with the point of vantage of leaderships – are best understood as rational agents who make the best strategic political choices they can in face of the constraints and opportunities provided by the democratic political process under capitalism. Given that choices are made in conditions of uncertainty as to whether they will be successful, leaders will select strategies which optimise the chances of achieving success. Once made, these strategic choices have powerful, if frequently unintended, consequences which cumulatively shape the contexts for, and contents of, subsequent strategic choices and predispose the adherents of the tradition to make them in a certain direction. The decision to participate in the electoral processes of bourgeois democratic states, once made, effectively predisposes Social Democrats at a later stage to seek multiclass rather than purely proletarian electoral constituencies. That decision in turn makes the subsequent choice of a reformist political strategy increasingly likely.

The defence of social democracy – the least worst option?

What political conclusions does Przeworski draw from his analysis? Przeworski in 1985 writes as someone committed to the construction of an alternative socialist order to capitalism. However, there is a studied ambiguity about his judgments on social democracy; has he come to bury or to praise it? His criticisms of the tradition are trenchant in identifying its failures and inadequacies either as an agency for socialist transformation or reformist alleviation of capitalism. Indeed it is tempting to read his historical triad – of electoralism, multiclass orientation and reformism – as a delineation of the spiral of decline and degeneration which we earlier suggested has characterised the trajectory of social democratic politics in the later part of the twentieth century. However, this is to misconstrue Przeworski's political purpose. His critique is circumscribed within a more fundamental argument which aims to sever the linkage Marxists seek to make between class struggle and the project for socialism. Social democracy, whatever its faults as a vehicle for socialism, none the less constitutes the best interest-optimising strategy open to the working class in pursuing their class interests. In so far as social democracy is the only rational 'game in town' available for the working class to play today, Marxist criticisms of its limitations and inadequacies as a vehicle for socialism are really beside the point. Working-class interests are not only not tied to achieving socialism: attempts to build socialism are likely to run counter to the interests of that class.

Przeworski's study thus has three goals. It advances a core historical thesis about the evolution of social democratic theory and practice. The historical analysis is itself intended as an exemplification of explanatory fruitfulness of RCM modes of analysis. It also aims to use a Marxist approach to the study of class politics in order to sever the connection which Marxists have traditionally asserted as holding between class struggle and the project for socialism. The three theses are necessarily intertwined but they also raise distinct historical, analytical and political issues. For this reason, I will take two separate bites at Przeworski's argument. The critique of his historical theses on social democracy will occupy the rest of this chapter. In the following chapter, I will criticise his more analytical theses on class and capitalist democracy and attempt to show that their defects flow at least in part from inadequacies in the theoretical assumptions and methodological tools of the RCM approach.

Three notes of qualification as to the limitations on this discussion need to be borne in mind. First, my concern is the adequacy or otherwise of Przeworski's 1985 study of *Capitalism and Social Democracy*; his more recent work, notably on the 'democratic transition', is not examined here.[12] Secondly, I am mainly concerned with Przeworski's use of RCM rather than with the wider AM position considered in its own right; others better qualified than I have already subjected it to critical scrutiny.[13] Finally, while we need to examine the assumptions underpinning the practical political lessons Przeworski derives from his analysis, these lessons are not themselves the primary focus of debate.

The sequence of strategic choices – logic or history?

A useful point of entry for our discussion is provided by Przeworski's three-fold set of strategic choices for it enables us to confront directly the problem of the status of his analysis. He insists that his sequence of choices – concerning participation, class orientation and reformist strategy – forms a series which discloses the developmental logic of the social democratic tradition; but what does this mean? Is it simply an expositional device to enable Przeworski to make some second order observations on analytical components entering into the historical explanation? Or is it intended as an empirically adequate historical periodisation of the trajectory of social democracy? The former, while it may be of some use to practitioners of games theory as an hypothetical illustrative device, adds little to our empirical understanding of the subject.

The latter claim is considerably more interesting for the purposes of constructing historical explanations, but it also suffers from some obvious empirical difficulties. To take the most glaring example, even in its earliest phases of development in the later nineteenth century, there were political currents in the social democratic camp which combined electoralism, multiclass alliances and reformism to varying degrees.[14] Moreover, such practices formed the subject of one of the central and defining debates between the 'revisionist' and 'orthodox' wings of the Second International. Eduard Bernstein's case was precisely that the three practices in combination provided the best strategy for achieving socialist advance.[15] It was precisely against such arguments that Rosa Luxemburg, in *Social Reform and Revolution* (1899) hurled her oft quoted anathema, 'He who pronounces himself in favour of the method of legal reforms in place of and as opposed to the conquest of political power and social revolution does not really choose a more tranquil, surer and slower road to the same goal. He chooses a different goal'.[16]

Przeworski can hardly be thought to be unaware of such basic facts of socialist history, or that both the practices and the debates profoundly shaped contemporary social democratic perceptions of the 'structures of choices' they faced. His silence here is rather indicative of a general tendency in his analysis to radically dichotomise ends and means and to treat the former as 'givens' which requires no direct or detailed scrutiny. This in turn flows from his game-theoretical focus on strategies to achieve goals rather than the goals themselves. However, his silence also serves to smuggle into his analysis a set of largely reformist assumptions about both the ends and means of socialist politics. This shows up clearly in the case of his non-account of the emergence of socialist theory and practice in the nineteenth century. His discussion of the subject amounts to a single, rather curiously constructed paragraph which opens the first chapter:

> The crucial choice was whether to participate. Earlier events resulted in establishing the principle of democracy in the political realm. Yet political rights were merely formal when accompanied by the compulsion and inequality that reigned in the social realm. As it emerged around 1850, socialism was thus a movement that would complete the revolution started by the bourgeoisie by wresting from it 'social power' just as the bourgeoisie had conquered political power. The recurrent theme of the socialist movement ever since has been this notion of 'extending' the democratic principle from the political to the social, in effect primarily economic realm.
>
> (*Capitalism*, p. 7)

The reformist character of Przeworski's assumptions here is evident. He assumes that under capitalism, the principle of democracy is established and that the socialist critique of capitalism is primarily concerned with inequality. Its main goal therefore lies in 'extending' democracy. We should also note the evasions and silences: what of class power and conflict?; what of capitalist exploitation, instability and crisis?; and what compulsions? Their significance becomes clearer as we move to consider his treatment of his 'crucial choice' of whether to 'participate'.

The 'decision to participate' and its 'structure of choices'

'The decision to participate' forms the linchpin of Przeworski's historical analysis. The question of whether to work within the electoral framework of capitalist political institutions has primacy, both historically and logically. The decision to participate taken by a majority of socialists in the decades between the 1870s and 1914, was critical for the subsequent evolution of their tradition. It is thus the 'prime mover' in Przeworski's analysis. Surprisingly, given what is at stake, Przeworski's treatment of the historical determinants of the choice to participate is cursory. He argues that by the latter part of the nineteenth century, socialists in all the industrialising states of Europe and the Americas confronted a 'structure of choices' between two strategic alternatives:

> As soon as the new bourgeois society developed its political institu-
> tions – first the bureaucracy and the standing army and then the pop-
> ularly elected parliament . . . the new political institutions had to be
> treated either as an enemy or a political instrument. The choice had
> become one between 'direct' or 'political' action; a direct confronta-
> tion between the world of workers and the world of capital or a
> struggle through political institutions.
>
> (*Capitalism*, p. 7)

The key issue for socialists was thus whether to take advantage of the opportunities for participation available to them within the political institutions of their respective capitalist states. While some rejected par-ticipation – the anarchist wing of the First International was a notable example – most socialists opted to engage in the game of electoral compe-tition characteristic of bourgeois politics.

Przeworski's explanation of this outcome is deceptively simple. His brief historical sketch is underpinned by a game-theoretic model. Socialists find themselves in conditions of uncertainty about the outcome of pursuing any particular strategy for socialism – not least because of uncertainty about the responses those strategies would elicit from both the ruling class and from political competitors organised on non-class lines. In this situation, and regardless of strategic preference, electoralism constitutes the interest-optimising strategy for socialists. In opting for this, they also opt to organise the working class in ways which seek to ensure that they maximise their electoral support for this strategy.

Now it is open to question whether this is in fact an historical explana-tion of the choices actually made by socialists, as distinct from a defence of the rationality of those opting for electoralism. However, let us treat it as a historical explanation and consider its problems. It is open to two lines of criticism. One, relating to its treatment of 'the structure of choices', occupies the rest of this section. The second, relating to the choices made and their rationality, is examined in the subsequent section.

Przeworski's account of the 'structure of choices' which capitalism presented to socialists is characterised by three core features. First, it is specified almost entirely at a political level – it is the State and democratic institutions which occupy centre stage. Secondly, it treats democracy as the more or less 'taken for granted' framework for discussion. Thirdly, it handles the decision to participate as a matter of autonomous choices by socialists; late nineteenth-century capitalist states just happened to present two faces – a coercive and a participatory one – and then left it to socialists to choose which they preferred.

All three features of Przeworski's analysis are open to challenge. First, he treats the political order as largely autonomous and ignores the wider capitalist context which shaped both its structure and functions. In particular, he ignores the balance of class forces in the latter part of the nineteenth century. (Though attached to game theory, he forgets that there is more than one class 'player' in the game.) Secondly, his assumptions about the prevalence of the norms and institutions of bourgeois democracy in the period are factually inaccurate and serve to obscure the ways in which the political structures worked in practice. Thirdly, the emphasis on the autonomous character of the socialist choices mis-specifies the balance between force and consent in shaping the 'structure of choices' which they faced. Let us examine each argument in turn.

It was the balance of class forces in late nineteenth-century capitalism which constituted the main determinant of the 'structure of choices' which confronted socialists and which largely shaped the choices they actually made. The political options open to both the ruling and subordinate classes were powerfully though differentially constrained by the strength of the other classes. Though the capitalist mode of production had deep historical roots, it was not until the latter half of the nineteenth century that extensive and intensive development of capitalist industrialisation across Europe and North America saw the emergence of an urban, industrial working class as the characteristic core of a 'proletariat' in the Marxist sense of the term. From the 1870s onwards, Europe in particular saw a rapid growth in trade unions and left wing parties which increasingly reached out beyond a minority craft/skilled élite within the working class to aspire to embrace the proletariat as a whole.

This pattern of development posed major problems for the ruling classes of Europe. Capitalist industrialisation was already subjecting them to internal crises and transformations as landed interests were obliged to renegotiate their traditional ascendancy over the State, in face of the political demands of commercial and industrial capital. It also confronted them, in an epoch of growing imperialist rivalries, with conflicts involving other national ruling classes which threatened to spill over into wars requiring the total mobilisation of their populations. It was under such constrained circumstances that the ruling establishments in each of the major capitalist states also found themselves faced with emergent proletarian mass movements. These posed 'social questions' for the regimes which were no longer capable of resolution by a blanket and continuous resort to coercion. As David Coates and I have argued else-where, it was in this context that a variety of ruling-class strategies emerged around the question of whether, how and for what ends work-ing-class 'participation' in the political institutions of the regime might be allowed or even encouraged.[17]

I have already noted that Przeworski's account of the emergence of democracy is cursory. It is also problematic. In his view, 'the principle' had been established by 'earlier events' before mass socialist and work-ing-class parties emerged in the latter part of the nineteenth century. By implication, political developments thereafter were largely a matter of putting this principle into practice by extending the right to political citi-zenship to the working class, or at least the male section of it. Now this is a by no means uncommon reading of the political context among reformist historians and political theorists, though usually somewhat greater play is made of the role of the working class in struggles to extend the franchise.[18] It is, however, a highly misleading one. The near univer-salisation of the institutions and practices of bourgeois democracy in industrial capitalist states is quite recent – the outcome of Allied victory in the Second World War. Nor was its selective adoption prior to then the product of some evolutionary trend intrinsic to the logic of the bour-geois social order as such. It was the much more contingent outcome – witness the widespread retreat from 'bourgeois democracy' into Fascism and Nazism in the interwar years – of political arrangements whose ori-gins lay in the much more pragmatic ruling-class strategies to manage and contain class conflict.[19]

One prior development which critically shaped ruling-class strategies here was the ways and extent to which they had transformed their bases of political rule from the pattern prevalent in Europe in the first half of the century. The old State structures had been identified with and con-trolled by a tiny ruling class anchored in a small minority of the popula-tion – predominantly the landed aristocracy though with some urban commercial and financial supports. The new regimes were organised on a more constitutional basis and represented a much wider range of capital-ist interests – industrial and commercial as well as landed. They extended their bases of popular support to encompass the urban bourgeois and petit bourgeois classes.[20]

These developments ensured that by the latter part of the nineteenth century, several options were available to the ruling classes for mediating the balance of class forces. One involved the incorporation of at least part of the working class within the framework of bourgeois electoral politics. The preferred outcome was to establish hegemonic political con-trol over sections of the rural and urban masses in order to defuse and frustrate the challenges presented by socialist and labour movements to the regime. Where this was not possible, the same strategy could try to manage and contain these challenges within the political structures, not least by a combination of limited 'redress of grievances' and where necessary, the modest 'paying of ransom'. However, this option was not the only or the preferred strategy open to the ruling class, nor was it in practice available in all the states experiencing the impact of capitalist industrialisation. In much of central, eastern and southern Europe, traditional autocracies continued to rule in the old ways. Whether by choice or necessity, such regimes placed continued reliance on tried and trusted combinations of political exclusion and occasional repression to handle the opposition of the rural and urban working classes, though with diminishing effectiveness by the turn of the century.[21]

In western Europe and North America, bourgeois political institutions and practices took a more secure hold. Even here however, the 'invitation to participate' to the working classes was carefully hedged around with severe constraints. In France under the Third Republic and in the Italy of Giolitti's 'transformismo', a restricted franchise either excluded the working class entirely, or attempted the segmental incorporation of their 'labour aristocracies'. In Britain, the latter gambit was essayed in 1866–67 but was thwarted by a broad working-class movement united precisely by their opposition to policies designed to fragment them.[22] In Imperial Germany, universal manhood suffrage gave socialists access to a constitutionally impotent Reichstag which was little more than a talking shop.[23]

Even where, as in Britain and the USA, the franchise increasingly approximated to bourgeois norms of democracy – at least for men – working-class and socialist involvement was powerfully constrained by a thicket of constitutional rules, institutional structures and informal political practices: the role of the Supreme Court and the indirect election of the Senate in the USA; the House of Lords and the 'common law' judiciary in Britain; the rural bias in the distribution of constituencies everywhere; the mixture of bossism and bribery, violence and vilification which hobbled socialist electoral challenges outside the national assemblies and the corruption and bourgeoisification which permeated them within. Such arrangements are part of that 'mobilisation of bias' which Marxist and radical critics argue are intrinsic to bourgeois democracy.[24] They also testify to the caution and pragmatism with which the ruling classes adopted democracy. It was less a matter of some underlying commitment to democratic principles than a question of their impact on managing working-class discontent.[25] The survival of these political arrangements was heavily contingent on the extent to which labour movements embraced the politics of reform rather than of revolution.[26]

We saw earlier that Przeworski heavily discounts the role of ideological domination and repression in the emergence of working-class and socialist organisations and strategies. However, while not sufficient, they are surely necessary components of any Marxist account of the wider structure of choices presented by capitalism and bourgeois democracy to socialists and workers. Przeworski's tacitly reformist frame of reference and his preoccupation with the rationality of the choices made by social-ist leaderships combine to produce an account which in practice margin-alises such considerations. Yet in the context of the balance of class forces in the late nineteenth and early twentieth centuries, they had cru-cial roles to play in the strategies adopted by various national ruling classes to handle their 'social problem'. Underlying the 'choice to partici-pate' presented to the working class was a structure of choice which worked – and to a degree was consciously designed to work – to 'steer' their political organisations into electoralist participation and away from other options. At one level, this involved a shift away from a blanket coercive response to any manifestation of class struggle into a more selec-tive approach whereby certain activities were designated as legal and oth-ers were outlawed. The coercive bias of the system was mobilised to push socialists towards electoralism and away from mass activism. A striking example of this as a conscious strategy was Bismarck's 'anti-socialist' laws which restricted the SPD to the sphere of electoral politics, but it was an important dimension of bourgeois politics everywhere.

At a more obviously ideological level, the emphasis on the legitimacy of participation in electoral politics served to de-legitimise in the eyes of workers those activities which fell outside of Parliament and outside the law. Crucially, it worked to reinforce the divide between 'political' and 'economic' struggle and to limit and de-politicise the scope of the latter.[27] It also provided a framework within which socialist politics could be confronted and combatted within the electoral arena in an attempt to create alternative foci for working-class loyalties. As David Coates and I have put it elsewhere:

> Time and effort was expended in the creation, dissemination and propagation of anti-socialist ideas, through the control of education, the encouragement of voluntary bodies (from political parties to patriotic associations and the activity of the churches). New and alternative hegemonic projects, particularly those emphasising nationalist and imperialist themes . . . were consciously constructed and canvassed; and national parties transcending 'mere' class inter-ests were built on them . . . or on older and less obviously capitalist themes – deference, Christianity, ethnicity . . . .[28]

Seen in this light, there is a certain implausibility – to put it no stronger – about portraying bourgeois electoral politics in the late nineteenth and early twentieth centuries as a process of extending a democratic 'invitation to participate' to workers and socialists. Rather, the multiple biases of the system were more or less consciously designed to channel their choices in the direction of electoral politics and away from more radical and confrontational strategies. Viewed thus, 'choosing to participate' was less a matter of 'making the most rational choice', than of 'taking the line of least resistance' in face of the tightly controlled political 'structure of choices' on offer in the late nineteenth-century capitalist states of Europe and North America.

Rival traditions and alternative rationalities

What were the political responses of socialists to this 'structure of choices' and how do we account for them? Here we can agree with Przeworski that the paths chosen by social democratic parties in the half-century prior to the First World War were powerfully shaped by socialist perceptions of the opportunities opened up by the 'extension of the franchise', and of the risks involved in pursuing more confrontational strategies. However, both the forces shaping perceptions and the judgments made by socialists in face of them are open to a rather different interpretation to the one he offers.

Developments in state structures and politics in the second half of the nineteenth century posed real dilemmas of state power for socialist strategy. The consolidation of centralised state power in command of technically effective military, police and bureaucratic resources seemed to render older insurrectionary models of revolution, derived from 1789 and 1848, outmoded. The lessons drawn from the failure of the Paris Commune by the parties of the Second International were that the epoch of 'insurrectionist' strategies was now firmly in the past.[29] At the same time, the availability of 'participatory' options opened up the question of whether the conquest of state power could be accomplished through the ballot box. Framing that debate, both poles of the ideological climate shaping socialist thinking in the period – Marxism and liberal radicalism – could be used to construct plausible arguments in favour of participation.[30] Universal suffrage was both a popular working-class demand and an important component of the social-democratic political programme. Struggles for the vote and advances towards its achievement testified to the growing power of socialist and labour movements and their ability to challenge and defeat their ruling class opponents.

Thus many considerations worked to persuade Marxists and socialists to reject the policy of 'abstentionism' advocated by the anarchists and to take advantage of the opportunities provided by the bourgeois state and politics for open and legal political activity.[31] For most of the parties of the Second International, the readiness to participate was, however, highly conditional and not a little problematic when it came to embracing the 'electoral tactic'. The majority rejected it as the strategic route to socialism but were divided over the extent and the purposes for which it should be deployed. Did it serve merely propagandistic and agitational purposes at the hustings and in the assemblies – 'speaking through the window' as the SPD conceived it – or could it be used to win real if limited gains for workers? If the latter were the case, how did the pursuit of such a 'Minimum Programme' of reforms stand in relation to the wider 'Maximum Programme' for socialism? Were there any circumstances in which socialist parties could enter into coalition with others as part of the process?

We cannot review here the complex story of the debates in the Second International on these questions.[32] We can agree with Przeworski that this was a period characterised by disputes as to how the electoral tactic might work in practice, one which provided an often painful 'learning curve' in the logic and limitations of electoral politics for socialists. However, we can question his view that the outcome was a pragmatic decision by a majority of socialists to opt for the game of electoral competition on the basis of instrumental calculations of the 'get in or lose out' kind. While we can conceive of socialist politics in the period as a complex process of testing out and clarification of the 'logic of electoralism', we must also recognise that this was framed by the larger debates on reform and revolution. Przeworski's assertion that opting for electoralism is explicable as the outcome of rational calculations in conditions of uncertainty only works if one first tacitly takes up a position in that wider debate.

There was not one, but at least three clear patterns of response by Social Democrats to the experience, each of which was perfectly rational within their own understanding of the constraints and opportunities which capitalism presented to them. Those who read the experience through the lens of a reformist analysis of the opportunities opened up by political democracy for socialist advance, responded by wholeheartedly embracing the electoral road as their central strategy. By contrast, socialists reading the same experience though a revolutionary framework, identified what they saw as the constraining and de-radicalising implications of bourgeois electoral politics and looked for alternative strategies to pursue the class struggle. There was also a third alternative which united Marxists of a formally revolutionary persuasion and more pragmatic trade union leaders in a common policy. Both feared that any radicalisation of socialist strategy would provoke a direct confrontation with, and defeat at the hands of, the capitalist state. They opted, therefore, for what was in effect a politics of immobilism, in which a combination of deterministic Marxist theory and passively 'electoralist' practice served to postpone hard choices about more activist strategies of either a reformist or a revolutionary kind.[33]

Part of Przeworski's case for concentrating on the first of these three alternatives relates to his apparent belief that it accorded with the preferences of the bulk of the organised labour movements of the period. In fact the situation was much more fluid. The decade prior to 1914 saw a strong and growing current away from 'electoralism' among workers in virtually all capitalist states of Europe and North America. One index of this was the rapid spread of syndicalist ideas and movements. The consolidation of electoral politics in the hearts and minds of the majority of the western working class was more a product of the interwar years. It was also at least partly shaped by the historic defeat and degeneration of the revolutionary tradition into Stalinism and its own contorted form of electoralist politics from the Popular Front period onwards.

The subsequent trajectories of the rival traditions reveal a complex dialectic of theory and practice in the face of the changing circumstances of the global capitalist order in the twentieth century. In that dialectic, there were certainly times and places in which the unintended consequences of their chosen strategies precipitated major shifts and transformations in both their ideology and practice. If we review the period from the First World War to the 1930s, this dialectic bears only an incidental resemblance to Przeworski's highly generalised and ultimately ahistorical account of both the 'structure of choice' and the choices made by socialists. In dealing grandly with the logic and limitations of an abstractly specified 'capitalism' and 'democracy', he fails to engage with the actual historical contexts or the political strategies pursued in the particular historical circumstances. One striking manifestation of this is that two core experiences of the first half of the twentieth century – war and revolution – play very little role in Przeworski's narrative. Yet these were precisely the historical 'forcing houses' which clarified the choices involved. They also provide instructive examples of the logic of unintended consequences which otherwise figure so prominently in the explanatory frameworks of RCM theorists like Przeworski, but which here subvert his substantively reformist analysis of the 'structure of choices' presented by capitalism.

In the historical development of the social democratic tradition, 1914–18 was the crucial catalyst. War and the revolutions in Russia which followed in its wake transformed the divisions between reformist and revolutionary currents within the Second International into rival organisations, programmes and strategies for socialism. In the process it clarified and redefined the choices at stake between them and laid out opposing rationales for selecting between them.

Let us consider the critical case of Germany. There, as elsewhere, the capitulation of social democracy to the war programmes of their various national ruling classes in August 1914 was motivated by many factors, not least by the 'social patriotism' of many on its reformist wing. However, among the more orthodox Marxist centre, it was shaped by the belief that the war was bound to be brief, so capitulation was merely a temporary 'bowing to the inevitable' which could be redressed once the conflict was over. However, the length of the war was to involve the leadership of the SPD in a sequence of events which they simply had not anticipated. Support for the war entailed support for the regime prosecuting it, at least for the duration of hostilities. That in turn required accepting a wartime 'social peace' policy and publicly identifying with the regime's patriotic war effort. As the war dragged on, they became a crucial weapon in opposing and suppressing the anti-war campaign of the Left and the industrial militancy of war-radicalised workers.[34] By the end of the war, the majority of the SPD leadership who stayed aboard for the ride[35] had been transformed by the logic of events into full blown 'social patriots' and national reformists. By the end of 1918, the majority leadership of the SPD countenanced the violent suppression of the revolutionary movement on the grounds that it threatened the achievement of representative democracy.

A similar dialectic can be traced in the critical months and years following the October Revolution of 1917 when neither of the options envisaged by the Bolsheviks – successful revolution in the West or defeat and destruction of the infant Soviet state – was realised. Instead a third, unanticipated, outcome – the survival in isolation of a Bolshevik regime in a hostile domestic and international environment – crucially shaped the 'structure of choices' within which the Bolsheviks were forced to operate from the early 1920s onwards. Though the choices made by the Comintern were not fully determined by this, it clearly contributed powerfully to the defeat and Stalinist degradation of the revolutionary programme by the 1930s. One not entirely paradoxical outcome was that in abandoning its revolutionary working-class orientation at all but a rhetorical level, Stalinist political practice in the West also ended up embracing an essentially electoralist politics. Faced with the triumph of Nazism, it belatedly abandoned the imbecilities of the 'class against class' Third Period, to embrace a Popular Front strategy which combined both electoralism and cross-class alliances in defence of the Soviet state. It was a combination which, despite the enormous and frequent shifts in Communist Party ideology from the 1930s through to the emergence of post-Stalinist Euro-communism in the 1970s, it rarely deviated in practice.[36] Even in its Stalinist form, the tradition managed to maintain some hold on the loyalties of radical and militant layers of workers in the West who were disillusioned with reformist social democracy. However, its more lasting impact was to discredit 'revolutionary Marxism' for the mass of the western working class, thus cementing their ties to reformist social democracy for much of the rest of the twentieth century.

Both the reformist and revolutionary inheritors of the social democratic tradition were agreed, by 1917–18, that one of the key substantive issues that divided them was bourgeois democracy. The choice, they agreed, was between evolutionary and revolutionary socialism and between parliamentary and insurrectionary strategies for achieving them. Reformists embraced democracy both as the indispensable means for achieving socialism and as an end in itself. Democratic institutions demonstrated that as capitalism evolved, class divisions could be transcended by community and national interests, articulated through political processes provided by capitalism itself. Electoral politics were therefore also a mechanism for educating workers away from the shibboleths of class antagonisms and class struggle. The Bolsheviks and other Left revolutionaries rejected this perspective. In their view, it was not simply a question of the structural limits on what bourgeois parliamentarianism could achieve within capitalism; it was that electoralism and parliamentarianism were themselves ideological weapons through which the ruling class disarmed and defused the class struggle and workers' commitment to it.

While reformists and revolutionaries were clear as to the choices involved, such clarity was not shared by the socialist movement as a whole. The survival and continued influence of the third 'orthodox Marxist' centre current we discussed earlier ensured that the role of the 'electoral tactic' within socialist strategy remained unresolved in the minds of many workers. Under the impact of wartime experience, this political current argued in support of a 'democratic socialist' third alternative, which combined support for revolutionary Marxism with a commitment to bourgeois democratic practice. This centrist current enjoyed considerable support during the critical conjuncture of 1917–23 and thereby frustrated Communist attempts to polarise issues in the minds of the mass of the western working class. The subsequent disintegration and dissolution of centrism into either the reformist Socialist or the Communist Parties was taken by both as proof as to the inherent incoherence of this political position.[37] Intriguingly enough, it is also the one key historical example in the period which appears to conform to Przeworski's specification of general dilemma for socialists involved in the democratic process in capitalism. Yet centrist perspectives and the problems they posed for their adherents arose not from pragmatic choices of means; rather, they flowed from a specific ideological position which turned out to be unsustainable in practice, at least in the circumstances of the interwar years.

The 'electoral dilemma' and cross-class alliances

I have argued that it was war and revolution which precipitated the development of alternative strategies for socialism in the early decades of the twentieth century. Each strategy provided a more or less coherent account of its vision of the socialist goal, and of the strategies for achieving it within the constraints and opportunities set by the capitalist social order. Each was in its own way a reasoned response to the situations faced; each provided a coherent rationale for the strategies adopted; each brought its own rationality to bear on the problems raised by their strategic choices. A useful way of illustrating the internal dynamics of these competing logics is to briefly examine the contrasting ways in which reformist social democracy and revolutionary communism handled Przeworski's second key sequential decision – of whether or not to enter into cross-class alliances to further their goals.

Przeworski argues that socialists, in advancing working-class interests in parliaments, found themselves espousing what was a minority cause, given the weight of the manual working class in the capitalist social structure. 'The majority which socialists expected to win in elections was to be formed by workers . . . but this proletariat was not and never became a numerical majority of voting members of any society' (*Capitalism*, p. 23). This faces them with an electoral dilemma:

> The combination of minority status with majority rule constitutes the historical condition under which socialists have to act. This objective condition imposes upon socialist parties a choice: socialists must choose between a party homogeneous in its class appeal but sentenced to perpetual electoral defeats and a party that struggles for electoral success at the cost of diluting its class character.
>
> (*Capitalism*, p. 24)

They can opt to preserve ideological purity in isolation, or to widen their electoral appeal to include other classes in order to win a majority. The former strategy severely limits the gains they can actually make on behalf of workers; the latter makes greater gains but at the cost of diluting their commitment to workers. The latter therefore represents the more rational interest-maximising strategy and this was in fact the route taken by social democracy. It is limited only by the existence of a trade-off between working-class and middle-class votes. If the outcome of this strategy is to embrace what is, in effect, a reformist position, this is in Przeworski's view the unintended consequence, not the cause, of the strategy.

Of course, it can be objected as a matter of fact that a majority of the parties pursuing such strategies were also committed to reformism and that reformism provides a pretty solid justification for such a strategy.

Indeed, an important historical confirmation of this was provided by those parties of the 'Two and a half International' tendency, who refused to pursue the strategies of cross-class alliances precisely because they saw them as reformist. More interestingly, we should note that Przeworski's formulation of the argument carries with it a number of 'taken for granted' assumptions about how class politics in capitalism work. Classes are multiple and sectionalised in capitalism. Class interests involve an agenda of specific demands which can be addressed segmentally; they are also inherently sectionalist in relation to the wider social order. Class interests can be aggregated together to build a coalition though this inevitably involves compromise and dilution. This strategy is none the less the most rational way of advancing class interests. Put this way, Przeworski's taken for granted 'structure of choice' turns out to be underpinned by an essentially pluralist account of class and politics. This is, of course, a reputable intellectual position to adopt, though as we will argue in the next chapter, such a conception of class is compatible neither with his proclaimed Marxism nor with the historical evidence. However, by pre-supposing that the 'structure of choices' works this way, his assertion of the rationality of socialists opting for pluralist interest-aggregating politics becomes simply tautological.

The point of course, is that strategies are crucially framed by one's reading of the 'structure of choices'; only in that context can we assess the rationality of the means–ends relationships involved. Marxists, facing the problem of class alliances, bring a very different frame of reference to bear, both in its definition and strategic resolution. One has simply to recall the debates between the Mensheviks and Bolsheviks in pre-revolutionary Russia or the interwar situation in Europe which prompted Gramsci's famous exploration and advocacy of hegemonic class strategies.[38] In a very different ideological framework, the Popular Front strategy of the Comintern in the 1930s was anchored in the operational assumptions of Stalin's rejection of revolutionary working-class internationalism in favour of a statist and nationalist 'socialism in one country' viewpoint.[39] Such views were rational within their own terms of reference. The more interesting political question is whether they were right or wrong in their assumptions and strategies and whether they advanced or undermined the cause of socialism.

The high tide of reformism and after

Przeworski's account of the reformist phase of the social democratic tradition is conventional, and deploys the familiar periodisation which uses the emergence of Keynesian economics as its yardstick. Prior to the

1930s, Social Democrats lacked a coherent economic policy to underpin their reformist impulses and therefore also lacked political credibility. Keynesianism endowed their reformist programme with a coherence and a legitimacy as well as indicating economic strategies for implementing them. The high tide of reformism came in the decades after the Second World War when Social Democrats were able to compete for office on more or less equal terms with parties of the centre and the moderate right. Crises in the 1970s, with their challenges to Keynesian economic policies, were also necessarily a crisis of social democratic strategy, though in Przeworski's view, writing in 1985, a temporary one.

Przeworski's account of reformism is perfunctory and at times appears to rely on a kind of idealist 'ideas as the movers of history' account which falls short of the rigorous demands of his own methodological framework. What is missing from it is any clear specification of the historically shifting parameters of the 'structure of choices' created by the global capitalist order in the period, and their constraining and facilitating consequences on the choices actually made by Social Democrats over the course of the period as a whole. For example, Keynesian ideas did not emerge in a vacuum, nor was their favourable reception by politicians guaranteed. The 1930s 'Slump', with its catastrophic collapse in global trade, produced everywhere a retreat into protectionism, isolationism and even autarchy – from Stalin's Russia and Hitler's Germany to Roosevelt's USA. In the process it gave renewed impetus to statism and strategies of corporatist planning on both the Right and the Left. The Second World War saw states mobilise for total war and accept a degree of central state intervention in their domestic economies which was unprecedented in the history of capitalism in the twentieth century. Victory against Fascism and Nazism was also accompanied by a rising tide of left wing popular radicalism everywhere, engendering a set of expectations about the post-war order which political leaders could ignore only at their peril.

The high tide of reformist ideology and practice came in the quarter of a century of the 'Long Boom' in the western world economy, following the ending of the Second World War. It was a period characterised by a combination of fairly effective state influence on national economies, slow but steady liberalisation of the global capitalist economic order and sustained expansion in output, employment and living standards.[40] In that context social democracy sought to fuse together three elements of the reformist tradition into a coherent strategy for state action. Keynesianism was to provide the basis for a policy of managing capitalism to produce economic growth and full employment. The fruits of that growth could be used to implement a policy of redistribution via social provision and the tax system. Such benefits would in turn enable organised labour, under the guidance of moderate trade union leaders, to pursue orderly and responsible collective bargaining in a framework which accorded legitimacy to the interests of both capital and labour.[41] Social democratic parties everywhere adopted the package though their opportunities for implementing it in government were conditioned by the readiness of parties of the centre and right to offer diluted versions of the same policies. Reformist parties were most successful in gaining and maintaining power in smaller European states like Austria and Sweden. Successes were more intermittent in West Germany, the UK, France and Italy, and they had very limited impact in the USA and Japan.

What became evident from the 1970s onwards was that the reformist belief that these strategies formed a mutually reinforcing package of viable and electorally popular policies was based on fundamental misconceptions. Once the particular conjunctural circumstances of the Long Boom gave way to renewed economic and political instability in the global capitalist order, the package disintegrated. Economic growth now appeared as a problematic outcome heavily dependent upon the pursuit of 'supply side' policies aimed at emasculating social provision and redistributing income from poor to rich. The return of mass unemployment was accompanied by a reinvigorated corporate capital able to drastically redraw the balance of power between management and workers, often with the reluctant co-operation of newly 'realistic' union leaderships. By the 1980s, the illusions of reformist social democracy were cruelly exposed by precisely those processes – the dynamic instability of market forces and the class antagonisms written into its productive system – to which its ideology was necessarily blind.

The last third of the twentieth century has therefore seen a downward spiral involving the dialectical interplay of a failing programme for reform by social democracy and a diminishing set of expectations about what can be gained from the political process among its working-class electoral base. The outcome – a combination of ever more 'moderate' social democratic politics with an ever more fragile level of working-class electoral loyalties – promises to complete the transformation of social democracy into a post-reformist electoral machine whose ties to, and claims on, the working class are at best tactical.

One of the few things that those calling themselves Marxists – whether 'traditional', 'neo' or 'post' – agree on today is that the massive changes taking place in the global capitalist order in the late twentieth century are profoundly transforming the constraints and opportunities for political action. On one side, 'post-Fordist' and 'post-modernist' readings of late capitalism point to a rejection of working-class oriented programmes of reform, in favour of a quite different electoralist politics geared to new agendas and expressing the needs of new social forces.[42] In contrast,

Marxists who see the globalisation of capitalist production as involving a widening and deepening of the contradictions of the system of class exploitation argue that this renders social democratic projects for 'national reformism' increasingly ineffectual, and can also work to undermine the appeals of electoralist politics as well.[43] In this view, the current malaise of social democracy is part of a wider process, which increasingly calls into question the ability of any bourgeois national political leadership and strategy to handle the contemporary crises and instabilities of capitalism within the existing institutional frameworks. The decline of reformist social democracy is simply one dimension of the wider dual crisis of legitimacy and competence facing capitalist democracies everywhere. The outcome is to render traditional social democracy, with its uneasy mixture of electoralism, reformism and cross-class alliance politics, increasingly irrelevant to the contemporary world. Placed within the context of these debates, Przeworski's book has a curiously dated feel for one published as recently as 1985.[44]

Summary and conclusions

Przeworski's account of the logic and historical trajectory of social democracy sees it as constituted by a sequence of instrumentally grounded strategic choices – to participate, to appeal for cross-class support etc. – which have unintended and cumulative consequences which lead it on a long journey from socialism to reformism. Against this, I have argued as follows.

First, the decision by socialists to 'participate' cannot usefully be treated as an autonomous choice designed to optimise prospects for socialist advance in conditions of uncertainty. Rather it was powerfully shaped by a combination of material and ideological factors, notably ruling-class constraints and pressures of the State structures, and theoretically grounded perspectives (the positive expectations of a reformist viewpoint, the lacunas and ambiguities in the Marxist formulations) which encouraged the participatory route.

Secondly, the experience of involvement within bourgeois political structures in the decades from the 1870s to 1914 precipitated fundamental debates about strategies for socialism. These turned in no small part on rival views of the logic and limitations of bourgeois democratic institutions in a capitalist social order. The reformist wing, precisely because of its analysis of the workings of state and society under capitalism – as a system of class inequalities which are in principle transcendable in and through appeals to wider community and national interests using democratic institutions etc. – embraced a principled commitment to bourgeois democracy both as a means of making socialist advances and as an end in itself. In opposition to this, the revolutionary wing, in stressing the fundamental nature of class antagonisms within capitalism, developed a critique of the inherent limitations of bourgeois democracy, whether considered as a forum or as an instrument for prosecuting the class struggle. Divisions between reformists and revolutionaries over the question of cross-class alliances were similarly grounded in substantive ideological differences over the nature of class relationships under capitalism.

Thirdly, the one historical 'paradigm case' which comes close to fulfilling the requirements of Przeworski's historical model is the political current which emerged from the politics of the orthodox 'Marxist centre' in the pre-1914 period and developed into the 'Two and a half International', which played an important role in the 1917–23 period. The substantive issue in the ideological debate between this current and the reformists and Communists focused precisely on their attempt to combine a Marxist specification of socialist goals with a commitment to parliamentary and democratic means. The fact that the combination proved unstable was a product of the problems inherent in their particular ideological position. It does not support Przeworski's attempt to treat the tensions between ends and means in this ideology as a paradigm of the dilemmas facing all socialists under conditions of capitalist democracy.

Fourthly, the historical logic of unintended consequences has undoubtedly played an important role in the trajectories of development of both social democracy and communism. However, our analysis of them involved a dialectic of ends and means which prioritised constraining contexts and processes – war, revolution, the operations of a global capitalist system etc. – which receive little or no attention in Przeworski's analysis.

Fifthly, Przeworski's treatment of the rise and decline of reformist theory and practice in the middle decades of the twentieth century one-sidedly focuses on the emergence of Keynesian analysis. His account fails to give serious consideration of the wider structures and processes – at the level of class forces, the nation state and the global economy – which provided adherents of that analysis with their opportunities to put it to practical use with some degree of success. Similarly, his lack of recognition of the scale and extent of the crisis of Keynesianism in the last third of the century flows from neglecting the ways in which those same structures and processes are now seriously constraining the possibilities open for reformist politics in the contemporary context.

My critique in this chapter has focused on the defects of Przeworski's historical analysis of social democracy. However these are rooted in the RCM mode of analysis which he brought to, and sought to exemplify in, the historical account. His analyses of structures of choices, of class actors, and of the logic of the interplay between the two have raised fundamental questions about the methodological and theoretical assumptions of RCM. These are the subject of the next chapter.

Notes

1. Since the 1970s this has been the general trend throughout the major states of Europe: the persistent electoral failures of the Labour Party in Britain and the SPD in Germany; the varying combinations of right wing policies and corruption which have characterised the performance of various 'socialist' governments or coalitions in Mitterand's France, Suarez's Spain, Nenni's Italy and Papandreou's Greece. Social democracy has failed electorally even in its Swedish bastion. The current (1995) revival in Labour's electoral fortunes in the UK appears to arise from a combination of the cataclysmic performance by the Major Conservative government and Tony Blair's eagerness to distance 'New Labour' from old reformism.

2. Lukacs, G. (1971) *History and Class Consciousness*, London: Merlin Press, p. 38.

3. The tendency is most marked in the pronouncements of British Labour 'modernisers' but is not confined to them. Blair's rejection of the old 'socialist' Clause IV of the Labour Party constitution was partially justified on the grounds that a text composed in 1918 was obviously unsuited to present-day needs. Hence its replacement by the hymn of praise to the Adam Smithian conceptions of the market quoted earlier. A case of back to the future presumably.

4. See Therborn, G. (1992) 'The life and times of socialism', *New Left Review*, 194, and the subsequent exchange between Therborn and Mouzelis, N. (1993) *New Left Review*, 200.

5. Braunthal, J. (1967) *History of the International*, London: Nelson, 2 vols. (The original German edition appeared in 1963.)

6. See for example, Miliband, R. (1961) *Parliamentary Socialism*, London: George Allen & Unwin; Coates, D. (1975) *The Labour Party and the Struggle for Socialism*, Cambridge: Cambridge University Press; Howell, D. (1975) *British Social Democracy*, London: Croom Helm; Panitch, L. (1976) *Social Democracy and Industrial Militancy*, Cambridge: Cambridge University Press; Hinton, J. (1983) *Labour and Socialism*, Brighton: Wheatsheaf Books. Perhaps significantly, historical approaches to Labourism from a Left perspective have largely dried up since the early 1980s. John Saville's (1988) *The Labour Movement in Britain*, London: Faber, is one of the few recent contributions.

7. Among the better examples of the genre are Paterson, W. and Thomas, A.H. (eds) (1977) *Social Democratic Parties in Western Europe*, London: Croom Helm and their (1986) *The Future of Social Democracy*, Oxford: Clarendon Press. See also Anderson, P. and Camiller, P. (eds) (1994) *Mapping the West European Left*, London: Verso. We are somewhat better served by comparative studies of labour movements; a notable recent addition is Kirk, N. (1994) *Labour and Society in Britain and the USA*, Aldershot: Scolar Press, 2 vols.

8. Przeworski, A. (1985) *Capitalism and Social Democracy*, Cambridge: Cambridge University Press. All direct quotations from Przeworski in the text refer to this volume unless stated otherwise.

9. See in particular Miliband, R. (1961).

10. See Louis Althusser's famous essay on ideology (1971) in *Lenin and Philosophy*, London: New Left Books. From a different perspective, Perry Anderson adopts a similar line of argument in his discussion of British Labourism in his 'Origins of the present crisis' reprinted in Anderson, P. (1992) *English Questions*, London: Verso. For a critique of the latter on this point see Looker, R. 'Shifting trajectories: Perry Anderson's changing account of the pattern of English historical development' pp. 16–20 in Barker, C. and Nicholls, D. (eds) (1988) *The Development of British Capitalist Society: A Marxist Debate,* Manchester: Northern Marxist Historians Group.

11. The series – 'Studies in Marxism and social theory' – was edited by three of the leading figures of analytical Marxism, Gerry Cohen, Jon Elster and John Roemer. For a useful presentation of the characteristic ideas of this school see Roemer, J. (ed.) (1986) *Analytical Marxism*, Cambridge: Cambridge University Press.

12. See Przeworski, A. (1991) *Democracy and the Market,* Cambridge: Cambridge University Press.

13. See Callinicos, A. (1989) *Making History*, Oxford: Polity Press, particularly pp. 64–76; Wood, E.M. (1989) 'Rational choice Marxism: Is the game worth the candle?', *New Left Review*, 177; Lebowitz, M. (1988) 'Is "analytical Marxism" Marxism?', *Science and Society*, 52, 2. See also the exchanges between Callinicos, Wood and Carling, A. (1989) *New Left Review*, 177.

14. Three obvious examples from the late nineteenth century are the 'Lib-Lab' current in the English labour movement; the Bavarian wing of the SPD under Wollmar; and 'Millerandism' in France.

15. See Bernstein, E. *Evolutionary Socialism*, 1899 English translation, London: Independent Labour Party 1909, in particular section 3: 'The tasks and possibilities of social democracy'.

16. Howard, R. (ed.) (1971) *Rosa Luxemburg: Selected Political Writings*, New York: Monthly Review Press, pp. 115–16.

17. See Looker, R. and Coates, D. 'The State and the working class in nineteenth century Europe' in Anderson, J. (ed.) (1986) *The Rise of the Modern State*, Brighton: Wheatsheaf Books. See also Looker, R. 'Shifting trajectories: Perry Anderson's changing account of the pattern of English historical development' in Barker, C and Nicholls, D. (eds) (1988).

18. See Marshall, T.H. and Bottomore, T. (1992) *Citizenship and Social Class*, London: Pluto Press.

19. See Therborn, G. 'The rule of capital and the rise of democracy' (1977) *New Left Review*, 103. There was, of course, nothing about the process in its origins which guaranteed the success of this policy or that it would be generally adopted. This was at least in part a contingent consequence of the actual success of the strategy, particularly in Britain. It was in turn greatly assisted by the success of reformism in securing the support of the mass of the working class in the West in the first part of the twentieth century. This view of the causal sequence holding between reformism and democracy reverses the one proposed by Przeworski.

20. There is, of course, much debate both as to the extent that this had taken place in Europe by 1914 and the dynamics of the processes involved. See for example Mayer, A. (1981) *The Persistence of the Old Regime. Europe to the Great War*, London: Croom Helm. With regard to Britain, see the critical examination of the long-standing debate between Edward Thompson and Perry Anderson in Barker and Nicholls (eds) (1988).

21. The explosive growth of social democracy in Tsarist Russia is a case in point.

22. See Hinton (1983), pp. 10–13.

23. See Looker, R. (ed) (1972) *Rosa Luxemburg: Selected Political Writings*, London: Jonathan Cape, pp. 34–40.

24. For a brief but highly suggestive discussion of the dimensions of power relations see Lukes, S. (1974) *Power: A Radical View*, Basingstoke: Macmillan.

25. Kaiser Wilhelm II's famous threat that he could send a platoon of soldiers to close down the Reichstag at any time of his choosing was perhaps the most public and blustering expression of an option that remained in the armoury of ruling classes everywhere.

26. See Looker and Coates (1986).

27. An unrelenting hostility to the use of 'industrial strength' to achieve 'political goals' has been a central feature of British Labourism from its inception.

28. Looker and Coates (1986), p. 109.

29. This view appeared to receive canonical endorsement in Engels's introduction to the second edition of Marx's *Class Struggle in France*. This was used in turn by Kautsky and the SPD leadership to justify their antagonism to mass action. See Nettl, P. (1966) *Rosa Luxemburg*, Oxford: Oxford University Press, pp. 754–5.

30. Marx's own writings on the consequences of an extension of the franchise in England were interpreted as licensing the participatory choice. See, for example, Marx's 1852 essay on the Chartists reprinted in Marx, K. and Engels, F. (1962) *On Britain*, London: Lawrence & Wishart, 2nd edn, pp. 358–69.

31. This was of course one of the key issues in the debates between Marx and the anarchists in the First International.

32. For a more detailed discussion, see Braunthal, J. (1967) vol. 1, part 3. See also Joll, J. (1974) *The Second International 1889–1914*, London: Routledge & Kegan Paul, 2nd edn.

33. What came to be known as Kautskyism was in effect the theoretical articulation of this position. See introduction to Looker, R. (ed) (1972).

34. See Schorske, C. (1955) *German Social Democracy 1905–1917*, New York: John Wiley & Sons; Nettl, P. (1966) chs 14–16. See also Berlau, A.J. (1970) *The German SPD 1914–1921*, New York: Columbia University Press, revised edn; and Harman, C. (1983) *Germany – the Lost Revolution*, London: Bookmarks.

35. Kautsky and the USPD minority 'jumped ship' in 1917 as the logic and direction of events became all too clear.

36. For an excellent polemical discussion see Claudin, F. (1975) *The Communist Movement from Comintern to Cominform*, English edn, Harmondsworth: Penguin Books.

37. This current – the so-called 'Two and a half International' – was most prominently represented by the USPD in Germany and the 'majority socialists' in France and Italy in the aftermath of the First World War.

38. For a perceptive analysis which picks up on both the Russian and Italian contexts of debate, see Anderson, P. (1977) 'The antimonies of Antonio Gramsci', *New Left Review*, 100.

39. See Claudin, F. (1975) especially ch. 4.

40. See Harris, N. (1983) *Of Bread and Guns*, Harmondsworth: Penguin books, ch. 2.

41. For some representative defences of this position, see Crosland, A. (1956) *The Future of Socialism*, London: Cape Press; Shonfield, A. (1965) *Modern Capitalism*, London: Oxford University Press; and Galbraith, J.K. (1974) *The New Industrial State*, Harmondsworth: Penguin Books. For a vigorous attempt to reassert the continuing relevance of the wider Keynesian-reformist tradition see Hutton, W. (1995) *The State We're In*, London: Jonathan Cape.

42. In the UK this perspective was most vociferously advanced by writers around the now defunct magazine *Marxism Today*. See in particular the 'New times' issue of October 1988. Currently, they find expression in Blair's 'New Labour' Party.

43. See Harris, N. (1986) *The End of the Third World*, Harmondsworth: Penguin Books, ch. 8.

44. A statement of his current post-RCM views can be found in the prologue to his (1991) *Democracy and the Market*, Cambridge: Cambridge University Press. It appears in a series entitled 'Studies in rationality and social change' edited by fellow ex-RCMist Jon Elster.

CHAPTER FIVE

Class struggle, capitalist democracy and rational choice: Przeworski's analytical theses

Robert Looker

Analytical Marxism and rational choice Marxism

The school of analytical Marxism (AM) and its rational choice Marxist (RCM) offshoot have complex intellectual and ideological roots.[1] In part, they emerged as a critical reaction to the two dominant traditions in Marxist scholarship in the post-war period: most immediately with the Althusserian structuralism which had been the major influence on Marxist theory in the 1960s and 1970s; and more indirectly with the tradition of 'western Marxism'[2] from Gramsci and Lukacs onwards, which had powerfully shaped the New Left in the 1950s and 1960s. Emerging in the 1970s and 1980s out of a predominantly 'Anglo-Saxon' philosophical tradition, the adherents of AM sought to use the tools of British analytical philosophy to reconstruct and re-ground Marxism upon its modes of discourse. Thus defined, AM was a 'broad church' movement embracing a diverse range of Marxist scholars – Robert Brenner, Norman Geras and Erik Olin Wright are all understood to have been influenced by AM – who none the less found stimulation from the enterprise. The foundational and exemplary text of the movement was G.A. Cohen's *Karl Marx's Theory of History: A Defence* (1978).

It would be a mistake however, to see AM as solely shaped by debates within Marxism. It was also powerfully influenced by the wider intellectual and practical trends of the period, and in particular by the twin crises of Keynesian economics and traditional reformist strategies and by the parallel revival of neo-liberal theories of economy and society. A political crisis and the need to rethink socialist politics and Marxist theory within it was thus allied with an intellectual readiness to look to what were, prima facie, unlikely sources of inspiration for Marxists.

Within the broad flow of the AM trend, RCM stood out as a more sharply defined current. It drew its inspiration from the revival of neo-classical economic theory and its application by political economists and others – in the form of games theory and rational choice models –

to the fields of decision-making and public choice.[3] The outstanding figures in RCM were Jon Elster, John Roemer and Adam Przeworski.[4]

The case advanced by RCM and AM drew much of its power from the sharpness of its critiques of what was seen as the conceptual confusions and explanatory weaknesses exhibited by Marxist predecessors. RCM in particular attacked the way in which the austere structuralism of Althusser reduced class actors to the status of mere 'bearers' of social relations and subsumed their consciousness under the rubric of ideology. The tendency evident in much Gramscian-inspired Marxism to explain everything in terms of ideological processes, was seen as similarly denying rationality to class actors and turning them into the unthinking victims of what Przeworski called a 'mass delusion, a hoax' (Capitalism, p. 135). Other targets for their criticism ranged from the propensity to discuss class and class-consciousness as if they were the properties of a trans-individual entity – Lukacs was seen as the prime villain of the piece here[5] – to an unthinking habit of explaining the roles of institutions and practices – the class nature of the state or reformist politics for example – in terms of their contribution to the maintenance of the capitalist social order.

Such critical shafts were not directed solely at the epigones of 'structural' and 'western' Marxisms. Rather they were seen as flowing from core methodological errors whose roots lay in Marx's own work. Seen from this perspective, Marx had to be regarded as at best a revolutionary guru whose substantive intuitions urgently needed rescue from the deeply flawed methodological framework in which he and subsequent Marxists had embedded them. A Marxism which aspired to satisfy contemporary standards of analytical rigour had first to purge its explanations of the diseases of functionalism[6] and teleology, collectivism (whether of the metaphysical or methodological variety) and culturalist subjectivism. Any satisfactorily reformulated Marxism required methodological underpinning by explanations which satisfied the requirements of causal explanation, methodological individualism and models of rational action.

Przeworski's contribution to rational choice Marxism

It is not my purpose here to attempt a general engagement with these intellectual currents. This has been undertaken by others better qualified for the task.[7] My focus is the narrower and selective one provided by Przeworski's use of certain of their characteristic themes to develop his analysis of class and its interconnections with the politics of reformism. The reasons for adopting this restrictive focus, however, partly reflect on a broader problem about the work of the RCM school itself. The undoubted fascination which analytical models of rational choice theory have exercised over minds with a bent for playing games has not been matched by any great wealth of substantive insights when they are applied, on occasion, to the real world. This has been particularly marked in the case of RCM, though even within the wider field of orthodox social science the use of rational choice models has been subjected to withering criticism precisely on the grounds of the poverty of their empirical applications and results.[8] In this respect, Przeworski's work stands out as one of the few serious attempts within RCM to put it to the test of applying it to historical and political analysis.

In interpreting and criticising his work, a note of caution needs to be struck. The task of establishing the precise shape and direction of Przeworski's analysis of class in *Capitalism and Social Democracy* is by no means a straightforward one. In part this flows from the nature of the volume: it is a collection of essays written over a number of years and addressing different issues and problems. This means that we first have to construct the overall line of his thesis from a range of texts whose arguments are not always entirely consistent. Where this is the case, I have concentrated on what I take to be his dominant motif while drawing attention, where necessary, to alternative lines of argument in the notes. However, there are some key issues on which Przeworski adopts divergent and even contradictory positions. In drawing attention to them, I see them arising directly from his attempt to combine elements – Marxist theory and rational choice analysis, socialist premises and reformist conclusions, neo-classical and Keynesian economic analyses – which in my view are ultimately irreconcilable. Handling a well-harnessed team of horses is problematic at the best of times; when the horses pull in opposite directions the enterprise becomes perilous in the extreme. In arguing that Przeworski fails the tasks he set himself, I am not therefore suggesting that this arises from inadequacies in his use of RCM categories and methods of analysis – though his methods of argumentation are open to question on occasion – but because he pursues them to their logical conclusions. The result is to expose their inadequacies as a basis for a viable Marxist form of analysis.

The shape and strategic purpose of Przeworski's class analysis

In the previous chapter, we examined the rational choice logic which Przeworski argues underlies the trajectory of the historical development of social-democratic theory and practice in what he terms democratic capitalism. In this chapter, we trace out and examine Przeworski's wider and complementary thesis that (working from premises rooted in the

Marxist analysis of class) he can show that there is what one might call an elective affinity between the working class and the politics of reformism and explain the logic of the connection.

Such a thesis, if proven, would be a matter of substantial import. At its widest, it would effectively sever the links, both theoretical and practical, which Marxists have sought to establish between Marxist theory, working-class struggle and the project for socialism. On the more restricted terrain of democratic capitalism, it would resolve a central problem in the study of working-class politics by delineating the structure and logic of the 'party–class–capitalism' relationship. It would also, incidentally, render largely redundant much of the criticism, developed in the previous chapter, of his historical analysis of social democracy.

The discussion will first summarise the three main components of Przeworski's argument and then offer a critique of them. First, we consider his theory of class and class struggle and its connections with reformist strategies and parties. Secondly, we look at his specification of the objective – economic, political and ideological – conditions which form the 'structure of choices' within which class strategies develop. Thirdly, we examine his treatment of the analytical problems raised in linking the two together. Having travelled out along the line of Przeworski's argument, we will make a critical 'return journey' concluding with some observations on class rationality and the project for socialism.

Class exploitation, class struggle and reformist strategies

Rational choice Marxist theorists in the main have approached the subject of class by rejecting the classical Marxist view that class is a system of exploitation whereby capital extracts surplus value from labour in the process of production.[9] John Roemer's 1982 rational choice model of class[10] – probably the most influential treatment of the subject developed by the RCM school – gave an account of class exploitation as a process of unequal exchange arising from the unequal distribution of property relations. Capitalist exploitation is thus equated with the distributional inequalities which flow from the unequal distribution of wealth intrinsic to an economic order based on private ownership of wealth. Exploitation is established by reference to comparisons between existing distributional arrangements and hypothetical but feasible alternative sets of socialist property relations. On this basis Roemer argues that workers have a class interest in choosing a socialist system of property relations over a capitalist one. However, he does not address the relationship between class exploitation and class struggle as such.

Przeworski, in his discussion of Roemer's model in Chapter 7 of

Capitalism, endorses its broadly distributionalist view of the logic of class relations with only minor reservations.[11] His main concern is to use the model to develop an account of class struggle within capitalism as a process focused on achieving redistributional outcomes within the existing social order. In the process, he amends Roemer's account in two major respects. First, he shifts the focus away from an emphasis on property and wealth to income distribution. Secondly, he rejects Roemer's view that the possibilities for income redistribution are severely constrained by capitalist property relationships and adopts a view which respecifies the constraints to allow for a much wider range of redistributional outcomes within capitalism. This leads Przeworski also to reject the linkage made by Roemer between class exploitation and socialism. 'Roemer's workers face the stark choice of individually maximising their wages or collectively struggling for socialism' (*Capitalism*, p. 223). In Przeworski's view, this fails to allow for the fact that patterns of income distribution are not simply given by the economic logic of capitalist class relations, but are also affected by the impact of workers' organisation, class conflict and the intervention of the State (*Capitalism*, p. 232). Historically, workers have significantly improved their collective distributional lot by struggling for reforms within capitalism. However if class relationships under capitalism are such that improvements are possible, it follows that Roemer's linkage of the struggles of workers for improved material conditions with the project for socialism has to be severed (*Capitalism*, p. 248). Indeed, given the risks involved in workers attempting to bring about the transition to socialism, workers interests are optimised by pursuing reformist strategies within capitalism to achieve their redistributional goals (*Capitalism*, pp. 235–8).

The detailed development of Przeworski's argument takes two routes at this point. The first examines the relationship between class struggle and reformist strategies and parties in order to demonstrate how reformism comes to be the normal form of class conflict under capitalism. The second examines the economic parameters which facilitate the emergence of this 'class compromise' between capital and labour.

Przeworski's core theses on the connections binding together class struggle and reformist politics are most fully articulated in Chapter 2 of *Capitalism* in the course of his main engagement with the wider Marxist tradition of analysis of these subjects.[12] Przeworski starts from what he sees as the core weakness in the classical Marxist theory of the working class, namely its preoccupation with Marx's 'class-in-itself/class-for-itself' problematic. This as 'a formulation in which economic relations have the status of objective conditions and all other relations constitute realms of subjective actions' (*Capitalism*, p. 47). He rejects this on the grounds that it involves both economic reductionism and determinism.

In the case of the former, he follows Althusser and Poulantzas in arguing that it is not the economic level alone but 'economic, political and ideological conditions [which] jointly structure the realm of struggles that have as their effect the organisation, disorganisation or reorganisation of classes'. In the case of the latter, he maintains that the course and direction of class struggle itself is also critically shaped by the strategic choices made by the collective 'class-in-struggle'. The working class are as much involved in making themselves as being made by objective conditions, to borrow from Edward Thompson's usage here.[13] In summary, then, 'classes must thus be viewed as effects of struggles structured by objective conditions that are simultaneously economic, political and ideological' (*Capitalism*, p. 47).

The argument so far is not unfamiliar and clearly relies at key points on Poulantzas and to a lesser degree, Olin Wright. Przeworski's novelty lies in the way in which he answers the obvious question – how these general formulations are put to work to account for the course of class struggle within capitalism. The working class is as much the product of, as the precondition for, class struggle. At the same time, there are a range of alternative class projects competing with each other, each one of which would ideologically define and politically organise the class differently. In point of historical fact, it was social democracy which succeeded in imposing its particular ideological and political stamp on the working class, by involving the class struggle in the direction of electoral politics: 'Political and ideological relations of bourgeois democracy lead to the organisation of the working class in the form of mass electoral parties. As a result, the process or organisation of workers as a class becomes fused with the process of mobilisation of popular political support' (*Capitalism*, p. 77). The 'class in struggle' – which is the only form in which class can appear as an historical actor in Przeworski's view – in effect fuses with the political parties which historically organised the class, that is, in the main, with social democracy. As we saw from the previous chapter, Przeworski argues that these parties were driven by the logic of electoralist politics, from socialist electoralism through multiclass alliances to reformism. It now follows from Przeworski's argument that this process also reshapes the working class as a politically relevant actor in terms of their collective identities and interests, modes of activity and organisation. The symbiotic relationship between reformist politics and the working class is thus the product of the historical organising, disorganising and reorganising of the latter by the former in the process of electoral politics.

The second leg of Przeworski's thesis on the interplay between class struggle and reformist politics within capitalism rests on his specification of the material parameters within which class compromises between capital and labour are constructed. His argument, developed in Chapters 4 and 5 of his book, first seeks to establish that, given that class interests are primarily concerned with matters of income distribution, there is in fact considerable space for redistribution within the constraints set by the requirements of maintaining the capitalist economic system. Secondly, he argues that in these circumstances, the interest-optimising strategies of both capitalists and workers will lead them to negotiate settlements which work within those constraints. Such settlements leave the property rights of the former and the profits they derive from them largely in place, while depriving them of exclusive control over investment decisions. Reciprocally, they contain the latter's pressures to improve their consumption levels within limits which ensure the ability of the system to maintain investment at levels which meet the future consumption needs of both classes. While crises generated by distributional struggles between capitalists and workers are theoretically possible, the historical evolution of patterns of class compromises has reduced the risk to an acceptable minimum, particularly since 'crises of capitalism are in no one's material interest' (*Capitalism*, p. 164). So while such class compromises can never be absolutely guaranteed, it is reasonable to expect them to constitute the institutionalised form which class struggles will take over the long term within democratic capitalism.

The structure of choices – capitalism, democracy, Keynesianism

Przeworski's accounts of class struggle, both game-theoretic and histori-cal, require some specification of the conditions which define the objec-tive components of the structures of choice, and which set the constraints within which classes in struggle make their strategic choices. We noted earlier that Przeworski rejected economic determinism in favour of a view which emphasised the combination of economic, political and ideo-logical conditions. We therefore need briefly to outline his delineation of capitalism, the state and ideology.

Przeworski characterises the capitalist economy as a system of class inequalities of wealth and income operating within an increasingly com-plex and differentiated occupational structure. The former view frames his distributional account of class exploitation while the latter accounts for the pursuit of multiclass alliances by social democratic parties. In so far as he addresses the question of the dynamics of the capitalist econ-omy, he focuses on the linked equations – governing the balance between consumption and investment on the one hand and the relative shares in consumption of capitalists and workers on the other – which set the parameters within which class compromises are negotiated. Przeworski's analysis is clearly located within a Keynesian problematic of how to ensure sufficient investment for growth and hence future consumption.

It will be evident from the earlier discussions that the democratic state is fundamental to Przeworski's accounts both of social democratic politics and class struggle within capitalism. This he explores in some detail in Chapters 4 and 5 of his book. Following Poulantzas, he sees the State as enjoying relative autonomy in relation to classes; indeed, picking up on Marx's classic discussion of the Bonapartist state in nineteenth-century France, he extends the conception by boldly asserting that 'democracy is the modern Bonaparte' (*Capitalism*, p. 143). In effect, democracy provides the central institutional framework within which class compromises are negotiated, legitimated, executed and enforced. 'Capitalist democracy . . . structures political activities as political participation and reduces political conflicts to short-term material issues. It simultaneously generates conflicts over material issues and reduces conflicts to such issues' (*Capitalism*, p. 145). At the same time, 'the organisation of the state as an institution and the policies pursued by this institution constitute an expression of a specific class compromise' (*Capitalism*, p. 202).

The theory and practice of democracy is also centrally implicated in the processes of ideological legitimation of the system. Following Gramsci, Przeworski sees the democratic state as central to the processes of ensuring hegemony, producing and reproducing the consent of workers to the system, in advanced capitalist social orders. It is the framework within which the working class and social democratic parties are organised into political activity and it is also the institutional and ideological expression of the class compromises which emerge from political struggle. It also serves to exclude and de-legitimate other forms of class struggle (*Capitalism*, p. 141).

The second key component in Przeworski's account of ideology is constituted by Keynesian economic analysis and practices which he examines in Chapter 5. 'Economic theories are rationalisations of the political interests of conflicting classes and groups' (*Capitalism*, p. 206), 'Keynesianism . . . provided the ideological and political foundations of capitalist democracy' (*Capitalism*, p. 207) and 'Democratic control over the level of unemployment and the distribution of income became the terms of the compromise that made democratic capitalism possible' (*Capitalism*, p. 206).

The structure of choices and the rational individual

The final component needed to complete Przeworski's analysis raises the question of how an RCM analysis conceptualises the process of interaction between class struggles and the objective economic, political and ideological conditions within which they take place. He explores this issue in the methodological appendix to Chapter 2 where he insists that explanations of the relationship between class actors and the objective conditions of action need to meet the requirements of methodological individualism. The structural conditions of capitalism are neither external material compulsions on, nor internal ideological norms and values shaping the motivations of, class actors. Rather they constitute objective 'structures of choice' within which the actors make rational choices in the light of their assessment of their own interests and their evaluation of strategies most likely to achieve their goals.

How does this bite on the specific issue of understanding class actors where it seems self-evident, on traditional Marxist arguments, that in the main they are positioned within a class independently of his/her will and acquire their class interests by virtue of that positioning? Przeworski answers this by constructing the example of a Mrs Jones who – married, white, catholic, a wife and mother, inheritor of a piece of land – none the less chooses to become a wage labourer and therefore to define her interests as those of a worker (*Capitalism*, p. 94). Przeworski's assertion here is that what explains Mrs Jones's position as a proletarian is her choice to adopt it. Or as he makes the point more formally elsewhere, 'social relations are given to the historical subject, individual or collective, as realms of possibilities, as structures of choice' (*Capitalism*, p. 73).

Methodological individualism and Mrs Jones

If I begin the critique of Przeworski's analysis with the Mrs Jones example, it is not simply because it is the easy target for ridicule which he correctly surmised it would be (*Capitalism*, p. 95). Rather its interrogation directs us to two key elements underpinning his analysis: his understanding of the constraints and opportunities facing class actors within the capitalist social order and the ways in which we understand and analyse the interplay between those constraints and actors. Both bear directly on the game theoretical frameworks and methodological individualist assumptions on which RCM rests.

How do we set about the task of explaining the choice which Mrs Jones makes? Two radically different lines of argument appear open here. The first anchors her interests in maximising her economic rewards and assumes that within the 'structure of choices' available to her by virtue of her situation – as landowner, wife, catholic etc. – she selects the wage-labour option as her interest optimising strategy. Such an account is clearly highly amenable to game theoretic calculations of strategy but just how we construct the game is heavily dependent on the tightness of the class constraints within which the game is played. If the constraints are drawn too loosely – the endowments supplied to Mrs Jones give her many realistic alternatives to wage labour – Przeworski is open to the charge of rigging the debate by situating Mrs Jones in a quite atypical location within the class structure. His example then fails to sustain the general argument because it mistakenly assumes that choices open to one person in a group are also open to members of the group as a whole. As Cohen has pointed out, even where wage labourers are individually free to choose alternatives, as a whole they are in a condition of collective unfreedom in this regard.[14]

Przeworski can, of course, avoid the fallacy of composition by drawing the constraints on Mrs Jones much more tightly. This has the virtue of according with the standard Marxist view that wage labourers, while formally free to sell their labour power, are none the less subject to the 'dull compulsions of economic necessity' inherent in their position in the class structure. However, to the extent that Przeworski does this, he empties the choice of real content because it is already effectively pre-determined by the specification of the 'structure of choices' in which it is made. Mrs Jones becomes an 'embodied structure', to borrow Ellen Meiksins Wood's useful phrase.[15] 'Freedom of choice' in these circumstances is at best the perversely Hegelian freedom to acknowledge necessity. (The point of course is not that workers have no options open to them but that their choices are sharply circumscribed by the structural constraints and opportunities open to those positioned by the class structure as 'wage workers'.)

Independently of the question of the tightness or looseness of its constraints, Przeworski's model seems open to a further objection. The picture of Mrs Jones rationally pursuing her interest-optimising strategies to maximise her income seems a particularly crude example of the kind of economic reductionism which Przeworski elsewhere rejects out of hand. He can, of course, avoid this by allowing – as in places he appears to do – that she exercises choice by selecting from among the social and personal identities available to her as wife, landowner etc. Economic reductionism is thus avoided and choice is preserved, but at the cost of making it a rather arbitrary act, for Mrs Jones's interests would then be consequential on her choice of identity rather than vice versa. Mrs Jones would in effect be practising a radically subjectivist 'politics of identity' and Przeworski would have embraced a post-modernist relativism antithetical to RCM assumptions.

There is support in Przeworski's text for both an 'objective interest' and a 'subjective identity' reading of his argument. Seen in relation to the discussion of Roemer's distributional theory of class in Chapter 7 of *Capitalism*, the former is the plausible view. However, read in the context of his account of the determinants of class struggle in Chapter 2, as we will see, the latter finds some support. This suggests there are some theoretical and conceptual confusions buried under the often convoluted articulation of Przeworski's theses on class struggle.

There is, of course, a third radical interpretation of the Mrs Jones example, reading it as an assertion that individuals must always be conceptualised as free to choose in relation to any or all social relations available to them. This would certainly be methodological individualism (MI) with a vengeance but it would also be open to obvious challenge. The 'individual' here becomes an analytic construct of a high level of abstraction where it functions as a socially and culturally empty bearer of instrumental rationality. In order to be 'individualised', i.e. translated back into the world of living, breathing human beings, MI would have to reintroduce into the description of individuals, references to all those interpersonal relationships and socio-economic positions – of class, gender, ethnicity, nationality, age etc. – which had been banished from the account of 'the individual' in the first place. In practice, MI could smuggle them back in under the guise of personal attributes and endowments. However, it is precisely a recognition of the individual as what Marx called an 'ensemble of social relations' which necessitates a methodologically prior reference to class structures and collectivities.

This does not, of course, resolve the problem of articulating a convincing Marxist solution to the problem of the relationship between structure and agency, but it does indicate the directions in which such solutions need to be sought.[16] Interestingly enough, it does not even exclude from consideration some relaxed variant of rational choice analysis, since the 'structures of choice'–'rational-actor' model is compatible with both MI and non-MI accounts of structure and of rationality. We could, for example, allow that while Mrs Jones's objective interests are in a real sense given by her position as a worker, her awareness of both her interests and identities are constructed in and through her set of social relationships. After all, the attributes with which Przeworski endows her – motherhood, catholicism etc. – are not simply or even primarily resources to be assessed instrumentally in the strategic game of interest maximisation. Rather they provide Mrs Jones with her sense of identities and solidarities and implicate her in shared practices and collective activities which will affect how she rationally defines and pursues her interests. This is not, however, a route which Przeworski can take without giving to social relationships an explanatory role which sits uneasily with his methodological individualism.

Put another way, the debate over MI is essentially a side issue in the context of Przeworski's RCM analysis. Our acceptance or rejection of it depends less on his problematic attempts to provide MI underpinnings for the abstract model, than in the way he applies it to the empirical analysis of capitalism. It is in his specification of the structures of choice and their degrees of constraints and opportunities for class actors that the real merits or otherwise of his game-theoretic model can be assessed.

Constraints on the 'rules of the game' of democratic capitalism

How well does Przeworski delineate the objective structures of choice in democratic capitalism? How accurate are his characterisations of the tightness and looseness of their constraining influences on class choices? As we have seen, Przeworski's specification of the objective conditions of capitalism offers us an 'either/or' choice – either economic determinism tout court or a voluntaristic perspective in which *economic, political* and *ideological* conditions combine to structure the situation in which the class actors in capitalism operate. In rejecting the former in favour of the latter he effectively excludes from consideration the debates among Marxists over recent decades on the relative priority of determination within the totality of structural conditions. The outcome appears at first sight to be an untheorised defence of pluralism, but a closer scrutiny of his account of the structures of choice in 'democratic capitalism' suggests a model in which economic conditions are marginalised and politics are prioritised in the construction of explanations.

The inmates of the prison – no, reform school – that is democratic capitalism are constrained in different ways and to different degrees by the objective economic, political and ideological features of the establishment. The system of private and unequal wealth distribution provides a strong perimeter wall for the establishment, but within the grounds, the economic regime is pretty relaxed and permissive of a wide range of redistributional strategies and outcomes pursued by competing sections – privileged and underprivileged – of inmates. Two key constraints shape the actual outcomes of distributional disputes. One is a set of prudential guidelines, courtesy of Keynes et al., which spell out the range of mutually acceptable compromises on offer. The other, and central, constraint is provided by the existence of an elected chief warder – the democratic state – which regulates, arbitrates and implements the process in the interests of the overall efficiency of the establishment. Within its walls, the inmates find life tolerable and even pleasant to the degree that they come to find conditions in reformatory far more preferable than running the risks involved in 'going over the wall'.

Once capitalist economic boundaries are set up, it is democratic institutions and practices which are accorded the central and tightly constraining role in Przeworski's account of democratic capitalism. The 'rules of the democratic game' – a recurrent image of his – set the social-democratic electoral game in motion and give it direction towards multi-class alliances and reformism; they shape the way in which the working class are organised, disorganised and reorganised; they become the institutional framework for negotiating and implementing 'class compromises', and so on. If Przeworski were offering a determinist account then his would be a model of political rather than economic determinism.

Przeworski makes many interesting comments on the logic of the democratic electoral game and its impact on party strategy. His observations on party strategy, class organisation and individual voting in Chapter 3 of *Capitalism* are particularly ingenious. However, this leaves unanswered the question of why this game comes to be played in a capitalist context. As we saw in the previous chapter, Przeworski barely addresses this question and when he does, his answers are contradictory. The second sentence of Chapter 1 proclaims that 'earlier events resulted in establishing the principle of democracy' (*Capitalism*, p. 7) but the hows and whys are left unspecified. Elsewhere he argues that the bourgeoisie, seeing themselves as the bearers of universal interests, create political institutions which 'express this vision of society' (*Capitalism*, p. 21). The implication is that while the bourgeoisie were mistaken in their self-image, the institutions they create none the less embody an authentically democratic and class-neutral framework for articulating and negotiating rival class interests. However, in a brief encounter with the Marxist debate between instrumentalist and functionalist theories of the State in Chapter 4, he rejects both approaches in favour of a view of the democratic state as the product and expression of class compromise between capital and labour (*Capitalism*, p. 202). Thus the democratic rules of the game explain the emergence of class compromise which in turn explains the democratic 'rules of the game'. Such are the explanatory miracles which can be accomplished with the use of game-theoretic modes of analysis.

Sarcasm aside, the circularity of the argument is indicative less of faulty logic than of a major lacuna in Przeworski's discussion, namely the absence of any serious or sustained encounters with Marxist theories of the capitalist state. His brief survey of Gramsci's concept of hegemony and Poulantzas's treatment of relative autonomy are focused solely on the question of democratic institutions and practices. Przeworski simply avoids the logically prior Marxist problematic of the relationship between the State and the ruling class.[17] This is understandable when one recognises that the latter concept has no existence anywhere in the work.[18] Of course, Przeworski need not endorse such concepts but, writing ostensibly as a Marxist, he is surely obliged to define his position in relation to them. As I indicated in the previous chapter, their absence seriously disables his historical account of social democracy. In fact

Przeworski's analysis is underpinned by a more or less coherent theory of the State; it just so happens that it is not a Marxist one. Rather it is one which operates somewhere along the pluralist/corporatist spectrum with powerful Keynesian inputs. Put another way, it is the kind of theory about the democratic state which social democrats are wont to rely on to legitimate their political practices.

If Przeworski's encounters with Marxist theories of the State are brief, his treatment of the Marxist political economy of capital is positively peremptory and dismissive – a point we will return to when we confront his analysis of class in the next section. His game-theoretic model of the capitalist economy is one in which rates of accumulation and inflation, levels of prices and employment and the distribution of income etc. are determined by actors, whether as individuals in the market or collective 'classes in struggle' (*Capitalism*, pp. 233–4). In other words, he rejects Marxist economic analysis in favour of the neo-classical model of the market as modified by Keynesian assumptions about the interventist role of the State.[19] We cannot argue here the rival merits of Marxist, neo-classical and Keynesian economic analyses. What we can do is look at the implications of Przeworski's position for the relative tightness of the economic constraints he places on the choices of class actors in democratic capitalism and see how far the picture can be sustained in reality. Having asserted, against Roemer, that capitalism allows for the possibility of redistribution of income, Przeworski translates this into a pretty open-ended outcome of the operations of workers organisation, class conflict and state intervention in modifying the original pattern of distribution established by the class system. In a democratic welfare state, satisfaction of class interests is determined as much by state policy as the market and many class positions are shaped more by political choices than economic processes. The only effective constraints here are prudential ones derived from the Keynesian parameters on the linked trade-offs between investment and consumption on the one hand and the class shares of consumption on the other.[20]

Against this view, traditional Marxists have argued that the possibilities for redistribution on any significant scale are severely constrained by 'the limits of the possible' set by the economic constraints of capitalism. Outside of quite narrow limits, class struggles and state interventions are in their outcomes and in their methods of achievement, profoundly threatening to the capital accumulation process and to capitalist control of it. Empirical data suggests that while governments have some impact on the distribution of incomes in society, this at best modifies rather than replaces market mechanisms.[21] Even in the heyday of welfare statism in the post-war decades of the Long Boom, reformism never managed to do much more than ameliorate the distribution of rewards largely determined by the market and the logic of the capital accumulation process. Their impact on the pattern of ownership and control of capital was even more marginal. At best, they created temporary 'no-go' areas for the market in some parts of the health, education and welfare systems.

The subsequent attack and roll back of social provision under capitalism, exemplified by Thatcherism in the UK, shows how fragile redistributionist tendencies are in reality. The experience goes a long way to provide direct empirical confirmation for the classical Marxist view that the State cannot supersede the capitalist determinants of class position and experience. Rather it works within its constraints and imperatives – the needs of capital accumulation, the maintenance of class power, and the requirements of the wider socio-cultural environment sustaining them. This is of course acknowledged in an indirect way by neo-liberal theorists of the New Right when they reject interventionism, welfarism and corporatism as disrupting rational market decisions, spawning a culture of dependency and reinforcing trade union power.[22] The New Right, in this respect, have a clearer grasp of the tightly constraining logic of the economic conditions of capitalism than Przeworski.

In turning, briefly, to Przeworski's handling of the constraining role of ideology, it is evident that he shares the general RCM distrust of what he portrays as 'sociological' approaches to the subject (*Capitalism*, p. 93), which explain away class behaviour in terms of processes of ideological domination which reduce workers to the status of 'perpetual dupes' (*Capitalism*, p. 3). Ideological conditions therefore play only a limited and particular role in his account of democratic capitalism; in particular they carry no great weight in providing some ethical or moral legitimation to the system. The components which figure prominently in his account – democracy and Keynesianism – are discussed in essentially pragmatic and procedural terms: democracy works; Keynesianism defines the mutually acceptable limits to moves within the 'class compromise' game.

This is not the place for a full discussion of RCM's account of ideology. Even if one shares the suspicion of dominant ideology theses and over-socialised models of consciousness, one cannot but be struck by the paucity of Przeworski's references to cultural dimensions of working-class experience or to major ideological forces – nationalism, imperialism, sexism, racism as well as Left alternatives to social democracy – which shaped class-consciousness and action in this century. When he does deal with the specific ideological influence of Keynesianism, his use of it is problematic. His discussion of the ways in which it shaped the patterns of class compromise in the decades of the Long Boom renders it virtually ideologically constitutive of the parameters of class struggle in democratic capitalism. One consequence is that when he has to account for the emergence of the New Right from the late 1970s onwards, he is obliged to endow it with epochal significance. 'The crisis of Keynesianism is a crisis of democratic capitalism' (*Capitalism*, p. 211) which presages 'a project for a new society, a bourgeois revolution' (*Capitalism*, p. 219), calling into question the links he sees binding capitalism to democracy. The point here is not that Przeworski, writing in the early 1980s, fell victim to the tendency among sections of the Left at the time to read Thatcherism and Reaganism as precursors to a new authoritarian state system.[23] Rather it is that, given the intimate linkages which Przeworski had constructed between democratic capitalism, Keynesianism and class compromise, the alarmist conclusion flowed directly from his analysis. If the conclusion turns out to be misplaced – and Przeworski in his later work clearly if implicitly acknowledges this[24] – then the premises from which it was derived are likewise open to serious question.

Class, class struggle and reformism – the closed circle?

We come finally to Przeworski's account of the working class within capitalism. I will examine in turn his treatments of class positions, class struggle and the class compromise, concluding with some more general observations on the ways in which his analytical and theoretical commitments work to exclude from debate many dimensions of class analysis encompassed by Marxist accounts.

Przeworski purports to offer a Marxist analysis of class positions in capitalism. In fact, he uses the language of Marxist categories to arrive at a position whose logic is anchored in largely neo-Weberian modes of analysis.[25] Though he makes recurrent if not always consistent references to class relations and structures, his interpretation of Marxist class analysis as a 'theory of empty places' redirects its analytical focus towards class as a stratification model. The result is to conceptualise the class structure as a complex aggregation of unequal positions. The key problematic becomes classificatory – which positions should be allocated to which strata? Applied to capitalism, the model produces an account of the evolution of the class structure from a simple and dichotomous pattern in the mid nineteenth century towards a complex pattern of positions differentiated in terms of occupation, consumption, authority, work etc. in the later twentieth century. On this account, capitalist development produces a trend from homogeneity towards heterogeneity in the class structure rather than towards class polarisation as envisaged in the *Communist Manifesto*.

Such developmental models are not unfamiliar. They are part of the stock in trade of Parsonian inspired accounts of the evolution of industrial society as a process of functional differentiation. Like them, Przeworski's variant rests upon some dubious readings of the historical evidence. For instance, it takes a certain disdain for the complexities of nineteenth-century class structure to assert that 'in 1848 one simply knew who were the proletarians' (*Capitalism*, p. 56). Its novelty lies in his attempt to derive the result from a Marxist analysis of the way in which 'capitalist development continually transforms the structure of places in the system of production' (*Capitalism*, p. 60). He does this via a highly selective engagement with the Marxist account of the capital accumulation process. Though the language is Marxist, the actual analysis is driven by very different – in this case Keynesian – assumptions.[26] Crucially, he rejects key components of Marxist economic analysis – the instability inherent in the capital accumulation process (*Capitalism*, p. 86) and the propensity to create mass unemployment and use it as a reserve army of labour (*Capitalism*, p. 89). Such ideas have no place in a post-Keynesian world.

In fact, Przeworski engages with Marxist economic analysis only on the very narrow front of the productive labour debate.[27] Here he follows Poulantzas's position – limiting the proletariat to sections of the manual workforce directly engaged in the process of production – and argues that the changing organic composition of capital results in such proletarian positions occupying a diminishing sector of the overall class structure. They become simply one component of a more heterogeneous class structure; one whose narrow and sectionalist producer interests are not necessarily antagonistic to those of the manufacturing bourgeoisie (*Capitalism*, p. 91). 'Surplus labour' generated by the capital accumulation process feeds into expanding non-producer 'middle class' positions, partly as a consequence of full employment policies pursued by democratic capitalism. In effect, the development of the capitalist economy itself and the emergence of Keynesian techniques combine to marginalise 'the economic' and prioritise 'the political' in the shaping of class positions and interests. As a result, reformist political projects come to act as key causal agents in organising, disorganising and reorganising the now heterogeneous 'working class in struggle' in advanced democratic capitalist societies.

We have already argued that the Keynesian assumptions underpinning Przeworski's economic analysis of capitalism have been largely discredited by the experience of the past two decades. The 'productive labour' thesis he seeks to link to these assumptions has likewise been subjected to convincing criticisms from Marxist perspectives.[28] We will also shortly explore some of the dimensions of Marxist class analysis which Przeworski's account simply fails to address. For the moment, however, I wish to examine the implications of this model for his account of class struggle in order to show the confused and even contradictory consequences that flow from it.

How does Przeworski build the bridge between the working class occupying the 'structures of places' and class struggle? One option open to him is to use Roemer's distributionalist model of class to ground the link on an objectivist account of class interests. Workers occupy positions defined in terms of the unequal allocation of rewards within capitalism. Being rational actors who possess a cognitive grasp of their situation, their class interests indicate that they should combine in struggle to change the distribution of rewards. Such an account would, however, commit Przeworski to rely on an economically determined model of the 'structure of places' of a kind which he elsewhere rejects as mired in the erroneous 'class-in-itself/class-for-itself' problematic. Perhaps for this reason, his account of class struggle in Chapter 2 of *Capitalism* adopts a more subjectivist model which emphasises the historically contingent social construction of class through political and ideological practice. Unfortunately, this opens the door to a view of class interests as contingent on the ideological and political specification of class identity and organisation, in which workers link their class interests with redistributionist strategies as a result of adopting the ideological perspectives and political strategies of social democracy. Once again, Przeworski's rational choice analysis has generated a model which appears to embrace the post-modernist politics of identity with its subjectivist and relativist connotations.[29]

The tension between Przeworski's two lines of argument can be resolved only at a major cost to the theoretical edifice which he seeks to erect. The 'subjectivist' account can be saved if we reground it in a framework which gives primacy to economic conditions in determining class positions and interests while allowing for their modification through interactions with political and ideological processes. This solution, however, also requires a reconstruction of his accounts of relations between class and party, capitalism and democracy – even the objective and the subjective – in ways which undermine Przeworski's substantive account of the logic of social democracy and his methodological commitment to RCM.

Another problem which arises from Przeworski's account of the class struggle is that it involves a thorough-going though unacknowledged *substitutionism*. It definitionally equates the class in struggle with parties in competition in the electoral game and thus conceptually subsumes class under party. In this reductionist conception, the working class exists as a politically relevant collectivity in democratic capitalism only in so far as they are organised electorally; class politics are expressed in the act of voting. Working-class politics are thus a function of the strategic choices made by party leaderships within the logic of the electoral game. The party is the active agent which organises, reorganises and disorganises the class. If for any reason the party ceases to be electorally effective, class loses its salience for political action.

Marxists have often criticised social democracy for seeking to substitute their parliamentary theory and practice for the consciousness and collective self-activity of workers in struggle. The party seeks to 'represent' the working class and act on their behalf, articulating and advancing their interests through the 'class struggle in parliament'. Historically, both reformist and Stalinist party leaderships have aspired, and often succeeded, in making over the working class in their own image and subordinating the class struggle to party needs. However, this is a long way from accepting that this is given by the very nature of the party–class relationship. Przeworski's conceptual substitutionism arises from the explanatory hole inherent in his theory of class, namely his exclusion of any conceptualisation of it as a structured relationship, anchored in the processes of production, which creates the circumstances not of our choosing within which, through collective self-activity, we make our own history. Przeworski can conceive class only as a set of empty places or as a collectivity mobilised for action by outside – party or union – agencies.[30]

Let us turn to Przeworski's handling of class compromises and the limits of reformism in democratic capitalism. As we noted earlier, his account of the objective structures of choice portrays the democratic 'rules of the game' as the key constraint on 'classes in struggle'. Against this, I argue for the traditional Marxist conception which sees the 'limits of the possible' within which reformist parties operate as flowing from the structural relationship of the bourgeois state to the capitalist economy. In addition to these external constraints, there are also internal contradictions in the relationship between the working class and reformist parties. Reformist parties present themselves as vehicles for advancing working-class interests. However, given limitations intrinsic to capitalism, those interests, whether pursued by political or industrial means, can be processed legitimately only to the extent that they are constituted as one of the many sectional interests competing for relative advantage within the social order. However, the working class are not simply one more interest group; they are central to the exploitative system of capital accumulation. Concessions to workers – particularly to organised labour – are therefore always problematic for capital. Economic gains for labour not only pose threats to the profitability of individual firms and national economies in the competitive environment of global markets; they also increase the self-confidence and combativity of workers and raise their demands and aspirations.

Reformist politics are thus positioned in a contradictory relationship to working-class interests and struggle. They are deeply implicated in a

system in which limited gains for workers require a corresponding acceptance of restraint, discipline and moderation, especially on the part of
organised labour. Reformist parties – and trade union bureaucracies for
that matter – require as a condition of achieving even limited success
that they act as 'policemen of discontent'[31] in the context of the wider
class struggle. They do not simply 'organise, disorganise and reorganise'
the class as an artefact of playing the electoral game. Rather they must
seek to manage and contain working-class aspirations and forms of
struggle. Their commitment to bourgeois democracy thus involves an
unrelenting hostility to extra-parliamentary forms of class struggle, not
as some technical consequence of the decision to participate, but as part
of the process of managing and containing class conflict in capitalist
democracy.

Przeworski equates working-class politics with voting. This is certainly an important dimension of their development within capitalist
democracy. However, the electoral game is itself only one of several competing forms of class struggle within capitalism. Przeworski's account
systematically downplays or ignores these alternatives. Thus he has little
to say about the complex interplay between industrial labour movements
and politics, even though these have been central to the politics of social
democracy. Nor do social-democratic politics exhaust the party-political
universe for workers, as the existence of competitors on the Left –
Communist, syndicalist, anarchist, Trotskyist et al. – testify. There is also
the subject which preoccupies classical Marxism – workers in struggle.
One of the paradoxes of the internal contradictions outlined above is
that even in the absence of revolutionary challenges to the existing social
order, apparently sectionalist class conflicts over redistributional outcomes can periodically transform themselves into something altogether
too radical for the capitalist social order. Such 'moments' are by no
means common – arguably the most recent one in Britain was the
1984–85 miners strike – but they do occur and recur in ways for which
Przeworski's analysis of class and class conflict can make no allowance.

Underlying these criticisms of Przeworski is my contention that his
analysis is deficient precisely because it breaks with the materialist
approaches to class and class struggle embodied in classical Marxism. He
does so by decentring 'the economic' and privileging political and ideological levels of discourse in his class analysis. I have argued that the
resultant model of class is both analytically and empirically suspect.
However, we need also briefly to consider the general case he advances
for making this break: in his view the classic Marxist position – the 'class-
in-itself/class-for-itself' problematic – is irredeemably bound to an outmoded and indefensible economic determinism.

What is striking about Przeworski's argument is the way in which he rigs the debate. In the first place, he collapses a range of distinct relationships and issues – objectivity and subjectivity; base and superstructure; idealist and materialist modes of explanation; economic and non-economic – into a simplistic choice between economic determinism or a kind of pluralistic voluntarism. Secondly, he equates the classical Marxist analyses of class with Kautsky, presenting the latter as 'the form in which . . . [orthodox Marxist thought] . . . has been perpetuated for nearly a century' (*Capitalism*, p. 48). Such assertions are inaccurate in respect of the history and intellectual subtlety of the Marxist tradition; they are also disingenuous in that they enable him to avoid a proper and detailed engagement with that tradition, offering in its place some questionable *obiter dicta* on Marxist theory, such as the assertion that 'the concept of the proletariat seems to have been self-evident for the founders of scientific socialism' (*Capitalism*, p. 55).[32] In part, the problems appear to arise from a certain confusion on his part as to the levels of debate involved. Marxist theories of class, because they refer both to structural relationships and intentional action, combine analyses which operate at different levels of abstraction. Przeworski, possibly because of his own Methodological Individualist stance, appears insensitive to this with the result that his readings of Marxism take on a 'straw man' quality, as when he pronounces that 'Marx's theory of accumulation, in *Capital*, has no logical place for class struggle' (*Capitalism*, p. 231).[33]

Przeworski's critique of economic determinism is conducted for the most part at a level of generality which signally fails to connect with Marxist explanations and relate economic processes to class. One example is particularly instructive. Przeworski characterises the 'class-in-itself' concept as a 'theory of empty places' and argues that 'at this level the occupants are "sacks of potatoes"; they share the same relationship to the means of production . . . yet they remain simply as categories, not as subjects' (*Capitalism*, p. 50). The 'sack of potatoes' metaphor, of course, refers to the famous passage in the *18th Brumaire of Louis Bonaparte* where Marx argued that the specific pattern of land proprietorship in post-revolutionary France positioned the peasants in isolation from each other and thus structurally disorganised them as a class. This contrasted with the ways in which the specific system of capitalist production created and organised the proletariat as a collective worker in the social division of labour. Structural conditions here facilitated the development of shared class interests and identities and provided both the circumstances and resources required to translate them into collective action. This analysis is no more determinist than Przeworski's rational choice model. What it does do, however, is to accord primacy to economic relationships and treat them as both constraining and enabling.[34] Put another way, Przeworski's rejection of economic determinism in the abstract consistently fails to engage with concrete Marxist analyses of the economic determinants of class and their connections with intentional class action. As a result, his own analysis is largely innocent of the ways in which the forms of organisation of capitalist production constrain, facilitate and collectively empower classes.

There is far more to class, both as lived experience and as struggle, than is dreamt of in Przeworski's MI philosophy. When he looks at traditional Marxist analyses of the economic determinants of class position, his analytical framework only allows him to see a 'structure of places'. Missing here is any sense of class as a relational concept, combining references to structures, positions and relationships, and locating and explaining individual and collective experiences, consciousness and activity by reference to them. The classical Marxist approach sees class relationships as arising from the structure of exploitation located within the process of production which has as its effects inequalities in the distribution of rewards, prestige and power. People are inserted into positions in these structures, often at birth and in the main independent of their choices. It organises the ways in which they experience life and shapes their judgments as to their interests and how best to pursue them. Przeworski rejects this conception because he sees it as determinist, denying people choice. The only choice to which his model sensitises him is the unreal one of whether or not to become a worker. The myriad experiences, problems and constrained choices involved in life as a worker – at work, in the market-place, household, community and state – play hardly any role in his conception of class. Once we address the shared experiences and collective activities of workers in the labour process etc., Przeworski's narrowly substitutionist and electoralist view of class politics collapses in face of the complexities and contingencies of the history of working-class struggle both within and in opposition to capitalism.

Marxist theory, socialist politics and rational choice analysis

Let us conclude by briefly assessing Przeworski's work by reference to its claims to be a contribution to a new paradigm for Marxist theory by a socialist, using rational choice models to illuminate processes of class struggle and politics.

Considered as a contribution to Marxist theory, Przeworski's project is highly ambitious. It seeks to describe and explain the logic of the interconnections between the working class, patterns of class struggle, and social democratic parties and politics within capitalist democracies. It promises to bring clarification and precision to an area of Marxist discourse all too prone to indulge in rhetoric and romanticism. However, the volume, for all its range of reference and the ingenuity of its arguments, fails to deliver on these claims. As we have noted earlier, he fails to engage with key theses central to his subject: namely with Marxist theories of the State; with the political economy of capitalist instability or with materialist analyses of class and class conflict. In their place we are offered highly selective borrowings of Marxist categories and strophes in order to reproduce what is in effect a social-reformist analysis. The account of the capitalist economy rests on largely Keynesian assumptions. The treatment of 'democratic capitalism' likewise depends on predominantly pluralist models of the State and the democratic process. His understanding of class and class conflict is essentially Weberian. Whatever his intent in *Capitalism and Social Democracy*, Przeworski's Marxism is merely gestural and cosmetic in its practice. Indeed there was always a certain implausibility about RCM as a programme to reground Marxism on categories and modes of analysis whose primary exemplification – neo-classical economies – yields an account of capitalism directly contrary to the Marxian one. Practitioners of RCM have over the past decade tacitly acknowledged this by increasingly abandoning any distinctively Marxist propositions in favour of a variety of alternative positions.[35]

Przeworski writes not only as an academic Marxist but as a socialist critic of the capitalist order.[36] However, his extreme pessimism as to agencies for its realisation result in a *faux de mieux* defence of reformism which serves to disconnect class struggle from the project for socialism. On the one hand, he rejects reformism as a route to socialism: 'Reforms would lead to socialism if and only if they were (1) irreversible, (2) cumulative in effects, (3) conducive to new reforms, and (4) directed towards socialism . . . So far at least they have not' (*Capitalism*, p. 241). None the less, reformism remains the most rational interest-optimising strategy for workers. Even if some feasible socialist alternatives were available[37] workers would be rational to reject them; the transition to socialism would threaten the economic gains they had achieved within the class compromises achieved by democratic capitalism (*Capitalism*, p. 239).

I wish to make two points in response to this argument. First, the originality of this thesis and its power to disturb rests on its claim to derive reformist conclusions about class struggle from an analysis grounded in Marxist theory. By contrast, to base such conclusions on a combination of pluralist, Keynesian and Weberian premises is almost banal; it merely asserts that if democratic capitalism conforms to reformist conceptions of it, then it is rational for workers to pursue strategies based on those conceptions. Przeworski's thesis amounts to little more than a sophisticated restatement of a familiar reformist line of argument, that the choice of reformism by social democrats on behalf of the working class is the outcome of a learning curve in response to the 'realities' and 'complexities' of capitalism and democracy.

In the second place, Przeworski's thesis rests on a number of assertions: the distributional nature of class interests; the possibilities open for class compromises within democratic capitalism; the historic role of social democracy in negotiating and institutionalising them. I have argued above that there are good grounds for rejecting these assertions. It follows that his conclusions are equally open to challenge. More particularly, his arguments neither engage with Marxist critiques of the role which reformism has played in managing and containing class conflict, nor do they address the structural roots of the contemporary crisis of reformist politics. Ironically, faced with that crisis, Social Democrats have largely abandoned the reformist politics he defends.[38] The case for a socialist strategy anchored in the classical Marxist conception of class exploitation and class struggle under capitalism remains undamaged by Przeworski's critique.

Let us turn finally to Przeworski's rational choice model. He presents it as a corollary of embracing a voluntaristic solution to the structure-agency problem, which reasserts that human rationality is the central motor in history. People choose to act the way they do, not because they are externally compelled or internally socialised so to do but because, given their situation, it is the most rational course of action open to them.

In my view, the main problem with Przeworski's rational choice model arises less from its general proposition than with the particular ways in which he seeks to advance and use it. In part, this is a matter of empirical argument: how adequate are his accounts of the structures of state, economy, ideology and class?; how tightly should we draw the constraints which they set on the choices open to class actors? In part it is a question of conceptualisation: are structures only constraining or should they also be understood as facilitating and conceptually empowering? Is analysis restricted to references to intentional actions and their consequences, or can we widen the scope to encompass the logic of structural relationships as well? My rejection of the answers which Przeworski gives to these questions in the above critique does not require a rejection of the model as such. Freed from the methodological strait-jacket of MI, there is nothing wrong in principle with a loosely drawn model of rational choice which explains the strategic choices made by class actors as involving a rational evaluation of alternatives in the face of structural conditions of action. However, the model then amounts to little more than a formalisation of the best practice of Marxist historians and political analysts.[39] What it is not is some 'new paradigm' for Marxist theory.

There is, however, one key feature of RCM models which has to be rejected. The model of rationality which they invoke is anchored in the utilitarian tradition, with its stress on instrumental calculations of the most efficient means to attain given ends. In prioritising rational calculative action, such analyses dichotomise ends and means and choices from debates about the structures within which they are made. Both ends and structures become 'givens' for the analysis, rather than issues which are themselves in debate for both the historical actors and historians seeking to explain their actions. Marxists – and they are not alone in this – have rejected such conceptions of rationality as both crassly de-humanising and analytically impoverished when applied to historical and political analysis. As we saw with Przeworski's account of the evolution of social democracy, the strategy is less concerned to investigate the historical contingencies shaping human choices, than with playing 'as if' games with the evidence. In practice, the RCM framework contributes very little to our understanding of history as processes of rational action. Its characteristic strophes – the 'prisoners dilemma' and the public goods/free rider problems – reveal a paucity of applications and generate few insights of substance. A historically sensitive analysis of human rationality needs to get beyond the utilitarian dualisms of personally chosen and ultimately arbitrary ends and 'interest-optimising' means to also embrace criteria of appropriateness and even morality.

The explanatory frameworks of the Marxist tradition do this. Their analyses of socialist political strategies in capitalism have characteristically been framed by three considerations. They start from a critical analysis of the capitalist mode of production and the bourgeois social and political order and locate the contradictions – its exploitative and oppressive processes and unstable and conflict-ridden dynamics – to which they give rise. The second element identifies an empirically realisable alternative social order in which capitalist processes are eliminated and their conflicts and instabilities replaced by a free, rational and democratically controlled socialist society. Finally, it is crucially concerned with agencies; with a working class whose position and mode of existence within capitalism gives them a fundamental interest in resisting, challenging and ultimately transcending its limitations and whose self-mobilisation as a collectivity – conscious, organised, active – empowers the class to bring about this transcendence through their practice.

Discerning the most rational course of action for socialists within this framework is not a matter of appealing to the formal rules of abstract games-theoretic models. Rather it involves historically contextualised debates in which critique, alternative and agency engage in a complex dialectic; debates in which the interplay of means and ends, and of contexts and strategies enter into the process of making rational choices designed to advance the cause of socialism. Faced with the fundamental contradictions and irrationalities of late twentieth-century global capitalism, there is an imperative need to reassert both the superior rationality of socialism and to reach the most rational calculation we can about the best means of bringing it about. For Marxists, the point of arguing about interpretations of our capitalist world remains that of locating and advocating the best strategy for changing it.

Notes

1. For a useful introduction to the school see Roemer, J. (ed.) (1986) *Analytical Marxism*, Cambridge: Cambridge University Press.
2. See Anderson, P. (1976) *Considerations on Western Marxism*, London: New Left Books, for a stimulating analysis of the tradition. In fact, RCM writers were prone to read the tradition through the lens of structuralist critiques of 'hegelian' Marxism, rather than making their own direct and independent assessments of it.
3. Key works in establishing and developing this approach to economic and political analysis include Arrow, K. (1951) *Social Choice and Individual Values*, New Haven: Yale University Press; Downs, A. (1957) *An Economic Theory of Democracy*, New York: Harpers; Buchanan J. and Tullock, G. (1962) *The Calculus of Consent*, Ann Arbor: Michigan University Press; Olson, M. (1971) *The Logic of Collective Action*, Cambridge, Mass.: Harvard University Press.
4. Elster and Roemer were prolific writers in the area of RCM in the late 1970s and 1980s though both had put varying degrees of distance between themselves and Marxism by the 1990s. For a characteristic expression of their views during their RCM phase see Roemer, J. (1982) *A General Theory of Exploitation and Class*, Cambridge, Mass.: Harvard University Press; and Elster, J. (1985) *Making Sense of Marx*, Cambridge: Cambridge University Press. Adam Przeworski's (1985) *Capitalism and Social Democracy*, Cambridge: Cambridge University Press, was the most explicitly political and historically oriented work of the school. This latter volume is the central subject of the discussion in this chapter and all page and chapter references given in the text are to this work unless otherwise indicated.
5. See Lukacs, G. (1971) *History and Class Consciousness*, London: Merlin Press.
6. This was a source of some dissension within the AM camp, given that Gerry Cohen's (1978) *Karl Marx's Theory of History: A Defence*, Oxford: Clarendon Press, provided a sophisticated defence of the legitimacy of a functionalist reading of Marx.
7. See Callinicos, A. (1989) *Making History*, Oxford: Polity Press, for a critique which is anchored in a more comprehensive defence of the classical Marxist tradition. Useful critiques can be found in Wood, E.M. (1989) 'Rational choice Marxism: Is the game worth the candle?', *New Left Review*, 177; Lebowitz, M. (1988) 'Is "analytical Marxism" Marxism?', *Science and Society*, 52, 2, along with other articles in this issue of the journal. See also the exchanges between Callinicos, Wood and Alan Carling (1989) in *New Left Review*, 177. As and when it is published, Marcus Roberts's thesis on analytical Marxism (Ph.D., Brighton, 1995) will make a valuable addition here.

8. For a highly critical survey of the empirical value of the wider rational choice school see Green, D. and Shapiro, I. (1994) *Pathologies of Rational Choice Theory*, New Haven: Yale University Press. However it does not directly examine the contribution of RCM as such.

9. In general, the AM school were inclined to analyse class relationships in terms of inequality and injustice. In part this flowed from their anchorage in the wider tradition of analytical philosophy as practised in British and American academies and more particularly the debates sparked off by Rawls, J. (1971) *A Theory of Justice*, Oxford: Oxford University Press. It also reflected their acceptance of the so-called neo-Ricardian rejection of Marxist 'value' analysis. (See Steedman, I. (1977) *Marx after Straffa*, London: New Left Books, for a statement of this view.) But see note 11 below.

10. Roemer, J. (1982) *A General Theory of Exploitation and Class*, Cambridge, Mass.: Harvard University Press. See also the special issue of *Politics and Society*, vol. 11, 2, devoted to a scrutiny of Roemer's thesis.

11. Surprisingly, Przeworski argues (*Capitalism*, pp. 228–9) for some reference to exploitation at the point of production to be included within the wider framework provided by Roemer. However, he takes this line solely in order to argue that variations in labour productivity establish possibilities for reformist redistributions of endowments within capitalism. It does not involve any focus on the exploitative character of the capitalist labour process or its implications for class politics at the point of production.

12. The chapter, which takes the form of a survey of themes and authorities from Kautsky to Poulantzas, is clearly intended to establish Przeworski's mastery of Marxicological debate. In fact it displays his propensity to indulge in *obiter dicta* to the full.

13. Thompson, E.P. (1963) *The Making of the English Working Class*, London: Gollancz, which Przeworski selectively cites (pp. 69 and 71) in support of his own position. In fact, Przeworski's substitutionist account of class struggle would in effect exclude the kind of analysis exemplified by Thompson.

14. See Cohen 'The structure of proletarian unfreedom' in Roemer, J. (ed.) (1986) *Analytical Marxism*, Cambridge: Cambridge University Press.

15. Wood, E.M. (1989) p. 59.

16. Callinicos, A. (1989) *Making History*, Oxford: Polity Press, is exemplary here.

17. Przeworski's handling of the issue is well illustrated by his throwaway line 'democracy is the modern Bonaparte' cited earlier. Though a remarkable piece of conceptual chutzpah, viewed as a contribution to the Marxist theory of the State, it is, shall we say, a somewhat undertheorised one.

18. The only reference I could locate in his work which comes close to this occurs on p. 12.

19. Callinicos (1989) pp. 68–9, makes the point that there is a general tendency among AM writers to distance themselves from both the labour theory of value and the tendency of the rate of profit to fall.

20. Przeworski's main preoccupation here is with the dangers of undermining the readiness of private capital to invest. There is no awareness of the classic Marxist emphases on the compulsions at work on capital to accumulate or on the contradictions and periodic crises intrinsic to the process.

21. See for instance, Abercrombie, N. and Warde, A. (1988) *Contemporary*

British Society, Oxford: Polity Press, section 3:3; and Westergaard, J. and Resler, H. (1976) *Class in a Capitalist Society*, Harmondsworth: Penguin Books, part 2.

22. See Coates, D. and Hillard, J. (eds) (1986) *The Economic Decline of Modern Britain*, Brighton: Wheatsheaf Books part 2, for New Right perspectives. For a useful discussion see Gamble, A. (1988) *The Free Economy and the Strong State*, Basingstoke: Macmillan.

23. See for example Hall, S. and Jacques, M. (eds) (1983) *The Politics of Thatcherism*, London: Lawrence and Wishart.

24. See Przeworski, A. (1991) *Democracy and the Market,* Cambridge: Cambridge University Press.

25. Przeworski's debts to Weber are partially acknowledged on pp. 64 and 76 of *Capitalism*.

26. For a revealing instance of this see note 11 above.

27. See Gough, I. (1972) 'Marx's theory of productive and unproductive labour', *New Left Review*, 76.

28. See for example Callinicos, A. and Harman, C. (1987) *The Changing Working Class*, London: Bookmarks.

29. Such a reading is supported at various points in the text as the following quotations indicate: 'The very theory of classes must be viewed as internal to particular political projects' (*Capitalism*, p. 67); 'Classes are not prior to political and ideological practice' (*Capitalism*, p. 70).

30. Przeworski does periodically acknowledge that class 'collectivities in struggle' are organised not only at a party political level but this has no impact on his substantive analysis. He attempts to avoid the charge of substitutionism by denying that parties should be conceived as 'external' to the class. However, this is merely a terminological solution which does not bear on the substance of the criticism.

31. The phrase is C. Wright Mills's – see his (1948) *The New Men of Power*, New York: Harcourt Brace, pp. 8–9. Lenin was even more pungent, speaking of them as labour lieutenants of capital.

32. Even a perfunctory glance at Marx's fragmentary treatment of class in the final chapter of volume 3 of *Capital* should be sufficient to dispose of this gratuitous misconception.

33. For an illuminating exploration of the intimate connections between the two see Lebowitz, M. (1992) *Beyond Capital: Marx's Political Economy of the Working Class*, Basingstoke: Macmillan.

34. Callinicos's (1989) discussion of these and related issues in Chapter 2:5 of *Making History*, Oxford: Polity Press, is particularly valuable.

35. Przeworski's now explicitly reformist position is spelt out in his (1991) *Democracy and the Market*, Cambridge: Cambridge University Press; Roemer (1994) advocates a kind of 'coupon socialism' in *A Future for Socialism*, London: Verso; Elster's distancing from Marxism was already evident in the 1985 work cited earlier.

36. See, for example, *Capitalism*, pp. 223, 237–8 and the Postscript. Note however his footnote on p. 239, 'I see myself as a follower not of Vladimir Ilyich but of that other great Russian socialist thinker, Georgij Konstantinowich Pessim.' Certainly in the main body of the discussion his pessimism about socialism is far more clearly articulated than his belief in the possibility of socialism; the latter appears grounded more on the consequences of automation than on any reading of possibilities opened up through class struggle.

37. By 1991, Przeworski had become an explicit advocate of 'democratic market socialism'.

38. In the context of recent debates in the UK, Przeworski's watered down 'workerism' would be too much for 'new social forces' advocates, while his 'traditionalism' would prove unacceptable to the 'modernisers'.

39. In one respect Przeworski's analysis is retrograde in relation to Marxist historical analysis. His application of the RCM model to historical situations tends to generate concealed paradigms – of the logic of democratic capitalism and class compromise – rather than historically contingent explanations. For example, the problems of explanation posed by the diversities and continuities of working-class movements – why, for example, were the working classes of most European states largely successful in creating autonomous political movements, while those of the USA signally failed to do so? why was the British labour movement virtually 'born reformist', whereas Marxist influences remained strong for much of the twentieth century in France and Italy? – constitute critical challenges to the kinds of generalised propositions advanced by Przeworski concerning the logic of political choices under democratic capitalism. Whether this failure is intrinsic to the use of RCM models as such, or is a consequence of smuggling substantively reformist assumptions about capitalism etc. into the account, is a moot point.

CHAPTER SIX

Roger Scruton and the New Left

David Coates

Marxism has been in retreat – in intellectual and political circles – for more than a decade now. Its quality and status as a source of explanation and argument has come under sustained attack; and indeed its legitimacy as an element in the teaching of history and social science has been more frequently challenged – certainly in the school curriculum, and increasingly in the university one. All this, of course, represents a definite shift in the balance of intellectual forces from that evident only 15 to 20 years ago. Then Marxism was a self-confident intellectual current. Though almost always a minority element in history departments, it was then much more dominant in the social sciences; and in both intellectual fields, its leading scholars enjoyed a sufficiently strong general academic reputation as to warrant a presence in most leading debates. The work of the Marxist historians (from Christopher Hill and Eric Hobsbawm, through Edward Thompson and John Saville, to Perry Anderson and Tom Nairn) was widely recognised as rich and important; as, in social science, were the writings of Raymond Williams, Ralph Miliband, Nicos Poulantzas, Herbert Marcuse, Jurgen Habermas and so on. Not any more. These days less radical intellectual frameworks prevail. New icons hold the undergraduate imagination; and the writing off of Marxism is highly fashionable. Some of the non-Marxist counter-offensive is itself stimulating and radical. The debate within the feminist movement, the emergence of a set of green issues and concerns; all this is to be welcomed. Less attractive is the stridency of the newly revitalised Right, whose writings – at their most polemical – bring back to mind the intolerances of the McCarthyite past. It is with one of those intolerances that this chapter is primarily concerned.

First in the columns of *The Salisbury Review*, and then in a collection entitled *Thinkers of the New Left*, Roger Scruton wrote a series of damning essays on the work of a number of leading left wing intellectuals. In doing so, he formulated in the clearest of terms the general critique of left wing scholarship to which we are all now subject. He also raised a series of specific criticisms of the Marxist historians, to which again many of us are regularly exposed in our daily work as teachers and intellectuals. So a dialogue with Scruton has its value: both as an opportunity once more to defend the validity of a Marxist history, and also as a moment in which to reflect upon the limits, as well as upon the strengths, of the Marxism we would defend. The structure of this chapter reflects those twin values. It will first lay out the Scruton critique of Marxism, then engage in dialogue with it, and then draw from it lessons (not for Scruton but for Marxism).

The Scruton critique

In the opening and closing chapters of his 1985 collection, *Thinkers of the New Left*,[1] Roger Scruton questioned the general value of a historiography deriving from what he termed the New Left, which he handled as a strand (and not the mainstream, as he observed, *Thinkers*, p. 6) of a broader Marxism. He then brought that general critique to bear on a bizarre collection of intellectuals – all labelled New Left – not just non-aligned Marxists such as Thompson, Williams and Anderson, but also orthodox Marxists, for example Althusser, liberals such as Galbraith and Dworkin, and a collection of the unclassifiable – Bahro, Foucault, Laing, Wallerstein, Habermas, Sartre, and the long dead Gramsci and Lukacs. Here we will restrict ourselves to Scruton's arguments on the New Left in general, and on the 'marxist historians' in particular.

The general critique

The Scruton critique was written from an explicitly right wing position: one variously described as *British Conservative*, 'a politics of custom, compromise and settled indecision' (*Thinkers*, p. 30) and as *The New Right* which, we were told, 'believes in responsible rather than impersonal government; in the autonomy and personality of institutions; and in the rule of law'. It recognises a distinction between state and civil society, and believes that the second should arise, in general, from the unforced interaction of freely contracting individuals; moderated by custom, tradition and a respect for authority and Law. Power, for the New Right, is an evil 'only when abused' (ibid., p. 203).

So here immediately, in one crystallisation, was a list of all the things which the New Left were not supposed to value sufficiently: *responsible government* (they were supposed to prefer the rule of the party); the *role of institutions as buffers against state power* (the New Left was supposed to treat the institutions of civil society as extensions of state power); and the importance of *traditions and customary practices* (the New Left was seen as pre-eminently concerned with change, equipped with too bleak a view of contemporary reality, and insensitive to the strengths of its existing practices). All this was taken to derive from the New Left's supposedly simplistic view of power – its preoccupation with power as coercion, and with the State as an agency of class domination. It was this naïveté which, according to Scruton at least, encouraged New Left thinkers to undervalue the importance (to individual freedom and social justice) of liberal political institutions and capitalist market forms.

So the basic criticism of the New Left which Scruton offered was that it lacked the insights of the New Right. More specifically however, the New Left stood condemned by him on four counts.

Firstly, according to Scruton, the New Left failed to recognise 'the extreme complexity of political realities' (ibid., p. 202); and in its willingness to simplify complex political tasks, demonstrated 'a kind of moral impatience' (ibid., p 201) and an associated arrogance – an 'assumption of a priori correctness' (ibid., p. 210). For Scruton, the New Left intellectual was typically a Jacobin. He 'believe[d] that the world [was] deficient in wisdom and in justice', and that the fault lay 'not in human nature but in the established systems of power' (ibid., p. 2).

Secondly, the imperviousness of New Left thinking to the complexity of reality, and to the necessary limits of human nature, meant – according to Scruton – that it was also closed to rational discussion. In Scruton's view, 'all of Marx's theories have been essentially refuted', and yet in the writings of the New Left, 'the central Marxist claims recur constantly ... neither refined nor qualified, but blankly assumed as the incontrovertible premises of social analysis'. That, we were told, occurred because we were not dealing here with 'a system of rationally held views'. Though Marxism claimed the status of science, it was 'clear to any neutral observer that these beliefs have been placed beyond science, in a realm of absolute authority which [could] never be entered by the uninitiated' (ibid., p. 5) – in the realm, that is, of ideology (ibid., p. 6), myth (ibid., p. 4), even fraud (ibid., p. 1). Scruton insisted that this 'failure to discuss with opponents, to open the mind to doubt and hesitation, [was] a rooted characteristic of the New Left' (ibid., p. 207).

Thirdly such New Left arrogance and imperviousness was, moreover, entirely negative and destructive. Though New Left thinkers enjoyed the freedoms of western society, and were the products of its most affluent period, they used that freedom and affluence only to criticise the order within which they flourished, discounting its virtues, ignoring its basically consensual nature and steadfastly refusing to specify in any detail the socialism with which it should be replaced. The Scruton 'voice' on this point was particularly scathing. 'Despite this devotion to goals, the radical is extremely loath to tell us what he is aiming at. As soon as the question of "the new society" arises, he diverts our attention back to the actual world, so as to renew the energy of hatred' (ibid., pp. 210–11): in this way 'turning attention away from the difficult task of describing the socialist future to the easy holiday of destruction' (ibid., p. 7).

Fourthly, Scruton assured the readers of *The Salisbury Review* that the quality of New Left scholarship and personnel was poor. Its writings in general were characterised by 'shoddy rhetoric' (ibid., p. 202) and by 'turgid prose and sheer intellectual incompetence' (ibid., p. 210). It had apparently been the unique achievement of New Left scholarship to make, 'fury respectable and gobbledegook the mark of academic success'. Quantity and quality here were obviously in tension, since it had only been 'with the hasty expansion of the universities and polytechnics, and the massive recruitment of teachers from this over-fished and under-nourished generation, [that] the status of the New Left was assured' (ibid., p. 7).

These four characteristics of New Left thought and personnel had two general consequences for the character of New Left scholarship, according to Scruton. The failure of New Left intellectuals to recognise the necessary complexities of social reality predisposed them to grant too great a causal role to their central category – namely that of *class*. In Scruton's view, Marxist scholarship was always 'tempted to identify classes as agents, to whom actions and responsibilities [could] be ascribed and punishment allotted' (ibid., p. 199). That in its turn put 'a hidden agenda' into left wing history (ibid., p. 4), obliging left wing historians to demonstrate that history was on the side of socialism. Defeats had to be explained away in that history only as setbacks on the road to a guaranteed future. New Left historians then produced history which was impervious to 'disquieting facts', to everything indeed 'which [had] happened in recent decades', a history which was only sustained to the degree that 'less talented intellectuals [could] still appropriate the past, and re-shape it in accordance with the necessary doctrine'. In other words, and according to Scruton, left wing history was, in its essential structures, simply myth.

The deep deficiencies of New Left scholarship to which Scruton alerted the readers of *The Salisbury Review* then also predisposed left wing historians to excuse, or excuse away, excesses carried out in the name of their chosen historical project. In other words, left wing historiography suffered from double standards; tough on right-wing authoritarianism, soft on communism. For once classes were seen as historical agents, with purposes and collective moralities, the road was open (according to Scruton) to the expropriation of classes, and to 'acts of retribution, expropriation and violence'. As he put it, 'this pattern of thought leads as logically to the Gulag as the Nazi ideology of race led to Auschwitz' (ibid., p. 199).

This was an important moment in the Scruton analysis of the New Left and its defects. Throughout his general critique, Scruton used the terms 'New Left', 'Marxist' and 'socialist' interchangeably, and took the eastern European state-socialist systems as unproblematic evidence of tendencies endemic to all forms of Marxist theory. In that way a rhythm of argumentation could be, and was, deployed; one that shifted repeatedly from theoretician to Soviet practice, and from theory now to practice at any point in the century. Yet such a rhythm could only slide over – it could not fully obscure – one particularly awkward point that might otherwise have struck at least the more perceptive of the readers of *The Salisbury Review:* namely that the vast majority of the New Left intellectuals under critique by Scruton were just as critical as he was of Stalinist totalitarianism. For Scruton to use the excesses of Stalinism as a critique of their intellectual positions, he had therefore to go one stage further – and assert that tyranny was a logical outcome of the application of their theoretical positions – whether they knew it or not. This is the key passage:

> It is difficult to assess the practical consequences of political theories. Nevertheless – it is not unreasonable to suggest that the New Left, in attributing agency to that which does not possess it (to class and society) has connived at the removal of responsibility from that which does – from the state and the party ... Nor should we dissociate the New Left from the attitude that communism has taken towards its opponents. The writings of Bahro, Gramsci, Lukacs and Althusser abundantly show that totalitarian thinking is implicit in the categories of social analysis that they employ. For such thinkers the opponent is never better than an opportunist. What he speaks is not reason but ideology ... His claim to truth is discounted by the class interest which speaks through him ... Whenever you encounter opposition, you encounter the class enemy, even if he is wearing some cunning disguise. This enemy is not to be argued with, for he cannot utter truth; still less is he to be the object of a compromise. Only after his final elimination from the social order will the truth be generally perceived ... The totalitarian structure of communist government is not an inevitable consequence of Marxist conceptions. Nevertheless ... the inhuman politics of communism is the objective realisation of the Marxist vision of society, which sees true politics as no more than a mendacious covering placed over the realities of power.
>
> *(Thinkers,* pp. 202, 205–6, 208, 209)

In arguing in that way, Scruton was well aware that he had 'lapse[d] from accepted standards of literary politeness' (ibid., p. 209). What he was less explicit about was that, having shut the door on a legitimate Marxist historiography in this way, he could then only approach historians operating within a Marxist tradition either as knaves or as fools. In fact he did both, as we will now see.

The Marxist historian as sentimental fool: Scruton on E.P. Thompson and Raymond Williams

Scruton was prepared to praise the quality of E.P. Thompson's history. He was less enthusiastic about that of Williams. Scruton was clearly drawn to the passion of Thompson's historical writings. Edward Thompson had, he told the readers of *The Salisbury Review,* a genuine 'gift for clear and imaginative writing' (ibid., p. 10). *The Making of the English Working Class* was 'an indisputable classic of social history, in which vivid imagination and energetic scholarship combine[d] with a vision of real emotional power' (ibid., p. 11). Moreover Thompson was clearly open to facts – willing to criticise 'even the received ideas of left-wing history'; and of course he received the full Scruton backing for his critique of Althusser. Scruton purported to see in Thompson's argument in *The Poverty of Theory,* 'the existence of a left-wing thinker ... determined to retain both common sense and intellectual honesty' (ibid., p. 15); and as such, one willing and able to dissociate himself from the general tendency of left wing intellectuals to close their minds to difficult facts.

Scruton also welcomed Thompson's treatment of class. He particularly liked his rejection of class as a collective agent, praising him for his attack on anthropomorphism in the 'Peculiarities of the English'[2] essay. Scruton also welcomed Thompson's emphasis on the way in which classes actively make themselves, drawing on religion, culture and their own past to build a sense of their own individuality and politics. The readers of *The Salisbury Review* were informed that here was real progress on the Left, 'this idea of class, as an entity formed by the interaction between material circumstances and the consciousness of social beings, [was] surely more persuasive than that provided by Marx' (ibid., p. 12). Of course it was progress – in Scruton's eyes – because (and to the degree that) it had 'devastating consequences for the theories of the New Left'. In the debate with Anderson, Scruton was with Thompson. Thompson, for Scruton, was simply vindicating the non-Marxist conservative vision of history. Again Scruton is worth quoting at length:

> Thompson's application ... presents a picture of the working class which no conservative need dissent from: the working class is deeply implicated in established social customs, political institutions, religious preconceptions and moral values, all of which unite it to the national tradition in which it grows ... History certainly does contain collective agents, which act as a 'we' and with a sense of common purpose ... what is it that brings men most effectively together as 'we', that enables them to combine their forces in a sense of common destiny and common interest? As Thompson makes clear, it is precisely those features which are not part of the material conditions

of a class that are here of greatest significance: language, religion, custom, association and traditions of political order – in short, all those forces that generate nations in the place of the contending individuals that would otherwise destroy them.

(*Thinkers*, pp. 12. 13–14)

So if the logic of Thompson's analysis was so profoundly conservative, why did he not go the whole way, and break with the labour metaphysic? There is no epistemological/political rupture for Thompson, according to Scruton, because Thompson remained a sentimentalist about the working class and its potential, and he remained that – like all New Left thinkers – because his own self-definition, as part of a movement of human emancipation, required it. Scruton again:

> Thompson's sentimentalism of the proletariat is integral to his self-image. He sees himself as part of the great work of emancipation ... In [the *Open Letter* ...] we witness the extent of the need which motivates Thompson's writing, the need to believe in socialism, as the philosophy of the proletariat, and in the proletariat itself, as the innocent patient and heroic agent of modern history.
>
> (*Thinkers*, pp. 14, 15)

Williams too – in Scruton's eyes – was guilty of similar sentimentalism, though here without the protective wall of Edward Thompson's willingness to confront uncomfortable facts. According to Scruton, Williams was able to sustain his argument that capitalism and consumerism were destroying community only 'because of a supreme act of sentimentalisation, whereby he [hid] from himself the basic facts of life and history' (ibid., pp. 59–60). He too subscribed to the 'long-suffering, tenderhearted workers of E.P. Thompson, who need only the abolition of the capitalist in order to live together in spontaneous brotherhood, sharing the fruits of their labour' (ibid., p. 60), but Williams lacked the Thompson rigour. His recent idiom was 'self-referential, vague and sloganising' (ibid., p. 62), 'the jargon ... of a writer who [had] imprisoned his thought in language over which he exert[ed] no intellectual control' (ibid., p. 65).

In other words, both men had come to believe the facticity of their own categories. Both had swallowed the music of their own prose; both talked of labour movements without establishing them; both gave the proletariat a historical mission which was a figment of their own organising categories. This was what Scruton meant by *sentimentality:* 'the active falsification of the world so as to ennoble the feelings of the falsifier', 'the making of the working class in the image of the left-wing intellectual' (ibid., p. 65). In his view, both Thompson and Williams were guilty of that, and ought to have their work rejected, as sentimental foolishness, because of it.

The Marxist historian as knave: Scruton on Christopher Hill and Perry Anderson

There was little glorification of a past proletariat in Perry Anderson's work, or in that of Christopher Hill, so the Scruton critique had to shift. Hill's sins were twofold. One was the sin of being rich and privileged, living in Oxford, and yet writing so disparagingly of the society that privileged him (and the class of which he was a part). This was a minor theme in the Scruton tirade against Hill's work, though it obviously stung. How else are we to explain the fire in this passage, 'thus, like the upper class radicals of the Fabian Society, they bent their energies to depriving future generations of the culture which they held in trusteeship and which they were determined should be enjoyed for the last time' (ibid., p. 130). Hill's bigger sin as a Marxist historian was that of distortion. He apparently 'proceeded to invent the seventeenth century in accordance with socialist requirements' (ibid., p. 129); particularly when writing about Milton:

> No work of Hill's is more blatant in its manipulation of facts than the recent study of Milton ... in which the defender of parliamentary government, constitution and free enterprise, is portrayed as a crypto-leveller, an armchair radical, suffering, along with the proto-socialists of his day, defeat at the hands of a ruthless establishment.
>
> (*Thinkers*, p. 142)

The main focus of Scruton's attack on the dishonesty of Marxist historiography is to be found in his chapter on Perry Anderson. Here too Scruton was obliged to concede quality. Anderson's work – particularly his *Passages from Antiquity* – was, 'erudite and imaginative' (ibid., pp. 131–2), 'influential and impressive' (ibid., p. 134). 'The range of Anderson's historical knowledge [was] extraordinary' (ibid., p. 135). *Passages* ... was 'a tour de force of condensed erudition and detail' (ibid., p. 137). Scruton conceded that for much of the time Anderson wrote good history, and congratulated him for drawing so heavily on non-Marxist sources. It was simply that the good history Anderson wrote was 'give or take a few marxisant asides, ... bourgeois history' (ibid., p. 137). Anderson was a good historian when he was not being Marxist. Anderson's sin was then to cheat, and to do so in two distinct but related ways.

First, Anderson wrapped up his good history in loaded categories. He adopted 'a marxist terminology pregnant with the desired interpretation', which carried unannounced into the writing 'a massive commitment to the marxian theory of history, including all that is contentious in it, such as the theory of exploitation and the distinction between superstructure and base' (ibid., p. 135). What Anderson did, according to Scruton, was, 'to rewrite bourgeois history in Marxese ... which [was] like rewriting a Haydn symphony with a continuous drum roll on the dominant, so that all is infected by a premonition of catastrophe, and nothing quite resolves' (ibid., p. 139).

Moreover, according to Scruton, Anderson held to a base–superstructure theoretical framework, when all his writing demonstrated the autonomy and determining role of superstructural factors. Anderson gave causal weight to law, to religion, and to politics, whilst insisting that this demonstrated, rather than falsified, a Marxist approach. Anderson could do this, in Scruton's eyes, only by deploying the 'usual device of Ptolemaic epicycles/Ptolemaic contortion': that is, by arguing that black was white. Anderson demonstrated in his writing that superstructures could determine bases, and that the distinction between the two could no longer be made; but then avoided any admission of this by 'cluttering [his] prose [with] untruths and apologies' (ibid., p. 141) and by using the uniquely Andersonian, 'device of emphatic meaninglessness' – the device of italicising a meaningless phrase/clause to avoid having to dump 'the ideological junk that has been piled up against those doors where facts might enter' (ibid., p. 141).

Where Anderson saw the 'dialectical relation between superstructure and base', Scruton saw the devious use of 'Marxist jargon' to mask a 'deep agreement with the fundamental proposition of conservatism, the proposition that history is on no-one's side' (ibid., p. 81). Anderson was no fool – no Thompson – so he must be a knave. Scruton's framework allowed an intelligent Marxist historian no other place.

It was not that Scruton – in surveying the leading Marxist historians of the post-war generation – caricatured the defining characteristics/tasks of Marxist history. He did not. These he listed quite adequately as: to explain the movement of institutions, laws and religions in terms of the transformations of an 'economic base' – that is in terms of the development and control of the means of production; to identify 'revolutionary periods' in which the 'forces of production' enter into conflict with the 'relations of production' and eventually overthrow them, and to show that those periods are also periods of 'class struggle'; to show that, during these 'revolutionary periods', there are radical discontinuities in all social institutions, of the kind foretold by Marx; to conform in some measure to the Marxian morphology, dividing the world into periods of 'primitive communism', 'slavery', 'feudalism', 'capitalism' and 'socialism', with each successive system being distinguished by its prevailing relations of production; and to substantiate the ideological claim (Scruton emphasised the term) that the movement of history is towards socialism, since socialism is implied, either as a natural consequence of preceding history or as the effective resolution of its conflicts (ibid., p. 135). What he did do was to give an entirely determinist and unilinear interpretation to those characteristics/tasks, insisting on a direct and simple determination of superstructure by base, and on an unproblematic and inexorable movement to socialism, as defining of Marxism: and he had to, because it gave him his one critical judgmental edge. For then, whenever Marxist historians explored the complexities and contingencies in those relationships, by that very act they invalidated the organising framework of Marxist scholarship, and in consequence retained their Marxist credentials only by being foolish or dishonest.

For Scruton, with his very narrow notion of what Marxist history involved, the very act of writing empirically sensitive history rendered Marxism discredited: so we who try to do it still can only be – in the end – some mixture of the fool and the knave: but are we?

The response to Scruton

The answer must be 'no'. It is just not true that all left wing historians are closed to dialogue with other traditions. Edward Thompson and Perry Anderson were (and are) not, as Scruton conceded. In fact, Scruton managed to sustain his own general characterisation of Marxism only by labelling Thompson and Anderson as 'bourgeois' whenever they did use broad sources; and then citing their openness to alternative perspectives as evidence of their sentimental or dishonest retention of Marxist categories. He couldn't have it both ways however. Either Marxist historians were to be dismissed because they were closed to alternative views, or they were to be congratulated for their openness and willingness to dialogue. Only Scruton's unquestioned premise of the uncontroversial superiority of conservative scholarship enabled him to criticise Perry Anderson for both being open and a Marxist; but that premise of uncontested superiority was an example of the very closed, ideological form of thought that Scruton wanted to lay at the door of Marxism alone. So in arguing in this way, he fell victim to his own form of critique; to the very sin of ideological thought to which he claimed Marxism was uniquely prone.

Nor did it advance a dialogue between traditions to collapse a variety of highly nuanced positions within one tradition, into a simplistic unity that was supposed to speak for the tradition as a whole. The Marxism that Scruton attacked was deterministic and reductionist in its theorising, and blindly pro-Soviet in its politics. It was the very Marxism that the New Left came into being to reject. It was therefore a grotesque distortion of the historical record (the test, you'll remember, Scruton used to dismiss left wing history in general) to imply support for Soviet tyranny to the majority of the very thinkers who broke from orthodox communism on precisely this issue. Scruton's collapse of New Left Marxism into Stalinist orthodoxy was legitimate only if there was something inevitable, inexorable, unavoidable in the use of a Marxist framework that led to Stalinism in practice and to determinism and economic reductionism in theoretical work. Yet that collapse was never argued for, only asserted, by Scruton – slipped into his analysis by his way of using evidence and categories. He moved from the party-class debate in Marxist theory to party domination of class in Stalinism. He collapsed Gramscian discussions of the role of civil society in buttressing capitalism into an argument about the preference of Russian Bolsheviks for party rule without civil liberties; and so on. Scruton, in other words, deployed the very slippages – of loaded categories, and the closing of eyes to uncomfortable facts – of which he accused Marxism.

Scruton, was also adamant that the Right did not have 'to bear the onus of justification'. It was not for his lot to 'show that the consensual politics of Western government [was] somehow closer to human nature and more conducive to man's fulfilment than the ideal world of socialist emancipation'. 'It [was] not for us to defend a reality which, for all its faults, [had] the undeniable merit of existence' (*Thinkers*, p. 210); but that too was to claim too much. It was quite valid to tax the Left for the lack of detail on its alternative. It was quite another to present a glorified vision of the reality that alternative would replace. Scruton accused left wing thinkers of double standards – hard on the West, soft on the Soviets. Yet this the New Left were not. They were hard on both. If there was a double standard, it was Scruton's; located in his attempt to shut out a critical relationship with western capitalism because its critics found it difficult to specify their alternative in detail. If science and not ideology is our objective as theoreticians, then on virtually any definition of the difference between the two it is vital to impose critical tests on realities as well as on futures; and Scruton did us no service by questioning the integrity and intelligence of those who try. If there was intolerance in this exchange, it did not lie with the Left, but with a mode of criticism – too often *ad hominem* in character – which in Scruton's hands raised doubts not about arguments but about the integrity of those who placed them.

So the specific form of the Scruton critique seemed to fall on its own terms. It was built on the very ways of thinking and arguing – closed, based on unquestioned premises, intolerantly ideological – which it found so defective in Marxism. However, the content of the Scruton attack could be considered independently of the form in which it was put, and ought to be, because it raised important issues about the value of Marxist scholarship – issues which predated the Scruton writings and will long outlast them.

In particular it raised the question of whether or not there is a 'hidden agenda' to Marxist historiography, and whether 'sentimentality' is an unavoidable feature of Marxist scholarship. It raised the question of whether we, as historians of Marxism and social scientists, do actually over-use our central category of 'class', by treating it anthropomorphically as Scruton suggested: giving it a collective agency in history, and freeing it from structural constraints to the point at which our use of it challenges the organising premises of the Marxism from which our mode of analysis springs. So we do need to follow Scruton this far, and look again at the detail of the debate between Thompson and Anderson on class and the appropriate mode of its study because we will find, when we do, insights and guidelines there for our own scholarship, guidelines which Scruton was too blinkered to see.

Knaves and fools on the question of class

As we noted earlier, Scruton gave unqualified support to Edward Thompson's view of class as an 'emergent phenomenon, which comes into being through the formation of a common class consciousness' (*Thinkers*, p. 13) – of classes as historical entities which in some basic sense 'make themselves'. We also saw that Scruton welcomed Thompson's scepticism about any anthropomorphic vision of historical processes – his antipathy to a view of class 'as a collective agent, which does things, opposes things, fights things and which may succeed or fail' (ibid., p 14). The Scruton criticism of Thompson was that, in spite of his scepticism, he fell back on just such a view of class in order to be able to 'attribute to the working class the historical role which left wing thought [had] always reserved for it' as a revolutionary opponent of industrial capitalism. According to Scruton, in Thompson's work 'the implication that the working class was bound together by its opposition to capitalism is brought in by sleight of hand' – a sleight of hand motivated by Thompson's already mentioned 'sentimentalisation of the proletariat'.

Anderson was criticised by Scruton on other grounds – for recognising the threat to the integrity of the Marxist theoretical and political project constituted by the Thompson emphasis on class-consciousness as defining of class. Anderson's position was successively characterised by Scruton as 'Muscovite', and as operating at that 'level of intellectual dishonesty [in which] the difference between science and alchemy no longer matters'. Anderson was quoted, to be rejected out of hand; even though the quotation merely cited Thompson's 'conceptual error' as being to: 'amalgamate those actions which are indeed conscious volitions at a personal or social level, but whose social influence is profoundly *in*voluntary . . . *with those actions which are conscious volitions at the level of their own social incidence,* under the single rubric of "agency" '.[3]

For Scruton, that statement was just 'emphatic meaninglessness' (*Thinkers*, p. 140). In his scorn Scruton failed to grasp that Anderson was here making an important distinction recognisable to much of sociology, Marxist or otherwise: between actions which, though voluntary in form are socially determined in origin, and actions which lack that degree of social determination. That distinction is central to a Marxist understanding of class; by failing to grasp its importance Scruton ignored the enormous insights into the proper study of proletarian history that can be extracted from the vitriolic exchange between his leading knave and fool.

So what can be extracted? The first thing that a re-examination of the Thompson–Anderson debate provides is an opportunity to clarify the nature of a Marxist approach to class, free of the vulgar reductionism with which Scruton sought to tar it. Indeed it is only possible to grasp the importance of the debate if we begin by emphasising the Marxist heritage that Thompson and Anderson held in common. That heritage was a materialist one. Marxism builds outwards from a materialist ontology. Production, that is, is seen as central to human life. To reproduce themselves, men and women act on nature, progressively transforming their environment into the artefacts necessary for human existence, and in the process changing both the natural world and the nature of the people who act upon it. Around that perennial process of production, Marx argued, settle stable social relations – relations which then give underlying shape to all other aspects of the social order which that production sustains. According to a Marxist reading of history, thus far those social relationships have settled into a class form: with each method or mode of production consolidating antagonistic classes – those who produce and those who do not; those whose labour generates a surplus and those who expropriate that surplus as their own property. In Marxism, such social relationships are seen to be structural in kind. That is, they are borne by individuals within any one generation, but are not created by those individuals. They are inherited by the individuals who bear them, and are then reproduced by the social practice of those class-bearing individuals. For this reason class positions can, and indeed in the first instance need to, be studied in isolation from the patterns of consciousness to which they give rise, and from the class practices through which they are sustained.

None of that seemed to be in dispute between Thompson and Anderson. Where they did differ was in the importance they attached to the role of explicit theorising in the telling of a Marxist history of class, and in the weight they placed on class situation rather than class action as the focus of study. In the debate between them, Edward Thompson was rightly cautious about talking of classes in too abstract and timeless a way. He was uneasy with broad historical generalisations which treated classes as subjects with their own motives and goals, or which marched whole classes up and down history in great strides with no apparent renewal of personnel, experiences or ideas. He disliked modes of analysis which rode roughshod over the losers as well as the winners in the working-class story they told, or which were quick to spot the 'real' class interests which actually lay beneath every variegated idea, action, political force or cultural phenomenon sustained by proletarian people. That unease derived partly from a recognition that in the hands of an historian the category of 'class' is an abstraction, a shorthand for a process that happens in the lives of ordinary people 'without volition or identity'. The substance of class is always simply men and women 'facing situations they did not choose, facing an overwhelming immediacy of relations and duties with only a scanty opportunity for inserting their own agency'.[4] For Thompson, classes have no sphere of existence other than in the lives of those who compose them. For him, 'when we speak of a class we are thinking of a very loosely defined body of people who share the same congeries of interests, social experiences, traditions and value systems, who have a disposition to behave as a class, to define themselves in their actions and in their consciousness in relation to other groups of people in class ways'.[5] A sensitivity to the historical detail of the lives of those people is then vital, since when in discussing class we find ourselves 'too frequently commencing sentences with IT, it is time to place (ourselves) under some historical control, or (we are) in danger of becoming the slaves of (our) own categories'.[6]

Thompson's unease was grounded in more than the sense of class as a metaphor. It was grounded too in the recognition of what a historian actually finds when returning to examine the experience of a proletariat. As he noted at the beginning of *The Making of the English Working Class*,[7] if we stop history at a given moment in time, if we drop a line down on one particular day, we do not initially see classes. What we actually see are a multiplicity of individual men and women in the pursuit of their own life goals, struggling individually (and occasionally collectively) to establish some degree of control over, ward off, contain or ultimately resolve, sets of problems, experiences and constraints that make up their daily material reality – the environment given to them, beyond their individual control, and in essence nothing more than the social ordering of the productive forces of their society. If we watch those men and women over a period of time, we see patterns in their social relationships, their institutions, their ideas and their behaviour. We see them making similar and persistent kinds of responses to their common experience of the social ordering of capitalist production: standard, similar and persistent patterns of behaviour, clusters of attitudes and values and sets of institutions that link them to other people in similar situations in their own generation, that link generations of people over time and space that experience similar problems, and that divide such people throughout time and space from other people with a different relationship to the means of production, and a correspondingly different set of life experiences, life chances, and problems and interests. These regularities of behaviour, attitudes and institutions which emerge from a shared and similar experience of the social ordering of material production over time came, for Thompson, to constitute the substance of a class.

On this argument, classes make themselves as men and women live out their lives, and therefore to study class was for Thompson (and is for us) to study an active historical process which unifies an otherwise disparate and unconnected set of events. A class becomes simply a group whose similar position within the social ordering of production generates for them certain specific regularities of behaviour, attitudes and institutions; and it can be studied historically because it can only be recognised in the medium of time – as sets of people responding to problems known to their predecessors in ways which draw much of their inspiration from the ways in which earlier generations also responded. The analysis of any class therefore, and certainly of the working class, requires that we locate common sets of material experiences over time; that we find the groups drawn into those experiences, that we locate their sets of initial responses, and the pre-industrial origins of these responses, and that we explore how these initial reactions shape later ones. Classes conceived in this way, as actors in the medium of time, are thus to be understood and studied through the sense of class which they gather to themselves, and through the traditions of organisation and behaviour which they consolidate. The core of a class becomes the traditions which it sustains.

There are powerful lessons here for us. Classes do exist in the medium of time. They are constituted, generation by generation, by clusters of men and women in the pursuit of their lives; and they do consolidate around themselves consistent patterns of attitude, organisation and behaviour; but such insights, though powerful, can also mislead. By themselves they are not enough, and do not take us to the heart of the problem with which in their different ways Thompson and Anderson were both centrally concerned; namely the range of working-class political responses over time and space. For those responses change over time; and they differ, country from country. Classes studied alone, and in their own terms, give us no clue to why that should be so. Indeed, why talk of classes at all if self-definition is the only guide? That sense of class has been missing, even in the English labour movement (and certainly in others) for significant groups of workers at particular periods. Are people then not to be understood as working class just because (and when) they vote Tory, identify with Ulster loyalists or hate workers of a different colour? Even Edward Thompson did not want to argue that. There is a materiality to class which predates consciousness, and which has itself to be studied. There is class experience as well as class awareness, a class experience determined by the productive relationships into which individual members of that class are involuntarily placed. The working class is not the only thing which has a history. The capitalism which created and sustains it has a history too: and for that reason, if the working class makes itself, it does not do so, 'just as (it) please(s), under circumstances chosen by (itself), but under circumstances directly encountered, given and transmitted from the past' (Marx, *Eighteenth Brumaire*).

Thompson's critics have made much of this point. His proper objection to bad theory, to 'violent abstraction', to the imposition of *a priori* theorising on living history, and to the forcing of historical data into predetermined moulds on occasions seemed to them to slip into an opposition to theory itself. This tendency to resist theory as such was reflected in *The Making of the English Working Class* in the underplaying of economic processes in the formation of class experience. 'It is not that economic relations and changes in ways of producing [were] absent' from Thompson's account. It was rather that 'their presence [was] *assumed* all the time. But the changes in economic relations [were] understood *through* their experiential or political effects, not, for the most part, in themselves'. The characteristic analytical move made by Thompson in *The Making* . . . according to Johnson, was 'to *assume* the force of economic changes, to insist upon the force of cultural and political processes too, but only to describe the latter in any detailed or active way'.[8]

Yet a full Marxist history needs to be able to do more than this if it is to explain the range of working class history and politics. It needs to be able to locate class positions and class experiences independently of the patterns of consciousness and activity to which they give rise, and it needs to be able to situate those class positions and experiences in the wider social and economic processes of which they are only a part. For in the absence of such a wider consideration, any historical account runs the danger of detaching an understanding of class from its objective anchorage in determinate modes of production, and of identifying it instead only with consciousness and culture. That in its turn would then encourage too narrow a focus of study, and would restrict the range of material which any adequate analysis of the working class has to stretch out to incorporate. This range has to be wide enough to take in the character, logic and development of modes of production, the interplay of old and new modes in particular social formations, the structure and character of all the classes created by those modes, the resulting legal and cultural forms of the dominant classes, the situation of subordinate classes other than the working class, and the determinants of the material situation and composition of the working class itself.

In other words, and quite contrary to Scruton's argument, classes have to be understood first as objective material relationships. Without an understanding of just this sphere of given social relationships, class analysis lacks anchorage and focus. As Perry Anderson said of E.P. Thompson, 'in the absence of any objective framework laying down the overall pattern of capital accumulation in those years, there is little way of assessing the relative importance of one area of subjective experience within the English working class as against another. Proportions are wanting. Selectivity of focus is combined with sweep of conclusion'.[9] As applied to the nineteenth-century working class as a whole, such a strategy of analysis would necessarily detach class struggle from the rhythms of capital accumulation, and explain it only in terms of a, 'simple dialectic between suffering and resistance'.[10] Attractive as that dialectic may be to the committed historian, it is something which a full Marxist analysis of class has to avoid. Proletarian life was, and remains, far more complicated than that.

The weight of Scruton's argument was that, between them, Thompson and Anderson demonstrated the vacuity of the entire Marxist approach to class; but a more sophisticated reading of the debate suggests rather that what needs to be abandoned is not a Marxist history, but both a reductionist and a sentimental one. Marxist historians have to recognise the complexity of class experience and determination, be prepared to demonstrate the superior capacity of Marxism to handle that complexity, and readjust (if necessary) their practice as historians in order to capture and explain the complexity of class lost in more reductionist treatments of capitalism and its contradictions. In fact, a full and adequate Marxist analysis of class has always to do three things. It has to situate class in the complex of forces creating class relationships, and thereby *situate the class as agent*; it has to problematise the dominance of class definitions, and thereby *confront the question of consciousness*; and it has to insist on the existence of classes even when those class definitions do not prevail, and thereby deal with the *question of the structural determinants of collective action*. High-quality Marxist scholarship can – and does – build itself around just those three tasks. Thompson and Anderson's work, taken as a whole, covered just that agenda, with Thompson's focused on the first two of those three themes, and with Anderson's stretching out explicitly to encompass the third. Scruton missed the totality of what they were about, and by so doing failed to grasp the strength of the overall approach which they separately deployed.

Scruton accused Marxist historians of treating the working class as a thing, as a free actor with a specific historic mission (and of course there was plenty of bad Marxist history available to him to sustain that view); but a sophisticated Marxist understanding of historical processes has been – and remains – just as critical of that error as was Scruton himself. It was Edward Thompson after all who was the clearest of all on this, insisting that the definition of class, 'ultimately . . . can be made only in the medium of time . . . [that] class itself is not a thing, it is a happening'.[11] Classes happen, he wrote, at a particular time and in a particular way; and if we are to understand them we have to study them first in their own time and place, as historical phenomena. What Thompson was less clear about was what we were to make of workers' capacities to live that history without adopting a class definition of their circumstances and interests. Yet as we know, it is just not inevitable that individual workers will unify their diverse life experiences around their experience as workers; that groups of workers will identify their shared experiences as constituting a class relationship, or that any class definitions so established will be given a specific revolutionary content in either theory or practice. Because class definitions have not always prevailed, and because revolutionary politics is a rarity in the general proletarian experience, Scruton would have us reject the whole theoretical framework and associated political project; but Marxism is not invalidated by the complexity of class. It would only be so were it unable to explain those complexities in ways that were consistent with its central propositions on the nature of modes of production and their attendant social formations. It can, and often has, generated explanations with just that consistency; explanations strongly associated with the very New Left figures Scruton chooses to condemn – with Anderson certainly, and of course with Gramsci.

There is therefore no need to apologise for the fact that a proper Marxist study of class carries with it an expectation that the proletarian experience will radicalise those exposed to it. There is enough empirical evidence on the tenacity and generality of class definitions to make the study of class and class consciousness of central concern to historians; and sufficient evidence of a tendency in proletarian politics for radicalism and revolution to sustain the importance of a set of Marxist questions on why that tendency has not yet been more marked. In any case, choices of theoretical approaches are determined by more than a process of ticking off proletarian politics against Marxist revolutionary aspirations. In the choice of a particular approach to the study of a class and its politics, complex judgments of many kinds are necessarily involved. After all, to use the term 'working class' – and to use it with a Marxist set of connotations – is to make a complex theoretical and comparative-empirical judgment about the overall character, history and imperatives of the world order, and about the comparative position and experience of different national social groups within it. To say, for example, that the American working class is a 'working class' is to say that it occupies broadly the same position in the social relationships surrounding production as does another working class in another capitalism. It is to say too that the American and the other national economy are part of the same world system, and contain broadly the same set of economic contradictions and social differentiations – so that to be 'working class' in one country has broadly the same meaning and significance as in another. All that follows from this, for the inclusion in our study of classes that do not define themselves in class terms, is that we will have to explain why those non-class definitions exist (and assess their significance for the subsequent development of capitalism) and make that explanation and assessment in ways which are consistent with our general explanation of class politics elsewhere.

Whenever Anderson explored the complexity of the wider social processes and forces moulding working-class development and politics, Scruton accused him of abandoning 'Marxist' for 'bourgeois' history; but the accusation was specious, for any Marxist historian concerned with the working class needs to come to the question of class and its history last rather than first. The first task of any proper Marxist analysis of class, as we saw earlier, is to map accurately the development of the capitalist mode of production and its attendant social forces, into which members of any one proletariat are inserted and to which they have to respond. If that mapping is to be done properly, it has to be done over time, by an analysis of the rhythms of capital accumulation, the stages of capitalist development and the overall shape of the emerging world capitalist system. As we do that, as we see the working class itself grow in size, organisation and activity, we will see too that its impact on those rhythms of development itself grows, so that working-class politics eventually becomes one of the factors shaping the capitalist world to which proletarian politics is a response. The proletariat was (and is) capitalism's creation; and if we are to grasp its true character and potential we need an understanding of the contextual forces creating it, and giving it shape. Marx long ago said that:

> history is nothing but the succession of the separate generations, each of which exploits the materials, the capital funds, the productive forces handed down to it by all preceding generations, and thus, on the one hand, continues the traditional activity in completely changed circumstances and, on the other, modifies the old circumstances by a completely changed activity.[12]

It is the recognition of this which commits us to a complex analysis of the interplay, over time and space, of society, class and party; to a probing of the constantly changing relationship between class situation and class-consciousness; and to an examination of the mutual interaction of capitalist trajectory, working-class experience and political response. It is that complex probing that constitutes the agenda of a full Marxist history of class.

The lesson we must take from the kernel of truth at the centre of the Scruton argument is not that class analysis is to be abandoned and a Marxist historiography rejected as inherently flawed. It is that the use of such an approach requires the most sophisticated and nuanced exploration of the totality of social forces released by the development of capitalism: an exploration firmly grounded on the recognition that – in capitalism as in other modes of production – the economic determines the social only ultimately, and in the last instance. It is also that Marxist historical scholarship needs to be defended for what it is – a historiography informed by a set of basic values and by a materialist understanding of the human condition. Scruton clearly lacks those values and works from a different (and to my mind, far more limited) ontology. That is his privilege. Histories have to be anchored in just those choices; but if it is his privilege, it is ours too and must be defended and fought for as such.

Notes

1. Scruton, R. (1985) *Thinkers of the New Left*, London: Longman; all subsequent page references refer to this text unless otherwise stated.
2. Thompson, E.P. (1965) 'The peculiarities of the English' in Miliband, R. and Saville, J. (eds) *The Socialist Register 1965*, London: Merlin Press, pp. 311–62.
3. Anderson, P. (1980) *Arguments within English Marxism*, London: Verso, p. 21.
4. Thompson, E.P. (1965), p. 342.
5. Ibid., p. 357.
6. Ibid., p. 357.
7. Thompson, E.P. (1963) *The Making of the English Working Class*, London: Gollancz.
8. Johnson, R. (1979) 'Three problematics: Elements of a theory of working class culture' in Clarke, J., Critcher, C. and Johnson, R. (eds) *Working Class Culture*, New York: St Martin's Press, p. 221.
9. Anderson, P. (1980), p. 35.
10. Ibid., p. 39.
11. Thompson, E.P. (1965), p. 357.
12. Marx, K. (1976) *German Ideology*, part 1, London: Lawrence and Wishart, p. 57.

CHAPTER SEVEN

Reading Alastair Reid: A future for labour history?

David Howell

> Unfortunately Marxism has all too often been wide of the mark in terms both of the answers it has produced and many of the central questions it has pursued

Thus, the social historian, Alastair Reid characterised the contribution of Marxist historiography to the understanding of the history of the British Labour Movement. He acknowledged the perspective's appeal – 'in terms of its intellectual rigour, its analytical clarity and its holistic ambition, it is currently without a real rival in the field'.[1] However, apparent virtues are essentially vices if their appeal results in misguided questions and erroneous answers. This rejection is one strand in a broader campaign against older approaches to labour history, and in some cases against the basic value of this field of research.

Alastair Reid's position has its attractions. His emphasis on the need to study in depth diversities of occupational experience and of local political tradition is one that should be endorsed. The same is true of his insistence that political action and language should be the subject of serious analysis and not be characterised as derivative from more fundamental economic factors. Yet such acknowledgements should not mean an easy rejection of previous positions, nor a ready acquiescence in the term of debates proposed by the revisionists. However, older models face serious problems and to deny this is foolish.

This chapter is a contribution to a debate about the methodology of labour history. It makes two fundamental assumptions – that the research field is one of continuing significance, and that its future necessitates an open debate about methods in which old icons and new prescriptions are subjected to the same critical standards. The analysis focuses on three significant features within Reid's critique: the general polemic; the scrutiny of a specific controversy – the rise of the Labour Party; and the advocacy of an alternative methodology.

Polemic

Within Reid's indictment, there are a variety of charges. Some focus on what he sees as the deleterious consequences of *a* – or perhaps specifically *this* – political commitment for historical research. He contrasts the 'stimulating and probing analyses' constructed by Marxist writers concerned with specific problems and particular periods with the failure to produce a broader successful synthesis – a 'coherent history'. This alleged failure is presented as more than a contingent matter: 'the only moment which can be celebrated with any degree of conviction by historians with revolutionary leanings is the first phase of Chartism and thereafter the whole development has to be analysed to explain what went wrong'.[2]

The actual trajectory cannot be adequately explained: 'even the most perceptive Marxist analysis will remain hampered by its author's own political opinions. In a country where revolutionary groups have been marginal, accurate interpretations of the overall development of the British working people are unlikely to come from those with revolutionary sympathies'.[3]

Thus Marxists are allegedly unable to appreciate the 'genuineness' of what 'they call reformism' since they view this as an aberration. Reid's response is the commendation of a 'thorough going revisionism' that will re-evaluate not only movements and personalities, but also 'basic approaches to historical explanation'.[4]

Some prior clarification is needed concerning the suggestion that, in some way that extends beyond the contingent, Marxist values impede the production of decent historical work. The range of possible relationships between political values and historical scholarship is not clarified. Is the argument against Marxist historians that they represent a specific manifestation of a general problem – that once *any* values intrude into historical research then the consequences will be negative? Alternatively the criticism could be directed specifically at the alleged impact of Marxist values on the grounds that experience demonstrates that their consequences for scholarship are particularly damaging. Reid's historical practice perhaps suggests that he would not subscribe to the first interpretation, but this remains unclear in his general presentation.

There is obscurity also about Reid's suggestion of a connection between Marxist values and research findings. The thrust of the indictment is that the connection is more than a contingent one from which strong-minded scholars could emancipate themselves. Yet Reid has acknowledged for example that John Saville's essays on late nineteenth-century labour figures 'are usually more nuanced than . . . Marxist generalisations might suggest'.[5] If the criticism extends beyond the contingent, it requires clarification. Is the claim that specific values constrain the range of questions, limit the selection of evidence which is deemed relevant, and prevent the tabling of significant explanatory hypothesis? If so, then a thorough investigation requires a comparison of how different value-positions promote contrasting research agendas within a shared field of enquiry. In addition, values arguably impregnate historians' characterisations of social actors and of actions. This appears to be one element in Reid's critique when he highlights 'a more or less crude smearing of the more moderate majority of trade union leaders and Labour politicians', and 'a narrow, intolerant and abusive conception of trade unionism'.[6] A distinction should be made. Social characterisations with some evaluative content are surely unavoidable in any historical and social scientific work. To attempt to make social action intelligible is to employ concepts which generate evaluations; indeed supportive evidence is provided in Reid's own historiographical practice.[7] The debate is over the appropriateness of competing characterisations, not over whether there should be any social characterisations at all. In general, the analytical underpinnings of this attack on the relationship between Marxist values and historical scholarship require much more specificity; the effective choices are not illuminated.

A more precise criticism is that the core Marxist model suggests an expected path of development for the labour movement, in the light of which the British case, and indeed those presented by most capitalist societies most of the time, appear as deviant. This critical position has generated its own research agenda and informs the edited volume by Eugenio Biagini and Alastair Reid, *Currents of Radicalism: Popular Radicalism, Organised Labour and Party Politics in Britain 1850–1914*.[8] The editors' introduction connects some of the above sentiments with a substantive historiographical agenda.

Their central claim is of continuity – 'in popular radicalism throughout the nineteenth and into the twentieth century'.[9] Thus the early Labour Party was marked fundamentally by this tradition; there was no significant break as between Radical Liberalism and Independent Labour politics that necessitated explanation. As Biagini and Reid present their negative thesis: 'Once we place mid and late-Victorian working-class Liberal and Labour activists back into their own political context . . . enough continuity in popular radicalism can be demonstrated to make the search for social explanation of major changes unnecessary.'[10]

This substantive proposition leads to the rejection of a dominant methodology. The link is made through a critical emphasis on the customary treatment of mid Victorian radicalism as a somewhat self-contained interlude between Chartism and the Socialist revival. This episodic judgment is related to the portrait of such radicalism as an anomaly in the context of industrial capitalism and therefore necessitating a special explanation. The appraisal contrasts starkly with the editor's continuity thesis. The popularity of the former is explained by the intellectual dominance of a framework which is subjected to uncompromising indictment:

> the Marxist assumption that the fundamental feature of capitalist society is class struggle, that all politics which is not a direct expression of the interests of one class is a direct expression of the interests of another, and that the only appropriate politics for a mature working class is state socialism of a more or less revolutionary type.[11]

In contrast Biagini and Reid tie their continuity claim to their own methodological precepts. Their starting point is the assumption that, 'popular politics needs to be assessed in the first instance within its own political context rather than in terms of what it "ought" to have been, defined for example in terms of its consistency with external norms of revolutionary rhetoric or with teleological models of historical development'.[12]

A historiographical problem

Equipped with images of adversaries and their own agenda and hypotheses, Biagini and Reid present and criticise earlier analyses of the shift from Liberalism to Labour. One school is identified with 'committed Socialists' such as Edward Thompson; its central claim that the emergence of the Labour Party can be explained through an emphasis on the formation of socialist groups and 'new unions' in the 1880s. The Party's advent was therefore:

> mainly the result of a major advance in working-class politics, which in turn was closely related to the latest developments in the organisation of industry. This led to an intensification of economic conflict, and to a growing sense of a separate working-class community which culminated in an increasingly sharp break with the 'bourgeois' Liberal Party and with 'middle-class' Nonconformity.[13]

The critique by Biagini and Reid attacks what they call 'the central assumption of these historians'[14] – that the 'new unions' differed fundamentally from the old. They suggest that the assumption is no longer tenable, since it is now established that the most durable 'new unions' were the ones most like the old. The centrality of the claimed assumption is perhaps exaggerated. Moreover, the proposition that surviving 'new unions' showed a significant convergence with the older organisations leaves open the possibility that the circumstances of their formation, their initial culture and early strategies contributed to a political shift. Thus, some surviving 'new unions' had a formal commitment to political independence, and in the rule-governed world of trade unionism that was significant.

Beyond this point of contention there is the more serious question of the vulnerability of this perspective to the editor's claims about content and method. Thompson is cited as an exemplar; his writings on this theme are few but they provide significant and influential claims. The first edition of *William Morris* (1955)[15] contains much on the fruitless search by Morris for an effective strategy. The most significant piece is 'Homage to Tom Maguire'[16] published in 1960 between *William Morris* and *The Making of the English Working Class*. The focus is on the creation of the Independent Labour Party (ILP) in the woollen towns of the West Riding of Yorkshire. There are also relevant comments in Thompson's celebrated 1965 polemic, 'The Peculiarities of the English'.[17]

All of these works emphasise working-class creativity, an insistence that socialist and labour organisations are constructed by conscious agents and are not the products of impersonal economic forces. This quality is acknowledged by Biagini and Reid; quite how such commendation can be reconciled with their dismissal of rival perspectives as teleological is unclear. 'Tom Maguire' is very much a product of those years when, having left the Communist Party, Thompson together with John Saville edited the *New Reasoner* as part of an attempt to construct a New Left alternative to both Social Democracy and Stalinism. In its columns Thompson explored the meaning of and prospects for a socialist humanism, always with the insistence that the prospects for a socialist alternative depend on creative and effective interventions. Here was precisely the insistence of 'Tom Maguire'; the essay explicitly attacked the claim that West Riding socialism was the result of economic pressures – 'economic hardship and President (*sic*) McKinley's tariffs'. For Thompson the claim is not just historically false but morally disreputable: 'It implies an appalling attitude of condescension towards those provincial folk who are credited with every virtue except the capital human virtue of conscious action in a conscious historical role.'[18]

The adversaries were not restricted to mistaken historians; they included Stalinists who had imposed the metaphor of base and superstructure as cast-iron paradigm.[19] 'Tom Maguire' is informed by a passion flowing not just from deeply held views of moral philosophy and historical method; the argument also resonates with a thorough commitment to New Left politics. This involved rejection of party machines holding instead to a belief that radical renewal would come from the initiatives of men and women realising the potential within their own communities. The essay's overture is a polemic directed against the domination of labour history by accounts of national decisions and strategies. This is not simply an attack on a limited historiography; it is also the rejection of a dominant strand in late 1950s politics. The belief that politics – including labour politics – was about élite management found a grotesque academic apotheosis as 'In Defence of Apathy' with the *End of Ideology* as back-drop. It was a challenge taken up by Thompson and other New Left writers not least in the 1960 collection, *Out of Apathy*.[20]

Such preoccupations locate Thompson far away from Biagini and Reid's mechanistic targets – the centrality of creativity, the sensitivity towards potentials which might not be realised, the portraits of activists, characteristic of their place and time, but with a capacity to see the possibilities for change. Yet the celebration of creativity is balanced by an unsentimental awareness of constraints – poverty, harsh workplace conditions in the dominant woollen industry, the ideological attractions of Liberalism. The image of Socialists working with the textures of their communities, contesting available spaces and ambiguous meanings but acknowledging structural limitations is a dominant motif.

Equally, Thompson's central historical claims do not fit neatly into the 'flawed' adversary projected by Biagini and Reid. Some emphases are at odds with the continuity thesis. Thompson refers to the cracking of the two-party structure, and the emergence of a third party with 'a distinctively socialist character'. He suggests that in Yorkshire the formation of a socialist party was based on 'a conscious decision', which was itself the consequence of a lengthy period of propaganda.[21] The West Riding breakthrough is located chronologically as following a series of 'false dawns'. Does this hint at a pattern of normal development which was finally realised in Yorkshire? Or at least in some Yorkshire communities! Leeds is characterised, at least in comparison with Bradford, as 'a remarkable case of arrested development'.[22]

Is this the teleological spectre hidden behind the celebration of creativity? Such a verdict needs to be placed against other considerations. Thompson sketches a brief but highly suggestive comparison of Leeds and Bradford. He claims that the former's employment structure was more diverse, its class structure less stark, its new unions in the short term more successful and the impact of skilled Liberal trade unionists more long lasting.[23] The validity of the claims requires testing but the comparative framework structured around the theme of political independence has the merit of generating worthwhile hypotheses. Moreover, Leeds's political development might have been 'arrested', but on the criterion of political independence, both cities arrived at broadly the same destination.

A key concern of Biagini and Reid is the characterisation of such an outcome. Despite Thompson's emphasis on the Socialism of the West Riding ILP and his indictments of employer Liberalism, his portrait of the region's radicalisation is notable for its nuances. The broader perspective is apparent in his later 'The peculiarities of the English'. His target, Perry Anderson, had dismissed the experience of the British Left between the demise of Chartism and the 1880s as a 'deep ceasura'.[24] Here is the classic target for Biagini and Reid, but it was also one for Thompson. The latter thus portrayed the mid Victorian years as a critical time when the workers 'having failed to overthrow capitalist society proceeded to warren it from the end . . . the period in which the classical institutions of the Labour Movement were built up'.[25]

Thompson presents much of this network as central to West Riding community experiences – co-operatives, chapels, friendly societies – and to a lesser extent, trade unions. Indeed the weakness of unionism in the dominant industry could render political initiatives more appealing. Thompson's portrait of the accompanying dominant Liberalism highlights its complexities. The millocracy could be thoroughly conservative on economic questions and was backed by influential sections of religious Dissent. Yet Gladstonianism could absorb old Chartists; Thompson provides a memorable vignette of Chartists toasting Gladstone in the mid 1880s at a Halifax temperance hotel.[26] Such absorption could highlight individual social mobility but perhaps said something about the complexities of Liberalism. There was within West Riding Liberalism the tradition, if not in the 1880s the actuality, of political independence for labour, expressed by fights within Liberalism between Radical and Whig. Thompson's images of Halifax radicalism in the 1860s, the interventions of Ernest Jones, suggest precisely the kind of continuity emphasised by Biagini and Reid. Indeed Thompson explicitly notes that to seek an unbroken independent labour tradition from Chartism to the ILP is mistaken. His posing of the key question is clear; the answer shows an awareness of the continuities: 'How far was the Yorkshire ILP an authentic socialist party? How far was it a late product of Liberal-radicalism, carried by a temporary tide of industrial and social unrest into independent political channels? The evidence is conflicting.'[27]

This target of Biagini and Reid shows awareness of, and explores the complex relationship between Radicalism and the emergence of independent labour politics. The exploration is balanced by an emphasis on innovation and a significant degree of discontinuity. On this side of the ledger the evidence marshalled by Thompson to suggest the intransigence of West Riding Liberal employers and caucuses is impressive. One response would be that the woollen district was atypical in the strength of conservative Liberalism; although by 1910, all sitting Labour Members had the benefit of local Liberal support or benevolent neutrality. Moreover, trade union weakness led to more significance for independent political initiatives than was the case in some other regions. Diversity is important, but such an emphasis is an important element in Biagini and Reid's case. Thompson's analysis of the complexities of the radical tradition suggest that in some circumstances it could be a tribu-

tary into a political initiative that was not just organisationally independent but explicitly socialist.

Throughout his New Left period Thompson considered himself a
Marxist, albeit one who placed strong emphases on cultural issues, on
political strategy, and on moral agency. Within 'Tom Maguire' economic
elements are present but as backdrop rather than decisive factors.[28] His
rejections of a simplistic determinism and a crude reductionism leave
open the elucidation of the relationship between structure and agency. In
contrast, a second target of Biagini and Reid is presented as a more
orthodox Marxist. They suggest that as a consequence, Eric
Hobsbawm's prime concern differed from that of Thompson. Whereas
the latter was preoccupied with 'the idea of the Labour Party as a channel
for the socialist activism of a minority', Hobsbawm's concern has been
more with the Party 'in its relationship to the position of the working-
class as a whole within the latest stage in the development of capitalism'.[29]

Biagini and Reid see the outcome as a more deterministic analysis of
the relationship between industry and culture on the one hand, and a
new sense of class unity and separateness on the other. They suggest that
this image was characteristically accompanied (from a socialist perspective) by a relatively pessimistic assessment of the facility with which this
class sentiment could be continued within the 'status quo'.[30]

Reid's principal critique of Hobsbawm's work pre-dates the discussion in the edited volume. He suggests that Hobsbawm's early analysis of
British Labour was informed by a developmental model not too remote
from the imagery of the *Communist Manifesto* with the expectation that
a conscious, organised and ultimately revolutionary working class
should emerge. Within this framework British exceptionalism is
explained, allegedly, by reference to a labour aristocracy and the contribution of imperialism. By the 1960s, Hobsbawm is seen as having abandoned this model with its consequential schedule of problems to be
explained, but yet retaining amended and discrete elements of the former
vision. These function not as contributors to a comprehensive and coherent framework but as valid characterisations of what had happened.
Reid suggests that such a radical revision was one facet of a deepening
pessimism about the prospects for revolutionary parties in advanced
industrial societies.[31]

If all that remains are some analytical fragments, with the grand
design shattered by an avalanche of events, this collapse has not been
restricted to self-consciously Marxist accounts of British Labour politics.
It applies equally to many accounts that presented the rise of a distinctive
Labour Party as a natural development – a privileged progression from
the Mid-Lanark by-election of 1888 and the formation of the

Independent Labour Party, to the arrival of Attlee in Downing Street. It was, after all, Hobsbawm in 1978, who raised the irreverent question – 'The forward march of Labour halted?'.[32] Controversial at the time, the intellectual challenge has become a political platitude. The question should provoke another – 'Was there ever a forward march anyway?'.[33] Hobsbawm's analysis has continued to suggest that in some sense there was. Biagini and Reid are sceptics and their scepticism challenges a family of assumptions that extend beyond the distinctively Marxist.

Reid's earlier critique emphasised both diversity and continuity – and carried a methodological admonition:

> Most of the available accounts of late nineteenth and early twentieth century popular politics have either assumed that changes in political attitudes were a direct reflection of transformations in the material conditions of working-class life or where such an economic explanation has been seen as insufficient or inadequate, 'culture' has been called in to provide the necessary social cement.[34]

The reference to 'direct reflection' is tendentious, but beyond the debatable characterisation of a rejected view, there is a serious empirical claim: 'It is only natural to assume that after a significant reorganisation of the economy and massive migrations from rural to urban areas, the working population would settle down and participate in increasingly shared ways of life . . . this view begins to seem increasingly implausible the closer it is inspected.'[35]

Biagini and Reid suggest that the research agenda fostered within this broad framework has produced findings that undermine its assumptions. For example, they suggest that emphases on mechanisation and de-skilling as causes of increasing working-class homogeneity have been exaggerated and that significant levels of workplace and labour market sectionalism remained. Similarly, older cultural forms seem to have displayed a significant level of endurance, eroding any claim that from the 1880s working-class culture was increasingly homogeneous.[36]

Such criticisms engage directly with the work of Hobsbawm which has stressed both economic and cultural changes as explanations of increasing working-class homogeneity. In the economic field Hobsbawm has employed a version of the labour aristocracy thesis suggesting that changes in the two or three decades prior to 1914 eroded the relative protection previously enjoyed by some skilled workers: 'A labour aristocracy threatened by technological and managerial innovation, increasingly pushed out of the old 'lower middle class' by the rise of a new white collar stratum . . . found itself both pressed into a common and apparently inescapable working-class universe, and radicalised in defence of its own privileges.'[37]

A political judgment on this claim must be nuanced. Early trade union affiliations to the Labour Representation Committee included several craft unions, most notably the Amalgamated Society of Engineers. Yet the wider significance of such attachments requires exploration. The decision to affiliate was taken typically without a thorough involvement by the membership. In the engineers' case, successive ballots showed an almost total lack of interest. Affiliations were characteristically the consequence of work by small groups of activists who drew political conclusions from their industrial experiences. Moreover, the precise character of such conclusions was often ambiguous.[38]

Beyond the claims about increasing homogeneity as a result of workplace changes, Hobsbawm suggests the development of a distinctive and uniform culture based around increasingly standardised patterns of consumption. Hobsbawm highlights evocative symbols and images – fish and chip shops, Wakes weeks at the seaside, flat caps, football on Saturdays, and for the supporters of successful teams the Spring pilgrimage to the Cup Final at Crystal Palace.[39] Here was a world, as he acknowledges, sometimes remote from and indeed despised by active trade unionists and committed Socialists. Such ardent self-improvers could be repelled by the enthusiasm of their fellow-workers.[40] Nevertheless, Hobsbawm's thesis remains that such cultural developments, together with his claimed economic changes were producing a form of class solidarity and distinctiveness that merits the employment of the term 'class-consciousness'. Although far removed from the combative ideal of many socialists, this identity is seen as having explanatory power at the political level.

Hobsbawm's depiction of working-class culture is gender-blind. Football crowds before 1914 were almost exclusively male. As the mass of cloth caps in contemporary photographs demonstrates, Hobsbawm's world of leisure occluded with that of the workplace; sport provided endless scope for workplace discussions; workmates shared leisure activities. To characterise these networks as evidence for an increasingly distinctive and coherent class culture is at best inadequate, and arguably serves to reinforce sexist stereotypes.

Similarly, the analysis tends to neglect working-class communities rather than workplaces as arenas for politicisation. Battles over housing provision – for example the Clydeside rent campaigns of the First World War and its aftermath – were typically free of the male and often craft exclusivity that characterised the region's workplace struggles. A successful campaign to redefine community identity in class terms could carry radical political implications.[41]

Awareness of such limitations inevitably diminishes the framework's appeal. Yet there is a more serious problem about the claimed links between the economic, the cultural, and the political. Within

Hobsbawm's own characterisation he focuses on the leader of the Yorkshire miners and later of the Miners Federation of Great Britain (MFGB), Herbert Smith, 'the man in the cloth cap' as symptomatic of the great cultural and political shift.[42] Smith is presented as a loyal supporter of Barnsley Football Club. In 1912, when Barnsley made their one Cup Final appearance, most of the club's supporters, if they could have voted at all would have voted Liberal. Even in the Yorkshire coalfield, a relatively distinctive male working-class culture did not generate readily an independent political party.[43] Elsewhere the linkages were weaker. Throughout the interwar period most soccer clubs visiting Stamford Bridge, and subsequently Wembley, did not represent communities where support for the Labour Party was dominant. Once time-lags and contingencies are brought into the thesis, then the basic formulation seems much less persuasive.

Yet it would be too easy to stop the analysis at this point, to acknowledge that Hobsbawm's characterisations and explanatory model are flawed and that therefore the field should be abandoned to the critics. The problem is that there remains something to be explained – the rise of a Labour Party, along with the growth and consolidation of national unions constructed out of the fragmented experiences of occupational groupings and communities. Hobsbawm highlights the theme in a portrait of W.P. Richardson, a miner from Usworth in County Durham, a man with a firm community identity articulated through Primitive Methodism, council work and local marriage. Richardson also helped to found a branch of the ILP, sat on the board of the *Daily Herald* and became treasurer of the MFGB. He became a national figure but remained in Usworth.[44] The individual biography is an industrially and regionally specific element in a broader canvas. The distinctiveness is there but through this is articulated a general development – the foundation of the MFGB in 1889, the eventual affiliation of the Durham Miners Association after long arguments in 1907, the federation's affiliation to the Labour Party in 1909 and three years later the first national coal stoppage. These developments can be understood in different ways. Some would emphasise the growth of a politicised MFGB which by the 1920s was a byword for loyalty to the Labour Party, and in some sense a vehicle and a focus for a relatively developed class-consciousness. Others would stress rather the development of an occupational solidarity. Miners increasingly saw themselves not as Durham miners or Yorkshire miners, but as miners. Such a change need not produce a cohesion which was the prelude to class solidarity but rather a sectionalism which was an alternative. In fact the history of the MFGB suggests the power of both tendencies, and at moments of crisis moreover, a demonstration that localism could erode national loyalties.

Beyond the complexities, the miners' case shows a relatively effective drive towards a more cohesive labour movement – an occupational variant on a general theme. It is a claim that parallels Thompson's comparison of Bradford and Leeds. Even within the coal industry there remained contrasting styles of politics, yet the contrasts fit into a broader picture in which changes have a pattern which demands explanation. The recognition and conceptualisation of this challenge is a major strength in Hobsbawm's presentation. In contrast Biagini and Reid face a fundamental problem on this issue. They proclaim the continuing influence of radical liberalism and yet have to acknowledge that Labour politicians have typically presented their politics as 'socialist'.[45] The problem is particularly acute since they stress the centrality of 'the political', focusing on what politicians said rather than what a dominant theory expected them to say. Yet their substantive position inhibits them from embracing the obvious conclusion – that these politicians referred to their policies as 'socialist' because that was what they believed them to be.

Hobsbawm is another writer within a Marxist framework who has a very clear view of the legacies provided by radical liberalism for the twentieth-century British Left. He contrasts the singularity of the Fabians with the continuing vitality of radical-liberal intellectuals; he insists on the legacy of secularist radicalism to the Social Democratic Federation; he claims that 'virtually all Englishmen [*sic*] of the Left were at least the illegitimate offspring of the radical-liberal tradition'.[46] The extent and character of the shift from Liberal to Labour may be a matter of controversy, but clearly he is no advocate of a sharp break. At a number of points Hobsbawm provides a significant counterfactual challenge to a thorough continuity thesis, in the shape of the National Democratic League. He sees its failure as symbolic of a significant change. Founded almost contemporaneously with the Labour Representation Committee (LRC) it brought together Lib-Lab and Socialist new unionists – George Howell and Tom Mann; Sam Woods and Bob Smillie. The early LRC rejected any formal link; by 1906 as the LRC expanded its parliamentary presence the NDL had disappeared. Hobsbawm sees the LRC's survival and the NDL's failure as symptomatic. Whatever the continuities here was a critical shift in worker's consciousness. Thus Hobsbawm:

> its politics were no longer implicit in a general belief in the rights of man, workers being merely one large section of a comprehensive 'the people'. The politics of Chartism, whether as an independent mass movement or as part of Liberal-Radicalism, fade out . . . The future lay with the Labour Representation Committee, and the essence of its programme, whatever it was, was that it specifically served the demands and aspirations of the working-class'.[47]

The challenge is in part one of characterisation – the extent and significance of continuities – but it also raises problems of explanation and methodology. It is time to turn more thoroughly to the critics' agenda.

Methodology

The earlier discussion of the developing politics of the Miners Federation of Great Britain provides a convenient starting point. The Federation was a relatively belated affiliate to the Labour Party, and down to the outbreak of war there remained a substantial section within the MFGB membership who were opposed to or uncertain about the significance of this connection. However, in December 1918 the expanded coalfield electorate showed enhanced support for the Labour Party. The post-war industrial struggles saw unsuccessful attempts by miners to transform state control into public ownership, and then to defend wartime and immediate post-war advances. Arguably this section of the working class experienced increased state intervention as positive. For miners the impact of the wartime state strengthened the appeal to them of proposals to nationalise their industry, an attraction deepened perhaps by the miseries that followed decontrol in the Spring of 1921. Such an account could be interpreted by Reid in a fashion that buttressed his general methodological position. A significant shift into Labour politics should not be explained in terms of 'irreversible transformations in the structure and culture of the working-class'.[48] Rather any explanation of political change necessitates an understanding in terms of specifically political events. In the case of the contribution of the First World War, he suggests that areas for investigation should include shifts in the character of the State's economic interventions, and alterations in the relationship between trade unions and the State.

Whether the dichotomous choice of explanations is inescapable, can be left aside for the moment. Instead Reid's conception of the state needs elaboration. His presentation of wartime collectivism is developed in opposition to the argument of James Hinton in *The First Shop Stewards Movement*.[49] Reid emphasises the diverse priorities of industrialists, claiming the implausibility of any thesis that the wartime state could act in their shared interests. Against this diversity he suggests that politicians and administrators had a clear priority: 'Rather than interpreting government policies as simple reflections of the interests of dominant economic groups, they should be seen as prioritising social stability at almost any cost . . .'[50]

The phrase 'simple reflections' is another bogus target, suggesting a reductionist perspective with little or no space for political creativity. The Marxist tradition of theorising about the State is diverse and is arguably vulnerable to criticism of its incoherence but, at the very least, the tradition cannot be identified with such crude reductionism. Moreover, this argument makes a problematic contrast between the economic interests of dominant groups, and the maintenance of social stability. The latter conception possesses intelligibility only in the context of a specific set of social arrangements. Thus any commitment to 'social stability' necessitates that consequential policies cannot be too radical; their justification is that they are thought likely to maintain many of these institutions and practices which give the society its character. The objective of maintaining stability could permit significant discrete reforms – for example the government's intervention in the market for private rented accommodation late in 1915, but it ruled out policies intended to transform radically and rapidly a pre-existing hierarchy.

This restriction is important because Reid develops a view of the State's role which has a strong resemblance to a liberal pluralist vision of state policies as the resultants of competing forces. Here is the style of Arthur F. Bentley – founding father of a group theory of politics.[51] Governments 'were themselves subject to competing pressures to influence the shape of their policies. From this point of view, it might be said that state activity represented the balance of forces in particular situations'.[52] The emphasis raises the question of whether 'the balance of forces' is skewed typically in a consistent direction. Reid argues that industrialists were often unhappy at their exclusion from wartime policymaking. This does not indicate of itself that government policies significantly infringed their interests – their resentments, however genuinely experienced, should not be taken as an authoritative verdict. Reid does not present public servants as passive recorders and implementers of policy verdicts that resulted from a clash of priorities. To develop the Newtonian imagery: 'the drawing of that line of balance was an active process conducted by various government agencies with their own histories, and often their own competing conceptions of the national interest'.[53] Within the tradition of Marxist theorising about the state, this theme raises important and difficult questions about the analysis of bureaucracy, about intra-bureaucratic competition and about whether such theorising can incorporate conceptions of interest that depend on position and resources within an administrative system.

Yet it is not clear that pluralistic fragmentation need be the final verdict. If Reid's emphases are applied to a more recent episode, the miners' strike of 1984–85, it becomes possible to develop a theme that has often been marginal to published accounts – the significant tensions that developed within and between Whitehall and the National Coal Board. Questions could then be posed about conflicts within Hobart House, the Coal Board's London headquarters, or between sections of that hierarchy and the Board's more traditional area directors. Equally, it would be worth investigating the relationship between Hobart House and senior officials at the Department of Energy – or between the various administrative networks and government ministers. Such an account would inevitably convey the image of a fragmented structure and exercise any belief in a tightly knit and coherent group whose shared agenda could be a key explanatory element: but can the stress on fragmentation be a thorough verdict? Whatever the differences amongst these groups, they were all opposed to a victory for the National Union of Mineworkers. Beyond the diversities there was unity on the most vital priority of all, thereby justifying a description of these groups as on the same side. Why those diverse elements could agree on this and why it was so important is surely crucial to any account. Similarly, to return to Reid's analysis, would there not be limits to administrative conceptions of the national interest, and would not such parameters be linked to conceptions of social stability and the preferred preservation of many pre-existing institutions and practices?

Beyond this analysis of the State, there is a more general thesis contained in Biagini and Reid's presentation of a major historiographical controversy:

> in the important debates over the Liberal's ability to adopt new social policies, over the speed with which Labour constructed an effective national organisation and over the implications of the franchise extension of 1918, the background assumption has generally been that the two parties were competing to gain support from an electorate increasingly dominated by an unambiguous sense of class.

In response they suggest that one merit of the arguments has been the demonstration of a negative methodological point: 'whatever underlying economic and social changes are assumed, reductionist explanations of political events will always be inadequate . . . the form eventually taken by popular politics will depend on the relative success of appeals from rival parties and programmes'.[54]

As Reid had earlier insisted concerning contests over community identity, 'none of the struggles or their outcomes had any necessary connection with a particular kind of politics'.[55] This needs clarification. What precisely is the claim of 'necessary connection'? Perhaps it is that conformity to specified cultural beliefs and values renders a particular form of politics uniquely preferable and therefore cultural dominance will have predictable political consequences. It is hard to believe that such a position could be advocated seriously. Hobsbawm's football-watching, fish-and-chips-eating male workers were not constrained decisively in their political choices by their reactions. How would Reid feel about a less limiting and arguably more plausible position, that certain cultural and industrial developments rendered specific political responses increasingly attractive?

In contrast to 'necessary connection' Reid proposes a pluralism which seems little more than agnosticism: 'The economic, organisational and cultural fragmentation of the working-class meant that it was neither inherently oppositional nor inherently incorporated, but was rather a constantly shifting mix of limitations and possibilities which could be mobilised into different configurations'.[56]

Once again there is the loaded use of an adverb – 'inherently'. Is it credible to refer to 'a constantly shifting mix of limits and possibilities' without clarifying the character of such limits? Should these be understood in terms of the discourse available to agents, or are there constraints which can have an impact, perhaps independently of an agent's conceptual framework?

Above all Reid stresses that 'the political' is as 'real' as 'the economic' and 'the social'. This claim is elaborated with reference to a characteristic dismissal of the alleged alternative: '*Any* sociological account of politics begins to collapse as it comes closer to the object under investigation. Over-arching social accounts just can't deal with the complexity and ambiguity of people's attitudes nor can they avoid presenting monolithic a-priori accounts to necessary connection which were actually quite diverse and uncertain'.[57] Thus in explaining the growing influence of the ILP on Clydeside during and after the First World War, Reid argues that emphasis should be given to organisational capacities rather than 'spontaneous pre-political class feeling'.[58] Equally, he insists that the explanation of political outcomes does not rest on the elaboration of chance and coincidence, but necessitates a sensitive exploration of a particular political world.

Such a defence of the autonomy of politics raises significant issues. An adequate account of any political action must illuminate why actors made the choices that they did – which choices seemed plausible, which would be stigmatised as illegitimate or irrational, and which were simply not perceived as available. Marxist accounts have often responded inadequately to this challenge; whether such inadequacy is endemic is another matter.

Reid's approach also permits a consideration of the place of constitutive beliefs within social understanding. The ideas that people have about social relationships characteristically help to constitute such relationships. Belief about the existence and the legitimacy of an authority structure do not simply assist in its maintenance; they also help to constitute it. Appropriate beliefs seem essential for the perpetuation of a military hierarchy, not just in the sense of supporting it, but also in providing and maintaining its character – beliefs about rank and the legitimacy of orders from duly constituted sources form part of the hierarchical net-work. A private soldier accepts an order in part because his relationship with a superior incorporates beliefs about hierarchy and legitimacy. If the beliefs alter, then the relationship will change – or indeed collapse with radical consequences. Changes in constitutive beliefs are crucial to the effectiveness of a mutiny. Once again it can be suggested that the emphasis pinpoints a weakness in some Marxist accounts where a sharper distinction has been made between social relations and beliefs about them.

Clearly Reid's perspective can capitalise on such difficulties, but his methodologically liberal approach has its own problems. When Reid asserts that, 'the world of politics is just as real as that of the economic and the social',[59] the underlying notion of 'the real' inevitably poses diffi-culty. As noted, the emphasis has the merit of focusing on choices made by agents according to their standards of information and reasonable-ness. In one sense, such accounts utilise 'real' factors; but can the analysis end there? Actors within the same culture, as determined according to agreed criteria, may have divergent views about political matters; equally the same actor's views may change radically over time. The conflicting claims may not just be about what ought to be, but also about what is or has been. How should an analyst committed to an explanation of political 'reality' assess such competing claims? Are they all to be counted as 'real', in which case a slippery slope to relativism beckons – or can there be grounds for adjudication between divergent positions? If the latter path is taken, then the 'reality' of the political or social sphere needs much more precise elaboration. Equivalent observations can be made about 'political reality' and constitutive beliefs. Granted that beliefs about relationships may help to constitute such relationships, can these be the sole constitu-tive element? If a slave believes that her relationship with her master is more egalitarian than would qualify typically for the master/slave couplet, this will illuminate the slave's behaviour, but it would be premature to endorse this characterisation of the relationship as definitive. Moreover, constitutive beliefs may be unstable. An individual may change, perhaps radically, his or her constitutive beliefs rejecting earlier ones as miscon-ceived. This may occur because parties to a relationship initially hold very different beliefs about its character, so that for each individual the rela-tionship is distinctive. There is the possibility of mutual education and thereby a change in beliefs, and therefore in the relationship.

This raises the critical issue of explaining political change. How far can Reid's pluralism and his emphasis on the reality of the political meet this challenge? Most political traditions have a developmental capacity that allows for change. Concepts and values may be applicable to novel situations, perhaps because they permit some contestability as to their meaning. Reid's view of Radicalism can be read in this way. Indeed the substantive claims about continuity and the methodological emphasis are mutually supportive.

Yet such an explanatory strategy has limitations. It has problems coping with radical shifts in political belief and allegiance which are seen as such by the participants. Certainly there are always likely to be elements of continuity even in the most apparently radical transformations, but the explanation of the latter is a challenge, unless the prospect is ruled out by stipulating that continuities are always dominant.

Reid's methodological response is captured in his critique of Hobsbawm's attempt to explain the rise of Labour and Socialist politics: 'he uses the existence of this party and its rhetoric of class as a final proof that such a working class did objectively exist'. Reid condemns this as question-begging: 'it short-circuits the whole inquiry into the social and economic background of political change by assuming from the start that there is a class basis and that this is directly reflected in the political language and style of the organisation under study'. The assumption is deemed responsible for an invalid argument utilising, 'the very organisations and ideas whose basis in economic and social life is being explored as themselves the key evidence for the existence of a class which cannot adequately be pinned down anywhere else'.[60] Whether the holding of an assumption in itself 'short-circuits' inquiry is debatable. Much depends on the tenacity with which the assumption is defended against inconvenient evidence. Any inquiry necessitates assumptions about significant relationships. Once again, the image is purveyed of an inflexible Marxism with the class base 'directly reflected' in the politics.

Even if Hobsbawm is vulnerable to Reid's criticism, there remain outstanding questions. If the rise of the Labour Party has to be explained, can this be achieved through Reid's commended methodology? A thorough emphasis on the world of politics allied to agnosticism about significant connections with the economic and the social, seems likely to produce little beyond the accumulation of case studies. Is the failure to pin down a class a contingent shortcoming or a methodological blind alley? Reid highlights 'an outdated theory of class'[61] as the principal weakness in Hobsbawm's presentation of labour history, coming close to the suggestion that class is just a ghost in the machine, a linguistic phantom whose claimed explanatory power is illusory.

The problem of course has dominated much Marxist historiography, producing memorable formulations, not least that of Edward Thompson:

> class happens when some men as a result of common experience (inherited or shared) feel and articulate the identity of their interests as between themselves and as against other men whose interests are

> different from (and usually opposed to) theirs. The class experience
> is largely determined by the productive relations into which men are
> born or enter involuntarily . . . [62]

The formulation has the merit of incorporating the emphasis on constitutive beliefs. People develop a specific class identity in part because of the beliefs that they come to hold about their relationships with others both inside and outside their class. Yet why assume, the sceptic will insist, that any specific interest claim will be effective, when the historical record suggests a variety of ways in which people with shared experiences came to understand their interests? Indeed this has been presented as one of the fundamental problems for a Marxist labour history – real-world workers have rarely arrived at the view of their interests that the theory would suggest. The point was made robustly by Max Weber: 'Above all the worker naturally hates his foreman, who is in constant daily contact with him, much more than he hates the factory owner, and hates the factory owner more than the shareholder, even though it is the shareholder who really gets money without working for it . . . '[63]

The concept of interest within Thompson's formulation can be attacked by a battery of sceptical arguments. The ultimate insistence is that references to interests possess only an extremely restricted explanatory capability; all they can provide is a clarification of choices on the basis that an agent considered an option to be in his or her interest. It is impossible to go further, since people can develop whatever conception of their interest they wish.

Any assessment of interests necessitates a conceptual framework, but as with substantive beliefs and social relationships, this recognition does not entail the claims of interest are constituted exclusively by that framework. Certain material features of the human predicament are unavoidable. There will be debate about how such basic needs should be pursued; there will certainly be controversy about interest claims that rest on assessments of social rather than biological need. However, recognition of such openness does not mean that so far as conceptions of interest are concerned, anything goes. Is it not empirically the case that within a particular form of society – for instance capitalism – the variety of claims has limits, and some claims acquire more plausibility than others? One explanation is that claims about interests are characteristically advanced by supporting reasons, and such justifications have to be intelligible within that society.

This explanation can be met with the sceptic's response that any notion of intelligibility is itself understandable only within a specific set of social conventions. Yet projects to advance proclaimed interests are tested typically not against the objections of sceptics, but against the consequences – either actual or hypothetical – for human happiness and misery.

Such considerations may be beside the point for those who insist that a critical problem for Marxist historiography is that within capitalist societies the dominant interest-claims with their attendant justifications have not been those anticipated by Marxists. Some have responded by incorporating time-lags, abnormal circumstances or wishful thinking to explain past and present. They are the proper targets of Reid's indictment; but such a vulnerable response is unnecessary. The purpose of a rigorous historiography utilising the rich and contested legacy of Marxism must be to explain the complexities and diversity of actual cases. This agenda can respond creatively to the demand that proper attention be paid to the domain of politics; but it will insist also that the problem of linkage between 'the political' and the class structure is an intellectual challenge and not a justification for an agnostic pluralism.

Notes

1. Reid, A. (1987) 'Class and organisation', *Historical Journal*, pp. 225–38.
2. Reid, A. (1987) 'Marxism and revisionism in British Labour History', *Bulletin of the Society for the Study of Labour History*, 1987, vol. 52, 3, pp. 46–8.
3. Ibid., p. 47.
4. Ibid., pp. 46, 48.
5. Reid, A. (1991) 'Old unionism reconsidered: The radicalism of Robert Knight 1870–1900' in Reid, A. and Biagini, E.F. (eds) *Currents of Radicalism: Popular Radicalism, Organised Labour and Party Politics in Britain 1850–1914*, Cambridge: Cambridge University Press, p. 215, footnote 3.
6. Reid, A. (1987) 'Marxism and revisionism', p. 46.
7. Biagini and Reid conclude their piece on 'currents of radicalism' at p. 19 with an acknowledged prescription – 'it seems to us that the Labour Party's ability to play a leading role in broad progressive movements in the future will be strengthened if it becomes more restrained in its tendency to legitimise its policies primarily in relation to "socialism", and if it develops more self-consciousness of, and more pride in, its relation to currents of radicalism'.
8. The volume's essays are organised around three related themes – 'Continuity in popular radicalism'; 'The Liberal Party and the people'; 'Radicals, Liberals and the Labour Party.'
9. Reid, A. and Biagini, E.F. (1991) 'Currents of radicalism 1850–1914' in *Currents of Radicalism: Popular Radicalism, Organised Labour and Party Politics in Britain 1850–1914*, Cambridge: Cambridge University Press, p. 1.
10. Ibid., p. 5.
11. Ibid., p. 3.
12. Ibid., p. 5.
13. Ibid., p. 12.

14. Ibid., p. 13.
15. The original version was (1955) *William Morris: Romantic to Revolutionary,* London: Merlin, a revised edition was published in 1977; see ix–xi for the character of the revisions to the original text. The second edition also had a postscript, pp. 763–816.
16. Thompson, E.P. (1960) 'Homage to Tom Maguire' in Briggs, A. and Saville, J. (eds) *Essays in Labour History,* London: Macmillan.
17. Published originally in 1965 in *The Socialist Register 1965,* London: Merlin.
18. Thompson, E.P. (1960), pp. 278–9.
19. This concern is evident in Thompson's writings (1957) in the *New Reasoner* – for example, 'Socialist humanism. An epistle to the philistine', *New Reasoner,* 1, pp. 105–43; and (1958) 'Agency and Choice', *New Reasoner,* 5, pp. 89–106.
20. See Morris Jones, W.H. (1954) 'In defence of apathy: Some doubts on the duty to vote', *Political Studies,* pp. 25–37; Bell, D. (1960) *The End of Ideology,* London: Collier-Macmillan; Thompson, E.P. (ed.) (1960) *Out of Apathy,* London: Stevens.
21. Thompson, E.P. (1960), p. 279.
22. Ibid., p. 302.
23. Ibid., pp. 302–3.
24. Anderson, P. (1992) 'Origins of the present crisis', reprinted in his *English Questions,* London: Verso, p. 23. The original location was *New Left Review,* Jan–Feb 1964.
25. See Thompson, E.P. (1978) 'Peculiarities' reprinted in his *The Poverty of Theory and Other Essays,* London: Merlin, p. 71.
26. Thompson, E.P. (1960), pp. 281–4.
27. Ibid., p. 311; for the campaigns of the 1860s see pp. 287–8.
28. See, for example, ibid., pp. 282–7.
29. Reid, A. and Biagini, E.F. (1991), p. 14.
30. Ibid.
31. Reid, A. (1987) 'Class and organisation'.
32. Hobsbawm, E. (1981) 'The forward march of Labour halted?' in the collection of the same title edited by M. Jacques and F. Mulhern, London: Verso.
33. Howell, D. (1990) 'When was "The forward march of Labour"?', *Llafur,* vol. 5, no. 3.
34. Reid, A. (1985) 'The Division of labour and politics in Britain 1880–1920' in Mommsen, Wolfgang J. and Husung, H.-G. (eds) *The Development of Trade Unionism in Great Britain and Germany 1880–1914,* London: Allen and Unwin, p. 158.
35. Ibid.
36. Reid, A. and Biagini, E.F. (1991), pp. 14–15.
37. Hobsbawm, E. (1984) 'The aristocracy of labour reconsidered' in his *Worlds of Labour,* London: Macmillan, p. 251.
38. For example, the Amalgamated Society of Engineers' votes were: first ballot 2 897 for affiliation, 702 against; second ballot 5 626 for, 1 070 against. See Howell, D. (1983) *British Workers and the Independent Labour Party 1888–1906,* Manchester: Manchester University Press, p. 92.
39. See his 'The formation of British working class culture' in *Worlds of Labour,* pp. 176–93.

40. See for example Waters, C. (1990) *British Socialists and the Politics of Popular Culture 1884–1914*, Manchester: Manchester University Press.
41. Melling, J. (1983) *Rent Strikes! People's Struggle for Housing in West Scotland 1890–1916*, Edinburgh: Polygon.
42. See 'The making of the working class 1870–1914' in *Worlds of Labour*, pp. 212–13. Also for one representation of Smith, Lawson, J. (1941) *The Man in The Cap*, London: Methuen.
43. Gregory, R. (1968) *The Miners in British Politics 1906–14*, Oxford: Oxford University Press; Baylies, C. (1993) *The History of the Yorkshire Miners 1881–1918*, London: Routledge.
44. Hobsbawm, E. (1984), p. 199.
45. Reid, A. and Biagini, E.F. (1991), p. 19.
46. For Hobsbawm's view of the Fabians see his 'The Fabians reconsidered' in (1964) *Labouring Men*; and for the secularist-SDF link his 'Hyndman and the SDF' in *Labouring Men*, London: Weidenfeld.
47. Hobsbawm, E. (1984), p. 211.
48. Mommsen, Wolfgang J. and Husung, H.-G. (eds) (1985), p. 162.
49. Published in 1973 and emphasising the radical potential of rank and file movements.
50. Mommsen, Wolfgang J. and Husung, H.-G. (eds) (1985), p. 162.
51. Bentley, A.F. (1908) *The Process of Government*, Cambridge, Mass.: Harvard University Press. See for instance, the discussion of the State in ch. 10.
52. Mommsen, Wolfgang J. and Husung, H.-G. (eds) (1985), pp. 162–3.
53. Ibid., p. 163.
54. Reid, A. and Biagini, E.F. (1991), p. 15.
55. Mommsen, Wolfgang J. and Husung, H.-G. (eds) (1985), p. 160.
56. Ibid.
57. Reid, A. (1986) 'Glasgow Socialism', *Social History*, pp. 95–6 (emphasis in original).
58. Ibid.
59. Ibid.
60. Reid, A. (1987) 'Class and organisation', pp. 237–8.
61. Ibid., p. 238.
62. Thompson, E.P. (1965) *The Making of the English Working Class*, London: Penguin, pp. 9–10.
63. Weber, M. (1978) 'Socialism' in Runciman, W.G. (ed.) *Weber: Selections in Translation*, Cambridge: Cambridge University Press, pp. 260–1.

Index

Compiled by Terry Wyke

abstentionism 150
anarchists 150
aristocratic power, persistence of 64
Althusser, Louis 93, 165, 170, 195, 199
AM, *see* Analytical Marxism
Amalgamated Society of Engineers 223
Amalgamated Society of Railway Servants 74
A Measure of Thatcherism (1991) 30–40
Aminzade, Ronald 59
A Nation of Homeowners (1990) 40
Analytical Marxism 165–6
Anderson, Perry 8, 194, 195
   critique of Scruton 199, 201–2, 205–12, 219–20
Anti-Corn Law League 104–5, 111
Ashton-under-Lyne 102
Affluent Workers in the Class Structure (1968–9) 60

Bagwell, Philip 74
Bahro, Rudolf 195, 198
Baines, Edward 111
Barnsley Football Club 224
Baron , Ava 10
Behagg, Clive 106–7
Bentley, Arthur F. 227
Berlin, Ira 88
Bernstein, Eduard 143
Bhaskar, Roy 99, 124
Biagini, Eugenio F. 216–33
   see also Reid, Alastair
Birmingham 64, 106–7
Birmingham Journal 78
Blackcoated Worker (1958) 60
Bloch, Maurice 124
Bolsheviks 153–4

Bradford, Yorkshire 64, 219, 225
Braunthal, Julius 138
Brenner, Robert 165
Briggs, Asa 69, 100
Bright, John 121
British Democracy at the Crossroads (1985) 20
British Election Study (1979) 26; (1987) 30, 37, 38, 51–2
British Post-Structuralism since 1968 (1991) 92, 93
British Social Attitudes (1987) 30
Buhle, Mari Jo 10
Burnley, Lancashire 40

Cannadine, David 71
Capitalism and Social Democracy (1985) 138–61, 167–90
Castells, Manuel 17
Chartism 69, 87, 215
   in Halifax 220
   language and class identity 87–9, 100–111
   and middle class 111–14
   network 78–9
   post-Chartism 116–19
   and women 114–16
Chartist and Republican Journal 102
City of Dreadful Delight (1992) 71
Clark, Anna 114
Clydeside 223, 229
class, *see* social class
coalmining, *see* trade unions: mining
Coates, David 2, 5, 7–8, 9, 147, 149, 194–213
Cohen, Anthony P. 65
Cohen, Gerry A. 165, 174
Comintern 153, 156
Communist Manifesto (1848) 180, 221

Communist Party 72
Communist Party Historians Group
　　60
Complete Suffrage Union 111
*Condition of the Working Class in
　　England* (1845) 108
*Conflict and Compromise: Class
　　Formation in English Society
　　1830–1914* 75
community identities 223, 228–9
Conservative Party 1, 20
　　electoral support 18–19, 23
　　voting intentions and car ownership
　　　42
　　and working class 45, 47–8
consumption
　　and class 6, 17–53
　　and political intentions 17–20
　　sectoral cleavages 17–25
Co-operator 116
Cook, Philip 73
cotton workers 73
Crewe, Cheshire 74
Crewe, Ivor 31
Crossick, Geoffrey 100, 118

Daily Herald 224
Davidoff, Leonore 64, 76, 77
decentring 93, 96–7
deconstruction 93, 97
democracy, bourgeois, spread of
　　147–50
democratic capitalism 176–80, 187
Dennis, Richard 71, 74
Derby 40
Derrida, Jacques 93, 97
deskilling 222
Devine, Fiona 6, 15–57
discourse 93, 97
Dobb, Maurice 59
Driver, Felix 79
Duke, Vic 16, 30–40, 40–42, 47,
　　48
　　class dealignment 31–5
　　social basis of Thatcherism 30–40
　　criticisms of 36–40
Dunleavy, Patrick 16, 17–30, 31,
　　36–7, 40–42, 47
　　social cleavage theory 17–25
　　criticisms of 25–30
Durham Miners Association 224

Dworkin, Ronald 195

Eagleton, Terry 122, 123–4
Easthope, Anthony 92, 121, 122
Edgell, Stephen 16, 30–40, 40–42, 47,
　　48
　　see also Duke, Vic
Edinburgh 70, 107
*Eighteenth Brumaire of Louis
　　Bonaparte* 59, 185, 209
elections
　　general elections (1979) 32; (1983)
　　　20–5; (1987) 32; (1992) 51–2
　　local government (1980) 29
electoralism 139–40, 142, 145, 147,
　　151, 152
Eley, Geoff 77
Elster, Jon 166
embourgeoisement 1
Emmett, Robert 110
Engels, Frederick 9, 70, 90, 91, 108
Epstein, James 66, 79
ethnicity 1, 88, 89

Fabians 225
factory colonies 72
false consciousness 100
Fielden, John 101
First International 145
First Shop Stewards Movement (1973)
　　226
food riots 61
football 223
Fordism 94
Foster John 63, 69
Foucault, Michel 7, 93, 195
Franklin, Mark N. 26–7, 38, 40

Galbraith, John K. 195
gender 1, 77, 95–6, 114–16, 223
Genovese, Elizabeth Fox 88
Genovese, Eugene 88, 125
Geras, Norman 165
Germany, social democracy 153
Giddens, Anthony 61, 75–6
Giolitti, Giovanni 148
Gladstone, William Ewart 220
Goldthorpe, John H. 30, 40, 48, 53,
　　60, 66–7
Goodway, David 106, 107
Gordon, Eleanor 10, 117

Gould, Roger 68–9, 72
Gramsci, Antonio 156, 165, 166, 177, 195, 198, 211
Granovetter, Mark 68
Gray, Robbie 100, 118
Greater Manchester surveys (1980–81, 1983–84) 30, 37–40
Gunn, Simon 64
Gutman, Herbert 88, 99, 125

Habermas, Jurgen 2, 194, 195
Halifax, Yorkshire 220
Hall, Catherine 64, 77
Hamnett, Chris 47
Harrop, Martin 25–6, 37
Harvey, David 94
Heath, Anthony 17, 51–2
hegemony 156, 177
Hill, Christopher 8, 9, 194, 201
Hinton, James 226
Hobsbawm, Eric J. 9, 59, 62, 63, 125, 194
    critique of Reid 221–6, 231
    labour aristocracy 117
'Homage to Tom Maguire' (1965) 8, 218
home ownership 26, 27, 29
    and voting behaviour 40–50
Howell, David 6, 8, 9, 214–35
Howell, George 225
Hunt, Lynn 99
Husbands, Christopher 16, 20, 40–41
    see also Dunleavy, Patrick
Huyssen, Andreas 95

'In Defence of Class' (1987) 101–2, 108, 109
Independent Labour Party 216, 220, 222, 224, 229

John, Angela 125
Johnson, Richard 209
Jones, David 114
Jones, Ernest 220
Jones, Gareth Stedman 63, 64, 71, 89, 118
    Chartism and class 90–92
    Chartism and language 93–9
    criticisms of 107–9, 119–26
    see also Languages of Class

Joyce, Patrick 64, 66, 72–3, 89, 116, 118, 128 n.22
    class 92–3
    criticisms of 92–9, 119–26
    see also Visions of People

Karl Marx's Theory of History (1978) 165
Katznelson, I. 62–3
Kautsky, Karl 185
Kentish London 70, 107
Kerr, Clark 71
Kessler-Harris, Alice 10
Keynesian economics 156–7, 157–8, 161, 165, 167, 171, 172, 178–9, 180, 181
Kiernan, Victor 9
Kirk, Neville 1–12, 86–134
Koditschek, Theodore 64

labour aristocracy 117, 148
    thesis 222
Labouring Men (1964) 117
labour movement 218–26
    in West Riding 219–21, 224
Labour Party 137, 138
    and consumption sector cleavage 21–5, 44–50
    electoral performance 15, 17, 19, 27, 36, 44, 47
    emergence 214, 216, 217, 226, 231
    and home ownership 44–50
    and miners 224, 226
    and 'new structuralism' 16–17
    and unions 73–4, 224
    and working-class support 15, 16–17, 18–19, 22–5, 49–53
    historical 'progress' 221–2, 225–6
Labour Representation Committee 223, 225
Laclau, Ernesto 123
Laing, R.D. 195
language and class 89–134
    and Chartism 100–119
Languages of Class (1983) 90, 91, 93, 95, 119, 123
Lash, Scott 66
Leach, James 102, 104, 105–6
Leeds 64
    socialism 219, 225

Letters to the Manchester Chartists
    (1844) 104
Liberal Party 37, 217, 220
Lib-Lab 225
Liberalism 116, 117–18, 216, 220
Liberal radicalism 225
'linguistic turn' 87–134
    theoretical criticisms 119–23
'Little Moscows' 72
locality 64
    see also space and class
Lockwood, David 60, 61
London Dispatch 78
Looker, Robert 5, 8, 9, 137–64,
    165–93
Lowery, Robert 111
Lukacs, Georg 137, 165, 166, 195,
    198
Luxemburg, Rosa 143–4

Macaulay, Thomas Babington 113
McCord, Norman 90
McDouall, Peter Murray 102–4, 106,
    107
MacIntyre, Stuart 72, 73
Maguire, Tom 218–21
Manchester 64
    Greater Manchester 30–40
Major, John 95
Marshall, Gordon 17, 30, 40, 48,
    49–50, 53
Metropolitan Tailors' Protection
    Society 107
Making of the English Working Class
    (1963) 2, 5, 95, 199, 207, 209,
    218
Manchester and Salford Advertiser 78
Mann, Michael 68
Mann, Tom 225
Marcuse, Herbert 2, 194
Marshall, John D. 72
Marxism 8–9
    Analytical 138, 143, 165
    historiography, critique and defence
        194–203, 214–33
    and labour movement 216
    Rational Choice Marxism 165–90
    and state 226–7
    see also Przeworski, Adam
Marx, Karl 59, 91, 107, 109, 113–14,
    166, 185, 206, 209

Methodological Individualism (MI)
    185, 186, 188
middle classes and Chartism 109–14
Miles, Andrew 67
Milan 59
Miliband, Ralph 1, 9, 194
Milton, John 201
Miners Federation of Great Britain
    224, 226
miners' strike (1984–5) 3, 184, 227–8
Montgomery, David 125
Mouffe, Chantal 123
Morris, Robert J. 64, 77
Morris, William 218
Musson, A.E. 88
mutuality 87

Nairn, Tom 2, 194
National Charter Association 78
National Coal Board 227–8
National Democratic League 225
National Reformer (1837) 113
National Union of Mineworkers 228
network analysis 5–6, 59, 67–8,
    69–75, 75–81
Newcastle-upon-Tyne 114–15
New Left 165, 217–18
    characteristics and critique
        195–203
    misinterpretations 203–5
New Poor Law 113, 114
Newport Rising 78
New Reasoner 218
New Right 2–3, 7–8, 179, 194, 195,
    197
    see also Scruton, Roger
new structuralism 15–57
    see also Dunleavy, Patrick
Northampton 70
Northern Political Union 112
Northern Star 78, 90

O'Brien, Bronterre 102, 104–5, 106,
    113
O'Connor, Feargus 78, 102, 104, 105,
    106, 107, 110, 111, 113
'Old Corruption' 90, 98
Oldham, Lancashire 70
Ossowski, Stanislaw 60
Outcast London (1971) 71
Out of Apathy (1960) 219

Owenism 116

Page, E. 26–7, 38, 40
Pahl, Raymond E. 17
Paris Commune 68–9, 72, 150
Passage from Antiquity to Feudalism (1978) 201
'Peculiarities of the English' (1965) 199, 219–20
Pilling, Richard 102, 104, 105, 106
Politics and the People (1993) 92
Poor Man's Guardian (1843) 104–5
populism 92
post-Fordism 158
post-modernism 1, 87, 88, 92–3, 93–9, 138, 158
    criticisms of 99–100, 119–26
post-structuralism 1, 2–3, 58, 93–9
    criticisms of 119–26
Poulantzas, Nicos 61, 170, 172, 177, 181, 194
Poverty of Theory (1978) 199
Prothero, Iorwerth 100, 106
Przeworski, Adam 5, 9, 138, 139–61, 173–90
    class analysis 166–73
    class struggle 169–71, 175, 180–86, 187
    decision to participate 144–50, 159
    democratic capitalism 176–80, 187
    and individual choice 173–6
    social democracy, criticisms 143–61
    and state 172, 176–80, 187
    'structure of choices' 145–50, 152, 156
    social democratic politics 150–54, 159–60
    working-class politics 183–4

race 1
radicalism, popular 216–17
Railway Review 74
railway and labour movement 73–4
Randall, Adrian 106
Rational Choice Marxism 143–61, 165–90
    and social democracy 140–42
    see also Przeworski, Adam
RCM, *see* Rational Choice Marxism
Reaganism 180
reformism 139, 142, 215

Reid, Alastair 8, 9, 88, 214–33
    criticism of Marxist labour history 214–17
    criticism of Thompson, E.P. 217–21, 231–2
    criticism of Hobsbawm, E.J. 221–5, 231
    critique of Reid 226–33
relative autonomy 177
Richardson, W.P. 224
Roberts, Robert 72
Roemer, John 166, 168–9, 174, 182
Royal Commission on Trades Unions (1867) 119
Rowbotham, Sheila 88
Runciman, W.G. 72

Salford, Lancashire 72
Salisbury Review 194, 197, 198, 199
Sartre, Jean Paul 195
Saussurean appoach to language 94
Saunders, Peter 16, 40–49, 53
Savage, Michael 5–6, 47, 58–86
Saville, John 2, 9, 108, 194, 215, 218
Schwarzkopf, Judith 114
Scott, Joan 96, 97
Scruton, Roger 8, 9, 194–213
criticism of Marxist historians 194–203
    Anderson, Perry 201–3, 205–12
    Thompson, E.P. 199–201, 205, 206–10
Second International 150–51, 152
sectoral consumption cleavages 6, 17–25, 30–40
semiotics 110
sentimentality 200, 205
Sewell, William H. 59
Siegel, A. 71
Sivanandan, Ambalavaner 88
Smillie, Bob 225
Smith, Dennis 75
Smith, Herbert 224
Slough, Berkshire 40
Social Class in Modern Britain (1988) 49
social class
    and Chartism 100–119
    class consciousness 60, 99, 166, 223
    class formation 59–65, 65–75

class struggle 142, 169–71, 175, 180, 182–6, 187
conceptualisation of 1–5, 63, 98–9, 166, 167–73, 206–13, 217–21
criticisms of 87–9
culture 222–4
dealignment 31, 35, 37, 40
decline of 3–4
defence of 4, 58, 59
demography 66–7
formation 59–65, 65–9, 69–75, 79–81
fragmentation 17, 36, 229
and gender 223–4
and language 87–134
and 'linguistic turn' 7, 87–134
and space 6–7, 58, 64, 65, 69–75
and Thompson, E.P. 4–6, 8, 60–62, 62–5, 206–13
and political alignment 6, 17–40, 49–50
and sectoral cleavages 17–30, 31–40, 41, 49–53
and social change 58
and state 172, 176–80, 187
structuralist conceptions 60–61, 63
substitutionism 182–3
symbols 66
social collectivities 65, 67–8
social democracy
conceptualisation 143–61
crisis 137–9
political parties 150–54, 159–60
and Rational Choice Marxism 140–42
and reformism 156–9
and war 152–4
Social Democratic Federation 225
social identity and space 69–75
socialism and SDP 150–54
in West Riding 218, 219–20
social mobility 60
social network analysis 59, 67–75, 75–81
social segregation 71–2, 74
Social Reform and Revolution (1899) 143–4
socialist politics 186–90
electoral dilemma 155–6
South Shields, Durham 70
South Wales Miners Federation 73

spatial analysis and class 58, 64, 65, 69–81
Sturge, Joseph 111, 112
Swindon, Wiltshire 74
Soviet Union
and social democracy 153–4
Stalin, Joseph 156
state, historical conceptions 226–7
structuralism, Althusserian 93, 100, 120, 140, 165, 166
'structure of choices' 145–50, 152, 156
syndicalism 152

Taylor-Gooby, P. 28–9, 38
textile workers 102–3
Thatcherism 179, 180
social basis 30–40
Thompson, Edward Palmer 99, 100, 170
class theories 2, 4–6, 8, 9, 58, 59, 60–62, 77, 87, 109
critiques 62–5, 95–6, 194, 195, 199–200, 205–11, 217–21
Thompson, Dorothy 10, 78, 88, 89–90, 100, 111, 114, 118, 125
Thinkers of the New Left (1985) 194, 195, 198
Tilly, Louise 59
trade unions 72, 80
cotton 73
new unions 217
craft unions 223
mining 73, 224, 227–8
railways 73–4
'Two and a Half International' 156, 160

Urban History Yearbook 70
Urban Political Analysis (1980) 17
urban sociology 71
urbanism 64
Urry, John 66
Usworth, Durham 224

Vernon, James 92–9, 98, 99, 119–26
Vincent, Henry 111
Visions of the People (1991) 92, 96, 119
voluntarism 140–41
voluntary associations 77

voting behaviour
 and consumption 17–40
 and property ownership 40–50
 and social cleavages 21–30

Walkowitz, Judith 71
Wallerstein, Immanuel 195
war 157
 and socialism 152–4, 155
Warde, Alan 29, 47
Weber, Max 232
William Morris (1955) 218

Williams, Raymond 9, 99, 119, 194,
 195, 200
women
 in Chartism 114–16
 historical neglect 223–4
Wood, Ellen Meiksins 174
Woods, Sam 225
woollen communities, socialism in
 218, 219–20
Wright, Erik Olin 61, 65–6, 165, 170

Zolberg, Aristide R. 62